Studying Business at MBA and Masters Level

Visit our free study skills resource at **www.skills4study.com**

Palgrave Study Guides

Authoring a PhD
Career Skills
e-Learning Skills
Effective Communication for
    Arts and Humanities Students
Effective Communication for
    Science and Technology
The Exam Skills Handbook
The Foundations of Research
The Good Supervisor
How to Manage your Arts, Humanities and
    Social Science Degree
How to Manage your Distance and
    Open Learning Course
How to Manage your Postgraduate Course
How to Manage your Science and
    Technology Degree
How to Study Foreign Languages
How to Write Better Essays
IT Skills for Successful Study
Making Sense of Statistics
The Mature Student's Guide to Writing (2nd edn)
The Palgrave Student Planner
The Personal Tutor's Handbook
The Postgraduate Research Handbook (2nd edn)
Presentation Skills for Students

The Principles of Writing in Psychology
Professional Writing (2nd edn)
Research Using IT
Skills for Success
The Student Life Handbook
The Study Abroad Handbook
The Palgrave Student Planner
The Student's Guide to Writing (2nd edn)
The Study Skills Handbook (2nd edn)
Study Skills for Speakers of English as
    a Second Language
Studying Business at MBA and Masters Level
Studying the Built Environment
Studying Economics
Studying History (2nd edn)
Studying Law
Studying Mathematics and its Applications
Studying Modern Drama (2nd edn)
Studying Physics
Studying Programming
Studying Psychology (2nd edn)
Teaching Study Skills and Supporting Learning
Work Placements – a Survival Guide for Students
Write it Right
Writing for Engineers (3rd edn)
Writing for Nursing and Midwifery Students

Palgrave Study Guides: Literature
General Editors: John Peck and Martin Coyle

How to Begin Studying English Literature
    (3rd edn)
How to Study a Jane Austen Novel (2nd edn)
How to Study a Charles Dickens Novel
How to Study Chaucer (2nd edn)
How to Study an E. M. Forster Novel
How to Study James Joyce
How to Study Linguistics (2nd edn)

How to Study Modern Poetry
How to Study a Novel (2nd edn)
How to Study a Poet
How to Study a Renaissance Play
How to Study Romantic Poetry (2nd edn)
How to Study a Shakespeare Play (2nd edn)
How to Study Television
Practical Criticism

Studying Business at MBA and Masters Level

Paul Griseri
and
James Wisdom

First published 2007 by
PALGRAVE MACMILLAN
Houndmills, Basingstoke, Hampshire RG21 6XS and
175 Fifth Avenue, New York, N.Y. 10010
Companies and representatives throughout the world

PALGRAVE MACMILLAN is the global academic imprint of the Palgrave
Macmillan division of St. Martin's Press, LLC and of Palgrave Macmillan Ltd.
Macmillan® is a registered trademark in the United States, United Kingdom
and other countries. Palgrave is a registered trademark in the European
Union and other countries.

ISBN-13: 978–0–230–50766–1
ISBN-10: 0–230–50766–2

This book is printed on paper suitable for recycling and made from fully
managed and sustained forest sources. Logging, pulping and manufacturing
processes are expected to conform to the environmental regulations of the
country of origin.

A catalogue record for this book is available from the British Library.

A catalog record for this book is available from the Library of Congress.

10 9 8 7 6 5 4 3 2 1
16 15 14 13 12 11 10 09 08 07

Printed and bound in China

Contents

List of Tables and Figures   vii
Acknowledgements   viii
Introduction   ix

1 Getting Started   **1**
    Introduction   1
    The idea of academic study   1
    Study at Masters level   6
    Tutors' and students' conceptions of learning and teaching   11
    Preparing to study   16
    Making time work for you   27

2 Getting the Most from Lectures and Reading   **34**
    Introduction   34
    Getting the most from classes   35
    Approaches to reading   48
    Accessing and using sources   52
    Online and other electronic sources   58

3 Examinations   **65**
    Introduction   65
    Unpicking a question   66
    Generating ideas   75
    Planning an answer   81
    Avoiding pitfalls   87
    Revision   92

4 Responding to Assignments   **103**
    Introduction   103
    Structure   104
    Argument   110
    Research   116

Presentation   121
Conclusions and recommendations   127
Originality and reflection   130
Managing time   134

5 **Learning in Groups**   **141**
Introduction   141
Understanding groups   142
Group effectiveness   143
When a group encounters difficulties   155
Electronic sources available to groups   160

6 **The Dissertation**   **163**
Introduction   163
What is a dissertation?   164
The scope of a dissertation   168
Clarifying the subject   171
Progressing the investigation   179
Concluding the investigation   183
Getting the work finished   191
What gets good marks in dissertations?   193
Working with your supervisor   195

7 **Researching for your Dissertation**   **198**
Introduction   198
Methods and methodology   199
Conceptualizing your dissertation   200
Proof   204
Research designs   208
Research approaches   212
Collecting and analysing information   217

Appendix   220
References   241
Useful Resources   242
Index   244

List of Tables and Figures

Tables

3.1   Key verbs   70
3.2   Practising exam answers   96

Figures

1.1   Lecture notes   20
1.2   Mind-mapping   25
2.1   Note- taking   41
2.2   Developing the knowledge space, 1   54
2.3   Developing the knowledge space, 2   55
3.1   A 'sunflower' diagram   77
3.2   Example of a network diagram   78
4.1   Question and answer structure, example 1   108
4.2   Question and answer structure, example 2   108
4.3   The Kolb model of experiential learning   132

Acknowledgements

A book of this kind is inevitably the result of a long series of experiences and experiments with different groups of students and colleagues. But to our recollection we have benefitted in a variety of ways from those mentioned below. Doubtless we may omit accidentally many from whom we have learnt a great deal, and to those we apologize for the omission as well as add our thanks.

Our thanks above all are due to students and teachers in the several higher education institutions with whom, over the last ten years, we have worked on Masters programmes, in developing study skills learning materials for Masters and professional programmes, and also in supporting teachers in the development of study skills in their MBA (and similar) students. These include teachers and students from, amongst others, London Guildhall University (now London Metropolitan University), University College London, BPP Professional Education, Malpas Flexible Learning Ltd (now BPP-Malpas), the Royal Military College of Science, Emile Woolf College, CSHS, the Isle of Man International Business School, Kingston University, and colleagues from the Staff and Educational Development Association.

Notable amongst the individuals with whom we have worked or gained valuable insights in this context are Jonathan Groucutt, Graham Pitcher, Chris Thomas, Andrew Edkins, Ron Matthews, Brian Blundell and Margaret Malpas.

Thanks also are due to Nina Seppala and Pedro Longart for help in sourcing material. Many thanks also to Alan Jenkins for permission to use material on learning outcomes in the chapter on examinations.

To all those mentioned above we are grateful, as also to our partners, Valerie Bott and Lyn Thompson, for their patience and support whilst we were writing this book. Needless to say, all responsibility for errors or omissions is ours alone.

PAUL GRISERI
JAMES WISDOM

The authors and publishers are grateful to the copyright-holders for relevant material reproduced in this book. If any have been inadvertently omitted, the authors and publishers will be pleased to make the necessary arrangement at the earliest opportunity.

Introduction

● What this study guide will do for you

Welcome to *Studying Business at MBA and Masters Level.* This guide will provide an introduction to the issues of studying on any of the range of Masters-level business-based courses, including:

- Masters in Business Administration (MBA)
- Masters courses, both MSc and MA, in occupational roles such as Marketing, Operations or Human Resources
- Masters courses focused on specific disciplines or aspects of business such as International Business, Technology Management or Organizational Behaviour
- Masters courses relating to specific industries or sectors, such as Financial Services, Manufacturing, or Public Sector Management

In each of these cases, there is a distinction between courses that are designed for people who have had some years' professional experience already and are looking to *develop* their career, and people who have gone more or less directly from their first degree to a Masters course and are thus looking to their Masters to help them *enter* their chosen career or become researchers into the subject. Each of these has its own specific features.

This book will make clear the difference in level and depth that is represented by Masters work, compared with undergraduate study or following a course required for membership of a professional institute. It will focus on the issues relevant to the study of business and management at this level, including many that are not covered by general books on study. It will address issues that are common to all kinds of Business Masters programmes, as well as dealing with issues that are specific to each category.

It will also discuss the main resources available to you – your lectures, the reading prescribed for you, using libraries and online sources, how to do yourself justice in exams, writing assignments, and working in groups. It will also deal with the issues of conducting research and, separately, how to go about your dissertation.

The guide is in three parts, each of which is related to one of the three phases of your study programme.

Chapters 1 and 2 have been written to help you deal effectively with the requirements you will have in the earliest part of the course. Chapter 1 deals with getting the level of study right, managing your time to get started effectively, as well as specific techniques and tools of study. Chapter 2 deals with getting the most out of reading and lectures.

The second part of the guide is attuned to the main part of the taught element of the course. Chapter 3 helps you prepare and perform at a high level in examinations. Chapter 4 focuses on how to do well with written assignments, and returns to the question of time management as the pressure of assessment through written assignment starts to grow. Chapter 5 addresses the issues of group work – both face to face and when communicating on-line.

The final part deals specifically with the questions of research and the dissertation. Chapter 6 looks at research – whilst this is clearly directed mainly at the work you will need to do in order to succeed with your dissertation, it will also be useful for earlier assignments. Chapter 7 takes this further to look specifically at what you will need to do to produce a successful dissertation.

How to use this guide

We have designed this guide so that it can be consulted as you need it, rather than intending it to be read from cover to cover. For example, many users may well go directly to the particular sections on exams and assignments, to see what help they can get from these. Others may feel they most need to adopt a strategic approach to accessing texts and getting the important points out of them quickly, and there are sections on this. Others might leave the chapters on research and the dissertation until later – though when you read these you may find they will have been helpful earlier. The important point is that **you** are constructing **your own** learning, and you should use this as a resource in whatever way it works best for you personally. We hope, therefore, that you can use this guide in a number of different and appropriate ways.

However, we would recommend a strategy for using this guide:

- Have a very brief skim of the whole book, chapter by chapter, just looking at the contents, the section headings and objectives, and the final summaries. Do this for each chapter. From this you will have a reasonable map of the whole.
- Work through the first chapter more or less straight away, going

quickly through areas about which you feel reasonably confident and paying more attention to material with which you are less familiar.

- Consider Chapters 2 and 3, again focusing on the aspects that feel most relevant to your own situation.
- Refer to the other chapters as and when they seem to you to be relevant, but ideally at least a month before you really need them.

Our main advice is to use this guide as a resource which you should feel you can dip into at any such time as fits your own learning process. We are all different, and we all learn in different ways, so it is entirely appropriate that one person may work steadily through this entire guide, and others might feel very confident about the material in certain places and so skim through it.

We are writing this personally and free use is made of the personal pronouns 'we' and 'you'. This is deliberate. We want you to feel that this is like a tutorial, where you can ask questions of the text and seek their answers, almost as you would from a tutor. Our hope or expectation is that you will use in it the way that you feel is most suitable. There is no best way, though from time to time we may make suggestions and recommendations.

Some of the material is in the form of a question, or something for you to consider, then we offer our answer or response. We think that the more you engage actively with these, the more valuable will be your learning. But we recognize that you are in control, and so you may just skim over them.

Much of this guide contains advice, and giving advice is always difficult. Offer someone advice too early and it can be meaningless ('What *is* he on about?'). To offer it too late can cause resentment ('I've struggled through this and you knew the answer all along . . . '). When you know the subject well advice can be so obvious as to be embarrassing, because we forget what it was like to be a novice. And there is the tricky issue of responsibility ('I have taken your advice, and just look where it has got me . . . '). Well, we give this advice with the best of intentions – please make of it what you will.

Another aspect of this is that you, the readers of this book, will include a wide range of individuals from different backgrounds, different intellectual cultures, different expectations and skills. A great deal of Masters study in business and management is based on the US and UK models, which emphasize an interactive approach to classroom discussion, and assessments based on dialogue, argument and debate. This guide is written with that style of education in mind – we do not claim it is the best, but it is the norm for study in this area.

Because the population of Masters students following business courses is so varied, there are various distinct needs for which we have catered. Some students will have had several years of experience in a managerial role, while others may have come straight from their first degree. Some may have entered a course without having previously studied at undergraduate level, having demonstrated their suitability to study a Masters on account of the level of their work experience. Still others may be new to the study of business, having previously studied another subject, and therefore may be unfamiliar with the breadth of study and thinking that is particular to this subject. Inevitably this will mean that you may find certain aspects relatively straightforward which other readers may find problematic or quite novel, and equally at other points some issues may be difficult for you that are less so for others. Following our points made earlier, use the material as it suits you – if something is pretty familiar then scan it quickly and then move on to areas that may be more challenging for you.

Bearing these issues in mind, this guide has been formulated to:

- provide a resource to support your progress through your Masters programme;
- enable you to study in a manner that is appropriate to Masters level;
- help you do yourself full justice in examinations, including revision and interpreting exam questions;
- develop good time-management skills;
- develop writing skills appropriate to an academic Masters course;
- help you produce good assignments, including the appropriate level of reading and discussion;
- provide techniques to help you get the most out of your reading;
- indicate ways to engage critically with texts;
- develop a focused approach to getting the most out of lectures and lecturers;
- develop a strong understanding of the practical and theoretical issues surrounding management research; and
- support you in completing your dissertation.

We also have one request: we hope this study guide is of value to you; if you have any comments on the book, please contact us at either of the following two email addresses:

JamesWisdom@compuserve.com
pgriseri.associates@virgin.net

So – start work, and we hope you find this helpful.

1 Getting Started

● **Introduction**

When you have worked through this chapter, you should be able to:

- identify the key aspects of academic study;
- describe accurately the distinguishing features of Masters-level study in business and management-related subjects;
- evaluate differences between tutors' and students' approaches to the learning process;
- make effective use of a range of techniques to support your study and learning, including approaches to the taking of notes and for working with reading material provided by your teachers, the use of graphical-textual methods to enhance your understanding of subjects, and strategies to help you read efficiently;
- identify the demands on your time and use a range of strategies to manage these.

Each of these outcomes is addressed in the following sections. We would suggest that you read and digest the content of the first three of these sections as soon as you are able to, as they provide the main framework of our approach to this book.

● **The idea of academic study**

In this section we are going to look at the nature of the task you are taking on, the kind of work that is involved at Masters level, and what this implies for your own activity.

Therefore, when you have worked through this section, you should be able to:

- describe the key features of academic learning;
- identify interrelationships between course-based study and professional and personal experience.

It may help to make notes on this section as you work through it – these can be in any form you think appropriate. This will help you formulate your own summary of the section, but this will also be useful to refer to when working through the section on preparing to study.

What does the word 'academic' conjure up for you? For many people, it suggests slightly eccentric or vague individuals, surrounded by piles of dusty old papers, pondering the meaning of some ancient volume. Of course this is a caricature – most academic work is not an arcane search into the obscure. But it contains one important truth – that the *discovery of new knowledge comes at least in part via the study of other people's thinking, as this is expressed in writing*. This is a central aspect of all work that purports to be academic. By participating in this course you are entering an environment which has the following features:

1   development of new ideas proceeds by way of *critical* analysis and discussion: i.e. that which challenges claims, recognizes strengths and explores areas for further development;
2   all participants in the academic debate have the same right to critique and question the work of any other participant;
3   no statement has any right to be accepted without question;
4   learning proceeds with reference to previous knowledge – by building on it, extending it, contrasting with it, refuting it, providing a wider explanation for it, or maybe by putting it into context.

But as well as the necessity for critical study, with a subject area such as management additional aspects come into play. Management is a study of *practice*. Therefore someone studying management needs to take account not only of existing learning but also to apply this to, and challenge, the context of practice.

For each individual, the study of management is different, because each of us has a different set of experiences which we bring to it and which gives some elements greater emphasis than others.

Consider

What different types of experience might be relevant to your study of management?

Response

You might have identified a wide range, which you might try to fit into one of the following categories:

Professional – if you have already worked as a manager, currently or in the past, this will provide you with cases where you have had to make decisions, carry responsibility, evaluate whether you are using resources appropriately to deliver the best results, and so on.

Bureaucratic – if you have had any kind of work experience, you will have found that in most work contexts there is some degree of bureaucracy (in the best sense of the word – meaning formally organised work), some amount of administration where the emphasis is on carrying out decisions that others have made.

Personal – much management literature ignores the very real impact that people's personal experiences have on their behaviour and development as professionals and as managers; in practice this frames their thinking and perspective at least as much as the experience they have derived from their paid employment.

Each of these perspectives can contribute to the academic process. Each may provide raw material as a basis for criticizing ideas and concepts that you encounter in your reading. Not that they can be taken at face value – it is not as if someone can justifiably say 'Well, I tried that technique and it didn't work for me, so it can't be any good.' One single experience cannot justify such a sweeping claim. But it would be the basis for raising a *question* about it. A statement that 'I tried that technique but it didn't work for me, so it needs a bit more exploration and investigation' IS a legitimate thing to say. This is what we mean by the idea that an individual's range of experiences can be a valid input to the academic investigation of what makes for sound management. They are part of what confirms or challenges theoretical approaches to management, and have their own – limited – validity because they reflect actual practices, which is what management theory is supposed to help explain and provide tools to enhance.

One important issue that we shall refer to on several occasions is the idea of *critique*. This means something rather more than criticism, a word which suggests identification of weaknesses and negative points. Critique, however, is meant to embrace both strengths as well as weaknesses. It involves the analysis of an idea down to its component parts, in order to estimate its value. This involves separating out the basic claim that someone is making, and distinguishing this from the evidence or arguments they adduce to support it. That is the analysis part. The critique element comes in with the evaluation of the arguments, and whether they do in fact support the claim that is being made, and how far they do so. For example, one question that might be raised as a challenge to an argument is whether what has been claimed is true in all contexts or only some. A great deal of academic progress consists simply in recognising that an idea works very well in one context but not in others. Other related questions might be whether a series of examples can or cannot be used as the basis for a generalization about all similar cases.

While it is important to develop this critical approach, you may find it hard to get into this way of thinking to start with. It may be especially hard if you have been educated in a culture where the authority of the teacher has been dominant, and where a student might feel that challenging an idea *could* be seen as challenging the person who suggested the idea. In fact this will not be the case. At this level all teachers of management and business related subjects will expect their students to critique ideas, and they will not take it as a challenge to their authority if you question ideas. Perhaps in different cultures the way you do this may differ – in some countries it may be less normal to ask questions directly in class during a lecture, whilst in others this is regarded as the norm. But the basic idea of learning by means of critical analysis and discussion is common to all intellectual cultures. Your tutors will be disappointed if you do not.

One simple exercise to develop your critical skills is to take a key idea from a text or a lecture, reverse its meaning, and then try to argue the new point of view. For example, on a previous page we asserted: 'much management literature ignores the very real impact that people's personal experiences have on their behaviour and development as professionals and as managers'.

You might question that by thinking: 'No, I suspect there is a <u>lot</u> of literature which builds on personal experience. What about the Action Learning work of Reg Revans, for example? I will look this up in the library and see what else has been written.' You can now take what you have found and write a text challenging or developing the original claim. Part of the process of becoming critical is to take risks, trying out ideas, playing with assumptions and thinking for yourself.

Critical, therefore, in this sense, means the identification of strengths and weaknesses in an argument as a basis for further investigation. On the basis of this one can estimate the value of academic arguments. The value of an idea, in this context, has two distinct senses:

- the validity of the theory in terms of its theoretical adequacy, evidential support, etc.
- the usefulness of the theory for practising managers.

As we shall see in later chapters, these often pull in different directions – the really useful ideas often have little strong evidence behind them, whilst the soundly researched ideas are often not appropriate for practice.

A further feature of academic study is that this process of critical discussion as a driver of future progress has no end point. Any idea can be and often will be subject to one form of challenge or another at any time. This means that *for all practical purposes, no idea is certain.* No theory or result is perfect, however strongly academics may feel about it. Uncertainty is a permanent feature of learning at this level. Each individual engaged with academic study has to develop ways in which they can entertain and work with those ideas that seem most plausible to them, but all of which they know are not conclusively proven, and are thus open to challenge and potentially to revision.

This implies a great deal about the relationship between teacher and learner. The uncertainty encountered at this level means that you cannot regard a tutor as a simple source of unquestioned knowledge. Their responses to questions should always be assumed to have a silent qualification at the beginning, something like 'As far as we have established so far . . .' Learning at this level is not a well-ordered process, and the relationship between learners and teachers is complex – sometimes you may find that your teacher in discussion is exploring ideas that are new to them as well as to you, and occasionally it might be you or a colleague on the course who is leading this new direction of thought. Hopefully this should dispel any idea that learning at this level is a matter of handing over a package of knowledge – this is not a simple transaction but a developing relationship in which you gradually become, if not a full equal to your tutor, at least a colleague in the process of learning.

● Study at Masters level

When you have completed this section, you should be able to:

- identify what study at Masters level means
- draw out the implications of Masters level study for your own actions as a learner

Activity

What do you think are the key features of learning at Masters level? List these out briefly.

Response

The table below gives the specification of what studying at Masters level means in the United Kingdom, as stated through the Quality Assurance Agency (it is an extract from the Framework for Higher Education Qualifications in England, Wales and Northern Ireland). This specification is very carefully constructed and the language is very precise. We strongly advise that you work through each of the sentences with a colleague or friend on the course, making sure you understand their meaning. The best test of your understanding is to attempt to create examples for each of them. We also strongly advise that you should engage with this exercise at intervals throughout your course, as your ideas about the specification will change as your learning develops.

Masters degrees are awarded to students who have demonstrated:

(i)   a systematic understanding of knowledge, and a critical awareness of current problems and/or new insights, much of which is at, or informed by, the forefront of their academic discipline, field of study, or area of professional practice;

(ii) a comprehensive understanding of techniques applicable to their own research or advanced scholarship;

(iii) originality in the application of knowledge, together with a practical understanding of how established techniques of research and enquiry are used to create and interpret knowledge in the discipline;

(iv) conceptual understanding that enables the student:

- to evaluate critically current research and advanced scholarship in the discipline; and
- to evaluate methodologies and develop critiques of them and, where appropriate, to propose new hypotheses.

→

Typically, holders of the qualification will be able to:

(a) deal with complex issues both systematically and creatively, make sound judgements in the absence of complete data, and communicate their conclusions clearly to specialist and non-specialist audiences;

(b) demonstrate self-direction and originality in tackling and solving problems, and act autonomously in planning and implementing tasks at a professional or equivalent level;

(c) continue to advance their knowledge and understanding, and to develop new skills to a high level;

and will have:

(d) the qualities and transferable skills necessary for employment requiring:

- the exercise of initiative and personal responsibility;
- decision-making in complex and unpredictable situations; and
- the independent learning ability required for continuing professional development.

Source: Quality Assurance Agency website:
http://www.qaa.ac.uk/academicinfrastructure/FHEQ/EWNI/default.asp

So the term 'Master' suggests that someone has achieved a degree of knowledge and understanding. They know this will never be complete but at least they will have covered the range of knowledge and developed understanding to a level that enables them to make good decisions.

It suggests that the individual would be able to cope with issues that arise from whichever part of the subject area, and at whatever level of complexity or difficulty. Hence, as well as possessing a systematic and comprehensive knowledge of the field, someone who achieves Masters level will possess:

(i) an ability to approach all relevant issues and concepts critically

(ii) sufficient understanding of the whole field to be able to establish fresh linkages and cross-references that go beyond those made explicitly within published material;

(iii) the ability to design and implement methodologies that test out and extend current theories;

(iv) the ability to deal with the application of theories and concepts in complex, unstable and dynamic situations;

(v) an approach to their own learning and development that relies on self-determined goals and self-evaluation via reflection on practice;

(vi) the capability to meet unusual and unforeseen challenges;

(vii) a degree of control over the subject matter that indicates the ability to generate their own theoretical approaches as appropriate;

(viii) the capacity to participate in the development of the subject via academic debate and critique.

These are challenging goals, but they are reflected in many discussions of the nature of Masters-level learning. We suggest you review them while discussing the QAA specification with your colleague. Their implication is that to be successful at this level it is nowhere near enough simply to respond to what is placed before you in lectures and prescribed reading. What is essential is to take a *proactive* approach to your learning. This requires

- reading on a wider scale than merely what is recommended;
- applying concepts in the light of your own experiences and practice as a basis for evaluating their strengths and weaknesses;
- preparedness to develop one's own approaches and criticisms;
- use of available material as *resources* to support learning in your own terms, rather than accepting these as the only source of the subject;
- an assertive approach to the use and validity of ideas to inform and support practice.

The English word 'Master' is derived from the Latin word *Magister* which is still used in several other European countries to denote this level of study – it suggests someone who contributes to knowledge in their own right, to whom others would go to receive advice and support in the field: An expert, a consultant. That is the condition to which Masters level study aspires, and although abstract and in some ways idealistic, it is the image that is associated with the possession of an MBA, MSc or MA qualification. In the next subsection we will discuss the idea of Masters level study in further depth.

What is a Masters in business?

There is another aspect of study at this level; there are different types of business-related Masters qualification, and three main categories can be distinguished:

- Specialist Masters, such as the MA in Marketing, which may be designed for career entry or for career development, or which may be taken by people interested in developing further research.

- Generalist Masters such as an MA in Management Studies, designed for career entry.
- Generalist Masters, the MBA most notably, designed as career development.

Each of these deals with a range of core subjects, and each will apply theoretical material to examples drawn from professional experience. In general the career entry programmes will be more theoretical in nature, and the career development ones more applied in tone, but this is a only matter of degree. Each type of programme will include *some* theory and *some* application to practice. It is the balance that differs.

All these qualifications, therefore, have some relationship with professional practice. As well as being an expert in your subject, someone who can act as a consultant, you also are expected to demonstrate *professional competence*. This means that you can deal with a wide range of management challenges that may present themselves to you in your professional work. It is no longer simply a case of knowing the range of theories and concepts in your field, but of being able to apply and *synthesize* all this knowledge as you deal with these challenges.

If you are studying in the United Kingdom, there is an important document which describes in detail the purpose of studying Business and Management at Masters level, the content of the courses, the skills you are expected to develop, and the standards which you are expected to reach. This is the 'Subject Benchmark Statement' for Masters awards in Business and Management, in which you will find that the purpose of the awards is:

- the advanced study of organizations, their management and the changing external context in which they operate;
- preparation for and/or development of a career in business and management by developing skills at a professional or equivalent level, or as preparation for research or further study in the area;
- development of the ability to apply knowledge and understanding of business and management to complex issues, both systematically and creatively, to improve business and management practice;
- enhancement of lifelong learning skills and personal development so as to be able to work with self-direction and originality and to contribute to business and society at large.

We strongly recommend that you review this document at various points during your study, both on your own and with your course colleagues. It has been written carefully and its ideas deserve to be closely analysed. You will find it becomes one of the major influences on your work.

(http://www.qaa.ac.uk/academicinfrastructure/benchmark/masters/MBAintro.asp)

Management studies are generally presented in an artificial way, splitting up the subject into separate areas, such as HRM, Finance, Strategy, and so on. But in the real world, the one in which you will have to demonstrate your own competence as a manager, issues do not pop up neatly labelled 'IT' or 'Finance and Marketing'. Usually a major issue will have elements that touch on each of the major aspects of management – in dealing with the finance issues you inevitably deal with the IT ones, or the people ones, or the marketing ones. It is as if you have to be able to look through a kaleidoscope and grasp all the different shapes and colours and know how they will all react if you were to shake it up.

Of course this is challenging for anyone who aspires to take a management role. We are considering what you should be able to do when you have completed the course, not what you can do when you start it. But the clearer you are about where you are headed, the more easily you can steer towards it. The main implications of all this for your approach to learning should be:

- that plenty of wide reading may be more appropriate than a lot of highly specialized in-depth knowledge;
- that a continuing focus on the practical implications of theory will be essential;
- remembering always that almost all theories are simplifications, and that therefore you have to add in aspects that the books leave out; and
- being always aware that each case and each situation presents the same types of problems but in unique ways, and that therefore there are no standard answers; although it is reasonable to have standard approaches and methods for embarking on investigation, it is essential to acknowledge that almost always these will lead in their own unique direction.

Central to all these requirements are two interlocked themes. The first is that much learning at this level is question driven. Not in the sense of a tutor's or a colleague's questions, but in the sense that you make progress in your understanding by continually questioning what is presented to you. In some cases it may be simply 'Is this argument convincing?' In others it may be more action focused, such as 'How could I use this effectively in a practical working situation?' In still other cases it may be more subtle, such as 'How does this approach link with other concepts I have been studying?'

These questions generate different ways in which you might work with an idea or concept, critique it and make it part of your own personal toolkit of management techniques. The 'toolkit' is a useful metaphor for what is needed at this level, for the apprentice may need someone else to provide the tools or tell them which tools to use; the master knows himself or herself what tools to use, and indeed may have designed some of them.

The second theme is that this questioning needs to be self-generated, though this may often happen in collaboration with others. You will encounter ideas in your studies; you will have material in a textbook or a lecture handout; but it is your reflection which generates the questions that develop your understanding and personal blueprint for action. So you have to consciously press forward the process of questioning; you have to supply the stock of questions that can be the basis for your developing understanding of what you read, hear or see.

A follow-on from this is that the theories you encounter will rarely answer all your questions satisfactorily. You will ask a question and normally get a partial answer, but some aspect may well remain open. This comes back to the flow of learning between the academic side of the course and its professional, experience-based side. Where you have a theory or idea for which you have only partially answered questions, that will be the place when you will need to say to yourself *'Well, let's see how this works when I try it in the real world.'*

● Tutors' and students' conceptions of learning and teaching

When you have completed this section, you should be able to:

- describe the links between what a teacher aims to do within, and what a student hopes to get out of, the educational process
- recognize the nature of key aspects of mature, autonomous, learning

Now we need to turn from what it means to be a Master in a field to what will happen whilst you are on the course. Learning should be your key focus. But learning comes by means of activities such as teaching, so it is reasonable to presume that there is some kind of parallel between the two. One might expect teachers to teach so as to maximize learning, and students to direct their learning in a one-to-one correlation with is taught. This might seem a rational approach – but is it really like this?

Question

What is learning? How would you describe or define what happens when you learn in higher education?

Response

Compare your own thoughts with the outcomes of a published study which gave the views of a range of students on what they thought learning in higher education is:

- memorizing;
- acquisition and utilization of facts and methods;
- measurable increase in knowledge;
- abstraction of meaning;
- interpretations of reality;
- personal development.

Source: Adapted from 'Conceptions of Learning' by F. Marton, G. Dall'Alba and E. Beaty, in *International Journal of Educational Research*, 1993, vol. 19 pp. 277–300.

These are all qualities or capacities that individual students have and wish to extend, and are potentially all present to some degree in all learning at whatever level. They may not be exhaustive of all the possible aspects of learning but they give a reasonable overview of the range of what students generally look for when faced with a learning opportunity, be it a lecture, a website, a book or journal, an assignment or exam, or a whole programme of study.

Now look at the results of another study (Dall'Alba, 1991), conducted at around the same time, by one of the authors of the student survey mentioned above. This survey was of the conceptions *teachers* had of what *they* were doing:

- presenting or transmitting information,
- illustrating application of theory in practice,
- developing concepts and their interrelationships,
- developing expertise,

- exploiting ways of understanding from different perspectives, and
- bringing about conceptual change.

There is some clear agreement at the earlier stages between the students' perspective on learning and the teachers' views of teaching, but at the richer end different ideas crop up. What they indicate is that the supply end of the educational process – what the teacher can deliver – is of a different kind to the demand end – what the student aims to get from their learning. Personal development, for example, is generally a legitimate feature of the learning process, but it is not something that a teacher can teach. What they can do is provide experiences, activities and challenges that may lead to that kind of development. Conversely, you as a participant just starting on a course may feel that all this talk of developing as an expert in a subject area is too high-flown. But from a teacher's view they will inevitably see what they are imparting as contributing towards your expertise. Bear in mind, by the way, that the Latin root of the word 'expert' simply means 'tried and tested' – seen in that light it may be an appropriate aim of a Business Masters course.

The point of this discussion is that *whilst there is some degree of connection between what teachers are trying to do and what students are trying to achieve within the educational process, they are not identical.* We will say more about this later in the guide when looking at lecturing and lecturers' different styles.

You as the learner should be the driving force behind what happens to your own understanding as you progress through the programme. Ideally this should always be the case, but very often at lower levels students have not developed the maturity to be able to take this proactive approach. At Masters level you are presumed to be mature learners, in the senses that:

- you can identify your own goals for learning,
- you can evaluate your own progress through the programme,
- you will relate what you learn directly to your own professional situation,
- you will take initiatives to develop your own understanding,
- you will take responsibility for your own learning, and for your own contribution to class and syndicate activities,
- you will manage the learning process actively, dealing with issues and problems autonomously (though still with a regard to the rules and regulations of the course),
- you will use your own experience – and that of your colleagues on the programme – as a resource to contribute to the debate about management, and

● you will use the tutor and all material supplied or recommended by the course team as a resource to be worked with, rather than as a fount of all wisdom.

Working with the other students on your course

Looking back over the topics we have covered so far in this first chapter, they are difficult and challenging. Ideas about the nature of academic study, of critical thinking, of the standards expected of Masters graduates, and conceptions of teaching and learning – we have tried to write about them clearly but they are not simple and straightforward. They need consideration, discussion and debate.

Students often say that they learn as much on their course from each other as they do from their tutors. On Masters programmes in Business, this may be even more true, as many of your new colleagues will have a wealth of experience on which to draw. As international travel has become more commonplace, in every country Masters courses now have students from all around the world. Each student will bring to the course different assumptions and expectations, drawn from their experience, their education and their cultural backgrounds. Everyone will have their ideas challenged. This can be exciting and rewarding – it can also be difficult and painful.

Nowadays Masters courses not only attract students from around the world, but also students of all ages – people who may have already had a successful career and who are very experienced in business. All students, whether they are classified as 'home' students, 'international', 'mature' or 'non-traditional', are apprehensive about starting a new course, they worry whether they are clever enough, or able to work hard enough, whether their memory is sharp enough, if they will be able to concentrate when reading, or if they will be able to write essays and dissertations, or keep up with the younger students. Do not believe what other students might say – everyone is very nervous about taking examinations.

One simple first step you can take – for yourself – is to start your time together by inviting your fellow students to debate and discuss the ideas and expectations we have outlined in this chapter. Such conversations would be very valuable. If they are combined with 'country evenings' – when students from different countries or areas of the world prepare short presentations with national food and drink – then these conversations will be sociable and fun as well.

There is one particular issue about working with other students which we want to consider early on in this book. Many lecturers tell us that they sometimes teach students who are very reluctant to discuss ideas in class, in seminars and in group tutorials. It may be that they do not speak English well, and are slow to form their thoughts in a foreign language. It may be that they are finding the whole experience very difficult (living in a new country, having few friends, struggling with the amount of work) and so are shy and withdrawn. Or it may be that they think that only the teacher is worth learning from, and that listening to other students will not help them. Our view, and many tutors' views, of academic study is that ideas are improved by being discussed and challenged, and that students learn better ideas by allowing them to be debated. We also know that each student learns more for themselves if they can state their ideas, discuss them and hear counter-arguments. So it is important to try to participate in academic discussion, both by putting in your ideas, and by listening hard to other peoples'.

The changing environment of higher education

As with all fields of endeavour, higher education rarely stands still, and at the time of writing this text it is in transition in several ways. One of these is the continuing impact of the internet and related forms of electronic communication, so that the use of Virtual Learning Environments (VLEs) is now standard when only a very few years ago they were unknown. This has changed the balance between class based and study away from the classroom, for example it is much easier now to have some access to a tutor when away from the classroom.

Another much more wide-reaching change is the shift from a teaching driven focus to one based on learning processes and outcomes. Most teachers in business schools, as much as in other parts of universities, are in a process of shifting their planning, delivery and accounting for student learning in the direction of measurement by learning outcomes achieved. John Biggs' (2003) book, *Teaching for Quality Learning at University: What the Student Does*, is the sort of text which is supporting this development. But all are at different places on this journey, and it is important for you to recognize that over and above the intrinsic differences in teaching style that you will encounter, there will be an additional difference based on the extent to which your teachers have made that transition. This implies that, as well as the uncertainties implicit in learning at Masters level, you will need to manage the uncertainties associated with changes to the philosophy and practice of learning. Ideas about learning, like ideas about every other subject, have always been contested and debated, so managing uncertainty is a task with which students throughout the ages have had to cope.

To summarize this section:
- Masters level is about developing expert-level knowledge and understanding about a subject.

- As well as your study and lectures, how you interlink your learning with your experience will be crucial for the process to work effectively.
- Questioning and application to practical problems are what drive the learning process at this level.
- Critique and reflection are essential components of the right approach at this level.
- What teachers teach and what learners learn are similar but not identical.
- At Masters level it is presumed that people will operate as mature learners, with all the autonomy this implies.

Having outlined what could seem quite a challenging task ahead of you, in the next section we start identifying the ways in which it can be made more manageable – indeed much of this guide is intended to help you do this.

● Preparing to study

As we saw in the previous section, Masters level study involves a high degree of knowledge that has to be critically examined and related to your own experience. In this section we shall look at some techniques to help you deal with this scale of study effectively.

> When you have worked through this section you should be able to:
>
> - identify the key tasks necessary for you to get off to a good start on the programme;
> - identify the value and use of mind mapping as a conceptual tool;
> - improve your reading efficiency; and
> - use notes and PowerPoint handouts as tools to develop strong conceptual maps of the subjects you study.

The first few days of any new situation can be daunting, in the sense that there is a lot of information 'thrown' at you, a lot to get familiar with, and people around who seem to know more than you about what's going on. So far as the latter is concerned, there should be such people – they are your tutors! Whilst it can often look as if your colleagues – other students – seem to have got on top of things more quickly than you, in general almost everybody feels overwhelmed to some extent or another. It is a reflection of the fact that there is a lot to deal with at the start of a course.

Activity

Write down the tasks that you think you need to achieve to get going on the course.

Response

Our view is that you will need to achieve the following:

- being clear about what is expected of you by the course team in a general sense;
- being clear about what is expected of you in specific terms – the modules, the milestones, what to do by when;
- being clear what library and computing resources are available to you, which ones are essential to look at now and which can be left until later;
- being sure you know the lecture timetable, the examination dates and the lists of dates for handing in assessed work;
- being sure you know what materials will be supplied by the course team, and when to expect these;
- making sure what to expect from online learning support, such as when electronic lectures slides may be available, and getting your electronic access organized;
- starting the process of identifying additional material that you will need to acquire, such as books, reports, etc., and whether there is likely to be any difficulty about getting access to these at the time you need them (this will be an on-going process, but it is important to get going on it straight away);
- thinking through what personally you hope to get out of the programme – what your individual goals are, over and above the goals of the course itself;
- being clear about what anyone else who has an influence over your life professionally or personally – your employer, perhaps, or a partner, children or other dependents, work colleagues, etc. – may expect of your participation on the course, both during it and after it is over;
- starting the process of identification of experiences that could potentially support your learning, in the manner described earlier (another ongoing process, but one you should begin now);
- having a clear view of how much time you will need to do well on the course, and negotiating with whoever else has some claim on your time to ensure that you can reserve enough to achieve your aim;

> - being aware of the really critical points in your study schedule – such as dates for assignment hand-ins – and the pressures that these can create;
> - making sure that your management of time includes not only sufficient quantity but also enough quality time to enable valuable learning to take place;
> - identifying the physical resources you will need to complete the course successfully (particularly space to study, notebooks/writing materials, computer and internet access, desk, peace and quiet or loud music, storage for learning materials), acquiring these and/or negotiating with relevant parties to ensure that these are in place; and
> - reaffirming with those around you their acceptance and commitment to allowing you the space to complete the course successfully.

This is quite a mixed bag, from the mundane to the more far reaching. Some of these are things you will need to go out and do yourself, whilst some need responses from others. All of them, though, are ultimately your responsibility. They emphasize that you have to approach the course as an active learner, not a passive one. We can now move on to looking at some of the issues directly related to the study activity you will need to embark on. The time management issues will be discussed in the final section.

One tip that has helped a lot of students in their early weeks on the new course is to find the resources which the university or college offers to support them. Many institutions have a Student Support office; sometimes it is called an Academic Writing unit. Most institutions have units to support students from overseas ('International Students'). UKCOSA – the Council for International Education – has helpful guidance notes on studying in a new country (http://www.ukcosa.org.uk/). You might find your institution offers 'Study Skills' classes, or has advice pages on its intranet.

Visual images and intellectual ideas

Much of the material you access on the course is presented in a format that was devised about six hundred years ago – that is, pages of successive printed text. Cultures then were highly oral in nature. People were more adapted to listening and remembering than in the modern world which, partly because of printing itself, has become more attuned to reacting to what we *see*. In Europe, printed books were laid out in lines starting from the top left corner and finishing at the bottom right. So today, many people feel that notes, for example, should look something like this:

- identify the key tasks necessary for you to get off to a good start on the programme

- identify the value and use of mind mapping as a conceptual tool

- make effective use of methods to increase your reading speed

- manage aspects of your time effectively as you get started on the programme

- use notes and PowerPoint handouts as tools to develop strong conceptual maps of the subjects you study

In other words, the material should be ordered rather like a printed book. Sentences follow each other sequentially; points are lined up one after the other; material flows from the top downwards.

But our ways of understanding do not necessarily follow these linear structures – they didn't really even in the fifteenth century. In reality we think in much more diverse ways than linear text allows. We link together words and texts with images, concept diagrams and other visual cues in highly sophisticated and subtle ways that psychologists are still trying to come to terms with.

Our own or other people's notes and handouts should reflect our own conceptual complexity and your notes after a lecture might well be more appropriately structured in a manner such as in Figure 1.1.

Clearly this kind of thing is highly individual. People will make notes of this kind in a manner that fits with their own personal style, their own personal shorthand, what is likely to attract their eye and fix their attention. There is no golden rule. But that is precisely the point about how we should represent our own thinking – there IS no golden rule that we 'must' do it in linear text. Equally of course there is no golden rule that says we should all record thoughts as mind maps or rich pictures. These are tools, and one should use them appropriately.

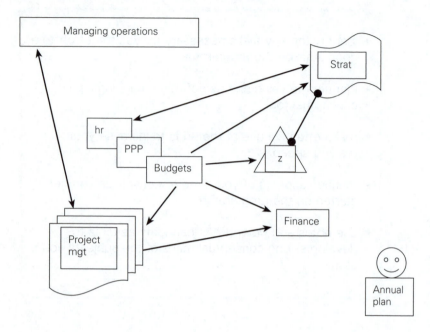

Figure 1.1   Lecture notes

Above all it is important, however you might choose to record your thoughts, not to impose a uniform approach on them. Each topic has its own logic, its own set of points. They will not all follow the same pattern, so you are well advised to represent them in their own terms, each having its own shape and design (and we mean this *literally* here – your set of notes for each topic can have its own visual shape, colouration, box and arrow style, or whatever you choose to use, on the paper).

Many tutors these days follow commercial practice and use PowerPoint as the vehicle for delivery of slide projections. This system also allows the tutor to hand out reduced copies of their slides with a space alongside for comments. Occasionally tutors may prefer to give them out at the end of a session, on the grounds that they do not want to distract students from the lecture itself and they can then focus on the image or text for the associated discussion. More often, however, tutors will give them out during the session so that participants can jot down ideas as these occur to them when looking at a particular slide. The risk here is that you try to capture the whole session in full detail, postponing thinking in the hope of later complete retrieval.

Activity

Refer back now to the notes we asked you to make for the section on the idea of academic work. You will of course have done them in a manner that felt right for you at the time. Review these now – look at your notes and write down a brief summary of the four or five key points that they say to you. Now compare with the commentary we provided, and evaluate the similarities and differences. Many textbooks contain summaries and key bullet points, and it is always a valuable exercise to compare your notes and summaries with those of the author(s). There are at least three benefits of this – one is that it provides consolidation of your learning, another is that it helps to differentiate your own thoughts from the author's, and lastly it helps capture things that seem obvious at the time but may not be so later.

Now find a colleague and compare their notes with yours, and vice versa. The pair of you probably will need to talk through things like personal abbreviations, the significance of scribbled personal pictures and diagrams, and so on. But again discuss what has been left in, what left out – and why in both cases. Also focus on what has been emphasized and what underplayed. Explore the reasons for these between the two of you. Even the way you 'doodle' shapes on your note page may tell you something about how you think and feel about a topic.

Try this exercise after an early lecture, and then occasionally as a refresher during the course. The point is to get you to think more assertively about even the simplest learning activity, such as taking notes. Establish what you want to get out of it and then evaluate whether you have done so. You may decide that your way of doing things is essentially fine. You may come to the view that you tend to put too much in or leave too much out, or that comments you put down at the time of reading are not very clear. The important thing is to raise your awareness of the impact on your learning of the style and form of the activity you undertake, be this note taking, summarising material, listing out key points or weaknesses of an argument or whatever.

Some tutors also post the lecture slides on the course web pages. If these are presented before the lecture, it is useful to prepare by working through them – then the most valuable part of the lecture is to hear how the tutor expands and develops the ideas. Many students also find these slides useful for revision purposes, either soon after the lecture, or in the days before taking an examination or completing an assignment.

These questions may look simple and obvious but they carry with them significant importance for your subsequent revision: What do you do with the

PowerPoint handout given at the start of the session? Do you summarize the lecturer's points by the side? Do you jot down fresh points that occur in discussion? What do you do with the image itself?

There are as many different answers as there are people who sit with such handouts in front of them. One approach, which we know some students have found useful, is that each slide should be treated as a paragraph in its own right. Every paragraph should be a single argument, a basic statement plus some support or elaboration. With each slide there should be one key point, which the other elements on the slide will either support with reasons, or will explain and illustrate in one way or the other. So one thing that you can do with a PowerPoint slide is to isolate the key point and use your own graphics and textual comments to indicate the relationships between the key point and the other ideas presented in the image.

As well as the PowerPoint handouts that you will be given, you will also inevitably receive full handouts at the end of sessions. These might be material from books and academic journals collected by the tutor, or maybe a brief literature review, or they may be interesting articles and other supporting or background material from popular sources such as newspapers, online news services or screen dumps from websites that the tutor thinks could come in useful.

What can or should you do with these? Don't just file them. As we shall argue with other textual material, you should aim to deconstruct them – find the key points and make sure that these are clearly emphasized, add your own commentary and note any links to other sources or ideas. As these are already in photocopied form, write directly on to them, and use highlighters, underlinings and asterisks to personalise them. Interrogate them with the questions you would apply to any source material.

Annotations in handouts and books (only your own, obviously) are perhaps best made in pencil to allow for development and change as you read and understand more. 'Post-it' notes are a much more flexible method of annotation, as they can sit securely in the book, but can be moved, removed or amended as appropriate.

It is worth noting that whilst electronic note-taking has the same aim as handwritten notes, the change in medium creates different opportunities. For example, some students prefer to use a spreadsheet rather than a word processing programme to take down ideas, because they have found it easier to later manipulate these, for example juxtaposing different cells. There is no best way to make use of these resources – the important thing is for you to try out different approaches and see what works best *for you.*

Reading effectiveness

On your Masters, you will need to do a lot of reading to complete the programme successfully. But it is simply not possible to read everything as thoroughly and as attentively as its authors would want. You have to get through a lot of material, and hence you have to develop techniques of working through texts effectively.

In the chapter on writing assignments we will discuss certain methods of getting content from textbooks quickly, without having to read carefully every paragraph. We will not duplicate these here, but some aspects will benefit from early consideration:

1   *Decide whether to read the material at all.* A very quick scan of the headings, key terms, and text used in any diagrams, bold faced or larger font text, should give you an indication whether the passage is appropriate. In this respect a text broken into sections and with relatively short paragraphs is much easier to decide upon than one that is full of long stretches of text.

2   *Decide what you want to get out of the text.* Whilst on this programme, it is best not to look at a text without having a question you need answering. That way, you will home in on what is relevant to your study, and you will know when to stop.

3   *Plan your reading time.* Get clear how much time you can allocate to reading at any specific time, especially how much time you can spend reading before fatigue sets in. A few minutes of real thinking are worth hours of page-turning.

4   *Get the physical environment right.* Some physical factors are so obvious that we ignore them – seating should be at an appropriate height (which may not be the same as the appropriate level for working at a computer – keyboards should usually be set lower than writing and reading desks). Lighting should be strong enough to read by but not at a great contrast with the ambient light levels of the room – both of these can cause eye strain, and with that comes fatigue and headaches. Some students can concentrate with unbelievable noise all around them, some need their own choice of music, while others need silence. Studying can be as varied as any other activity and trying to maintain an identical environment each time might be counter-productive. Whatever approach you choose, treat yourself to some luxuries – it is going to be a large part of your life for a while and you might as well try to enjoy it!

5   *Know what you can get through.* Look through each chapter or section that you intend to read. Make a quick check on the length of

the item. You will do some work on the course to help you understand what your reading speed is and how you can enhance it. On that basis you should be able to evaluate how much you can get through in a fixed period of time. As a very rough rule of thumb, many people find that with practice they can manage the following speeds:

- familiar material – about two and a half minutes for a page of continuous prose on single spaced A4
- difficult or unfamiliar material – about double this.

6   *Set yourself clear targets, and work in bite-sized chunks.* Given this range, you can see that a section of about 20–25 pages of well spaced material that you feel fairly familiar with, with a number of diagrams, illustrations, headings, etc., should take you less than an hour, whilst a densely written chapter of the same length, with some unfamiliar or difficult argument, and few diagrams, might take more than two hours. In this latter case, it would make sense to break this into smaller chunks. The main thing is to have some clear and realistic targets and then create some motivation to achieve these. The motivation might be nothing more than a personal promise of a drink or a snack – these apparently trivial issues matter more than the attention they usually get! But it is important to create a sense of achievable challenge and subsequent success – this is a crucial motivation builder.

Understanding and remembering

Many people, when they start their Masters course, worry about how they will be able to remember all the facts and figures that they will be presented with. The short answer is that they shouldn't bother! At this level it is not generally a matter of memorising lots of factual material, so much as understanding what you can do with it all. In the rest of our lives we have to remember some things, but most other really useful material is kept in manuals for reference. The one serious exception to this on your course is the factual knowledge you will need to recall in an unseen examination – the golden rule here is to get clarity about this from your tutor (see Chapter 3).

If the things you need to remember are associated with understanding, it is best to develop approaches to learning and thinking, rather than for memorizing. There are techniques for learning directly, such as mnemonics, and these might be useful for learning short lists and similar collections of material that can be expressed in a word or two, but they do not help much at Masters level.

One approach which students have found helpful is to develop a visual representation of the concept which depicts its structure and inter-relationships. This will be much more readily absorbed by the mind and more easily accomplishes the connection between 'right-brain' and 'left-brain' activity that is essential for learning at a deep level.

You start with the key word of the topic – and write it in a balloon in the centre of the page

Then you add further balloons for each idea that is suggested to you by the main concept

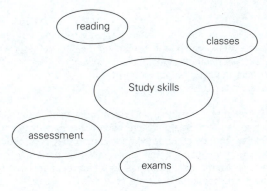

Connections are drawn in as appropriate, and additional balloons that represent further associations

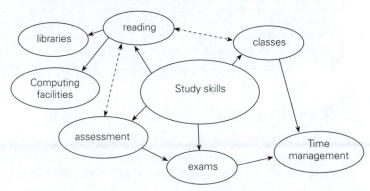

Figure 1.2 Mind-mapping

The main methods for achieving this are to link text and graphics. One way is the technique of mind-mapping, an example of which is shown in Figure 1.2.

This approach is often added to by means of personal symbolic icons. Some people find it useful to add in geographical icons such as crossed swords to indicate a point of conflict. This kind of 'rich picture' is often attributed to Peter Checkland (1984), whose book *Systems Thinking, Systems Practice* is a clear example of the links between text and visual as a means of expressing concepts – see especially chapters 6 and 7.

Creating links is a meaning-fixing activity. If you go through the activity of creating a mind map or rich picture then you will find that the very activity will help consolidate your learning. But be warned – it will fix your understanding of the topic in the manner in which you have done the mind map. If you later change your view then you may have to re-do the mind map (this might be no bad thing, however).

Activity

With a colleague, identify a subject about which you both think you know very little. Now do mind maps on this subject. Agree a time for this – say ten minutes. Add additional balloons for every separate idea that occurs to you, whether directly linked to the main topic or to subsidiary ones.

You will most likely find that you know more than you initially thought! Many people start off by thinking 'I don't know anything about this' but find that when they come to do a mind map they can produce rather more than they expected. This is particularly important when you come to sit exams, as sometimes your first reactions about which questions you cannot answer are not reliable.

Compare your mind maps. You will doubtless have quite different products. One may have quickly done a great deal, the other may have thought more about the topic and consequently done just a few balloons. Each of these is fine – after all these are YOUR mind maps. Try to recount to each other the thinking you had as to why you included certain points and excluded others.

Summary:

In this section we have briefly referred to a range of potential techniques to help you learn more effectively, but in practice these are all very much a matter of what works for the individual.

● Making time work for you

The final, and perhaps most telling, issue to deal with in this introduction is your use of time. In fact this is a sizeable topic, so we shall deal with some of it here and some of it in Chapter 4. In this section we shall look at the issues that are most directly relevant to you when you start the programme, whilst in Chapter 4 we will look at the issues that affect you as you are progressing through the course. The issue of managing the limited time you have when you do an examination will be dealt with in the chapter on exams.

How good are you at managing your time? Most of us have a self-image that is based on various experiences in the past. Professional life tends to force even less well-organised people to work systematically and plan the use of their time. There is to some degree a matter of style involved – some people approach issues slowly and in a more relaxed fashion, others are very tightly focused and direct. All the same, on a Masters programme it is essential to be highly effective in the manner in which you use time.

Question

What do you think are the key symptoms of a poor use of time?

Response

We suggest the following:

- key deadlines are missed;
- the individual has many people waiting for an answer to their enquiries;
- the individual is always busy;
- the individual is paralysed and unable to act;
- priorities are not clear or not followed;
- the individual is often unusually prone to aggressive or defensive behaviour.

The management of time is an essential aspect of management competence. When people do not manage their time effectively, it's more than their own job that is affected. Usually it places pressure on those who work closely with them – people waiting for information to be passed through, subordinates who are often expected to work harder or for longer in order to cope with the manager's ineffectiveness. And bad time management can damage personal life as well. A person who is under pressure because of their mismanagement of time is likely to be difficult to communicate with, may well work long hours or bring work home that they do not satisfactorily resolve. In some cases excess levels of stress can even be linked to the dangers of coronary heart disease.

Activity

Think back over the activities of the last couple of weeks. Try to recall how many of them you completed to your satisfaction, how many are still outstanding, how many ended up being so rushed that they were not well done.

Now check back with other people who were involved with these activities and see if your impression is the same as theirs.

Response

If there is a disparity between perceptions of the way you manage time, it can be instructive to think why. More important is the issue of being rushed. It is not necessarily a bad thing to be very busy. It is problematic if it distracts you from giving tasks and activities the time they need.

Activity

A useful additional method of getting an idea of how well you deal with time is to keep a diary or MP3 recording of all the activities you carried out over a specified time period – often a week is selected as it gives a reasonable range of potential demands. It is essential that you look at the whole of the week, not just study-related activities or work-based activity. Personal life must also be added in, as on this course it is likely that much of your study will be taken out of personal time. One problem is that filling out a diary itself takes time, but the analysis often surprises people and is therefore worth the effort.

Response

Of course, what you find out is specific to you and your range of responsibilities and commitments. The important thing is how you can learn from it. Once you have made a record of your activities, analyse them for patterns. How often do you work on your own in your office? How often at meetings? How many times did you do work related to the course – and for how long each time?

Once you have some idea of the patterns of time usage in your life as a whole, then look at your reasons for the activities. Many of them may seem be fully justifiable, but when you have identified the amount of time you need for the course you may have to look carefully at these in order to see where time can be saved.

Activity

What are the demands on your time? Identify each area that requires time from you – for example work, family/personal life, travel to and from work, eating and other domestic activities, leisure/fitness, sleep, and the course. Try to make an estimate of the time required for each of these – the previous activity will give you some indication.

A part-time course may well take up at least 15 hours of your time each week, beyond the timetabled attendance (that's one hour each evening and two periods of five hours each at weekends). A full time course is usually compressed into a shorter period – often a calendar year, and you will probably need to *at least* double the number of hours per week that you will need to commit to the course.

Now add these hours up – it is when they exceed 168 hours per week that you might need to apply some of the ideas of good time management!

The most important moves are to:

- prioritize,
- eliminate unnecessary activity,
- work more efficiently – e.g. avoiding duplicating activities,
- negotiate for more study time from those who have a call on your other types of time.

You might be interested to know how the lecturers who have designed your course have gone about it. While there is no formal agreement about this, most UK universities work on the basis that full time postgraduate students have approximately 1,800 hours for studying in any calendar year. That is notionally 40 hours per week for 45 weeks. Most Masters courses are currently valued at 180 credit points, so the simple calculation is that a credit point might be worth about 10 hours of study. Each lecturer knows how many credit points their own module is 'worth', and therefore the number of hours (in college and in private study taken together) an average student should spend studying. So, for example, if a one-year course has 10 taught modules of equal credit value, the study and assessment for each module should run for 120 hours, which could be made up of between 20 to 40 hours in class and 100 to 80 hours for private study and writing the assignment. Some students may need longer, others may complete their work in less time, but this rough calculation is a way of guiding you in working out what to expect. Most Masters courses are 180 credits (perhaps using 120 credits for the taught course and a further 60 for the Dissertation). Check closely with your course handbook to find the actual hours for your particular course.

Prioritizing

The classic issue here is that what is *urgent* is not always what is *important*. Every commitment can be mapped on to a grid as can be seen here:

	Urgent	Not urgent
Important		
Not important		

For each of these there is an appropriate strategy, such as:

	Urgent	Not urgent
Important	Act now	Plan time for this
Not important	Delegate or do it very quickly	Ignore

The main conflict here is that unimportant but urgent issues take up too much time and there is little time for the long-term priorities. Your course is a perfect example of this. An assignment may be due five weeks away, whereas if you are in employment, a task such as completing the weekly staff returns may have to be done by Friday. So the assignment takes a back seat. The assignment may well come up the priority list as the due date approaches, but this leads to the 'Sunday night panic,' which is highly undesirable for several reasons: (a) something unexpected may happen on the night that prevents completion (b) when you are really pressed for time, computers and printers seem to have a sixth sense to let you down and crash

(c) most important of all, you will not have the opportunity to reflect on the first draft of your work and learn as much as you could from the experience.

As well as putting aside anything that is neither urgent nor important, you can work towards a resolution of at least part of this issue by breaking a task into component parts and planning time for each of those. It is then easier to keep progress going on a task that has many components if each of these has a psychological identity of its own.

For an assignment, then, you might break up the tasks as follows:

- preliminary reading of the basic material,
- searching for further reading material,
- reading additional material,
- drafting the outline of the answer,
- consultation with others to compare notes,
- writing up the first draft,
- reviewing the first draft – ideally with colleagues on the course,
- writing up the final version, and
- printing off, binding and delivery.

Each of these has its own appropriate time-scale and it is therefore easier to assign them a degree of urgency as well as importance. For example, if you let slip on the second stage it will be very difficult to catch up, as hunting for books and articles takes a significant amount of time – often a text has to be ordered and delivered from a remote location. It is particularly useful to arrange collaboration with others as there can then be a degree of peer pressure to meet common deadlines and targets – quite apart from the considerable benefits from working together. The most effective approach is to work back from the deadline in a simple form of project management – if it takes two days to print and deliver, and four days to write the final draft, then it will need to be with your colleagues for review at least 16 days before the deadline (to give them 10 days to fit the reading into their schedules), and so on.

While most students on most courses make good progress through their assignments and assessments, some get into difficulties. Within your programme handbook and module guides you will find regulations about the number of pieces of work you should submit and the timetables by which they should be finished. If you are a student who is returning to university after years in business, or if you are a student whose previous education has been outside the UK, it is especially important for you to find these regulations and realise what they exactly mean – recent UK graduates will be familiar with them already. Usually, all modules have assignments and deadlines, and in some institutions the regulations covering work not submitted, delayed submissions or opportunities to re-take examinations can be very strict. If you get into difficulties with time and workload, keep your tutors fully informed, and then they might be able to use their 'extenuating circumstances' regulations. They want to teach you, not fail you.

As the course progresses

As you progress through the programme, you may find the way you manage time changes. If your course has been well-designed, you will settle into a rhythm of reading and writing. Or you might find that many of the assignments are issued for similar deadlines, and you will have to be very well organized and focused to make the best of your work.

You will also, as your understanding of the subjects of the course improves, be able to distinguish more quickly between what is useful for you and what is not relevant. As your intellectual frameworks develop, you will find that you can understand material more quickly, and your notes will be produced more quickly and more efficiently.

Whilst you will save time in these respects, what you will also find is that collaboration brings many benefits, and therefore you may well spend more of your learning time with your colleagues. This can be time-consuming, as it takes five people longer than one to get through something – the difference is that the end product is often of higher quality. One way, though, in which working with others can still help you to manage time is to share reading – each member reads a different text and brings their summary of it to the group, so that each member of the group gets the benefit of five pieces of reading. We offer other ideas for group activity later in the text. In whatever ways the pattern of your work changes, it is sensible to run the time management analysis exercise at intervals to keep on top of the pressures.

Summary:

In this introductory chapter we have looked at the nature of academic writing, study at Masters level, the special nature of a management course, and the differences between the expectations of students and teachers.

We looked at the use of notes, and we have also looked at some of the key things you need to get started on the programme, including the management of your time, the best approaches to deal with the volume of reading and the use of visual imagery as an aid to understanding and memory.

In the next chapter, we shall look at one of the key aspects of your experience of the programme – getting the best from reading and lectures.

2 Getting the Most from Lectures and Reading

Introduction

Many students regard attending lectures and reading textbooks as their main learning activities. It is more productive, however, to see them as *opportunities* – experiences from which we can learn. Neither lectures nor reading will teach you automatically. It is *your approach* to learning from them which determines what you will get out of them, far more than the quality or quantity of the learning experiences themselves. With a Business or Management Masters course, the additional challenge is to be able to apply your knowledge and understanding to concrete organizational realities.

In general, what you learn can be measured as a contribution to:

- your ability to complete assignments satisfactorily and pass exams; and
- your personal and professional development.

So far as personal/professional development is concerned, everyone has different aspirations and plans, and we will leave you to focus on these for yourself. We assume, however, that everyone has a vested interest in doing as well as possible in the assessment programme, so there will be reference to this in the text.

This chapter will address the following areas:

1 **Getting the most from classes**: what you can gain from the taught elements of your programme in terms of general learning.
2 **Approaches to reading**: the range of reading based sources available to you.
3 **Accessing and using sources**: the management of and extraction of value from different sources.
4 **Online and other electronic sources**: accessing and using material via the world wide web, and the academic sources available.

● Getting the most from classes

When you have completed this section, you should be able to:

- identify the key activities necessary to prepare effectively for participation in a class;
- describe the different approaches to teaching adopted by lecturers, and identify strategies for maximizing the learning to be gained from class attendance;
- identify the appropriate activities to undertake after a class to get the most benefit from it.

Preparing for a class

What is a class? It is a broad term that can cover many different kinds of teacher-to-group interactions, including: formal lectures, discussion based lectures, small group tutorials, seminars, practical workshops, demonstrations and guest lectures. We will generally use the term 'lecture' in this chapter to focus on classes where the teacher is responsible for the content and for the direction of the discussion. Before anything else, you should get clear whether the teaching session or class you are going to attend is a lecture, discussion, seminar, or whatever.

Remember that when you are studying business at Masters' level, you will be expected to develop general intellectual skills to a high level, showing originality in your ability to apply knowledge to business realities, demonstrating sound judgement, and dealing with complex issues. Your engagement with what happens in class should be focused on developing these skills as well as mastering the knowledge gained during the class.

Before you attend a class, there are three key questions you need to address:

- What is the 'real' syllabus of the module?
- What does the lecturer expect to do, and what contribution is required from you as a student?
- What place does this session have in the overall scheme, and what kind of conceptual context will be assumed?

The 'real' syllabus is not necessarily the same as the official one. Syllabuses can change over time. Tutors change, and this can change the emphasis on different aspects of the content. Business practice changes and the content of a syllabus will often reflect this. Usually syllabuses are slightly updated on a year by year basis, so that what is covered in the fifth year that a unit is taught may differ significantly from what was originally taught. Unless a text-book is revised frequently it will begin to look out of date after a few years.

Course documents are also only an approximate guide to what will be taught. Schemes of work often refer only very briefly to what is to be covered. A session title such as 'Logistics' may cover the whole field, may deal with just the key points, or may focus on just one or two typical issues, leaving you to learn about the rest from private study.

For these reasons, we advise that when preparing to attend a session you need to draw on the full range of available cues as to what the session will be about.

Activity

Pick a session title from a scheme of work on one of your taught units.

- Before looking at any textbooks or other materials, write down briefly what you think it is likely to cover.
- Now cross check your understanding with the main recom-mended textbooks, module guides and supporting materials.
- Using any gap between your understanding of the topic and the coverage of the textbooks, identify two or three key learning objectives for yourself – *'When I have attended this session, I should be able to . . .'*

The objectives of teaching are extremely important. Most people think of teaching in terms of the activities of the teacher, but in fact the most impor-tant thing should be the outcomes that each learner achieves. Many lecturers today will describe what they are trying to do in terms of *'intended learning outcomes'*. These are statements in very clear terms that set out what a student should be able to do as a result of participation in the course and the successful completion of the assessments. They should provide a clear link between what happens in a classroom and in your private study time, and what you will be assessed on. There should be overall outcomes for the unit, and possibly specified outcomes for each session. You are strongly advised to make sure you clearly understand the intended learning outcomes of a module or a session. The overall learning outcomes for a unit or course are your keystone for understanding how you will be assessed.

Before approaching any learning event, especially a teaching session, each participant should have a clear sense of (a) what they hope to get out of it, (b) what the teacher hopes to achieve by delivering the session, (c) how the outcomes of that session will fit together with the outcomes of the unit as a whole and even (d) how it contributes to the broader outcomes of the whole programme.

There are three layers of objectives for any session:

- the overall unit and course intended learning outcomes, which will help you to put this specific session into context;
- the teacher's aims, which will be common for all the students in the class; and
- your personal objectives, which will help you tailor the session to your own needs.

Teachers often aim to cover a certain amount of content in a class. They will have determined how much content by reference to the number of teaching hours allocated to this subject over a term or semester, the depth which they want students to reach, and the number of topics to be dealt with. As well as covering specific topics, they will also want to express academic values that they want you to emulate, such as critical analysis, building on other people's ideas, acknowledging sources, making managerial judgement etc. Be careful, though – just because a teacher has 'covered' a subject does not mean of itself that you have learnt it.

A further issue that you should consider before attending a class is the level of technical or theoretical language that the teacher will expect you to understand. Teachers inevitably have to make choices about the kind of language that is most suitable for the delivery of their content. By and large the later a session is in a sequence of lectures, the greater is the assumed background of prior knowledge, and therefore the more complex the terminology that the teacher will use without explanation. Good teachers often vary the speed with which they cover topics, taking early sessions slowly, trying to build up your understanding, but sometimes dealing with later topics swiftly on the basis that you have already grasped the basics.

One useful way of keeping track of how your knowledge builds up in a sequence of classes is to keep a section of your notes solely to record your understanding of key terms. This becomes your mini-reference for the foundational concepts of a subject area. It can also be your starting point for exam revision. Often you need do no more than highlight some words, and then later review and record their meaning in the context of what else you have newly learned in that session.

Another way to help keep track of the overall 'shape' of the content of a course unit is the use of simple summary texts. The further you go on the academic ladder the more you tend to know about increasingly narrow fields and the more comfortable you are with specialised books and articles. But everyone needs to have some quick and simple reference points to remind them of the whole subject. It's like finding your way around an unfamiliar city – we need to know the details of our own location, but in order to understand that properly we need to have a much larger map that covers the whole terrain, though inevitably in less detail.

For this reason, it can be very helpful to have a short, simple book (perhaps even a chapter from an encyclopaedia) that condenses down the key areas of the whole of a subject to a few essentials. This is not a substitute for detailed study of the larger academic textbooks. It is rather an *aide-mémoire*. It does not need to be perfect – though it is essential that you know how comprehensive it is. It is there to help you map out where each topic goes, what the inter-relationships are, and therefore what concepts and what language is likely to be assumed by the teacher when delivering a lecture.

A common question is: 'How much preliminary reading should we do?' It should be clear enough that if a tutor says that it is essential to read a specific article before turning up at a class, then their plan is to work on the subject matter of that article. It is less clear when a tutor says it would be 'useful' to read certain things before attending the class. Our guidance is that you should try to read in advance, that you should try to encourage your classmates to do the same (to make sure the questions and discussions are really useful), that you should attempt to integrate your reading into your comments, your questions and your discussion in the class, and that you should encourage the lecturer to build on the knowledge that you are bringing to the session. Many lecturers find a hard part of their job is to be constantly introducing brand new topics to students and would much prefer to be able to use their sessions to develop and manipulate the ideas and knowledge that they know their students have. By reading in advance you will ensure you will get the best from the time spent with your lecturers.

So, before attending a taught session, you should:

- be clear about the overall syllabus and the place of the session within it;
- set yourself personal learning goals for that session;
- ensure that you have sufficient grasp of what has been taught in the course till now that you will be able to follow the lecture; and
- establish what the teacher expects from you in the way of preparatory work, and make sure you do any essential reading or case-work, and at least try to briefly skim read a relevant chapter to get a feel for the rough outlines of the topic to be discussed.

Different approaches to teaching and learning in class

The 'transmission' model of lecturing may be represented as in the diagram:

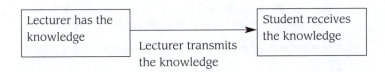

This model of higher education presumes that lectures are the driving forces of learning (in fact, research in higher education over the last two decades has suggested that *perceptions of assessment* drives learning). The model depicts the teacher as the active participant, and the learner as a passive receiver of what the teacher 'transmits'. It can even result in assessments in which the lecturer checks how much of what they have transmitted the student has remembered.

But in reality there should be a much wider range of intellectual connections going on than this suggests. This should especially be so with Masters level learning, where you are not just receiving information but should be probing it, questioning the research that supports it, testing out its applicability in different contexts, and so on.

One can depict what might happen in a lecture along a dimension. At one end is the transfer of information which the student might remember. At the other end is the possibility that students engage with ideas to the point that they change their understandings and concepts. Each end is more suited to a different kind of class, so a transmission lecture is focussed on delivery by the teacher, but is not so well-designed for conceptual change, which is focussed on the needs of the participants. A teaching session based around a lot of small group work and occasional full class discussion will probably help with developing concepts, but may be inefficient where the lecturer thinks that covering a lot of straight knowledge is required. This model of teaching is derived from the work of Prosser and Trigwell (1999).

You will have deduced from reading this chapter so far that we believe Masters-level students have a major role to play in shaping their own learning. Whatever may have been your experience as an undergraduate, or however you may have been taught before, Masters-level learning is about working with new knowledge, questioning it, shaping it and challenging it. This raises one key question, which relates to how active you should be in a class.

The SOLO model

A very useful model that helps to clarify what we have been discussing is the SOLO model, which stands for Structure of Observed Learning Outcome, devised by John Biggs (2003). His model identifies at least four different levels of learning:

Uni-structural: where only one specific aspect of a topic has been grasped.

Multi-structural: where several aspects have been grasped, but are understood in isolation from each other.

Relational: where the various aspects of the topic have been understood as being integrated and in relation to each other.

Extended abstract: where someone is able to generalize from their relational understanding, apply the idea in new contexts, formulate a more abstract rule or concept that subsumes the topic.

In all study, some uni- and multi-structural learning is necessary simply to get going. But at Masters level you should always be looking to achieve relational learning, and towards the end of your course you should certainly expect to move into extended abstraction.

We will discuss later on how you can use this model to help you understand more clearly the intended learning outcomes of a course, the teacher's aims for a particular session, and the main purposes of assessments.

You can read more on this model of teaching in Biggs, J. (2003) *Teaching for Quality Learning at University: What the Student Does.* 2nd edn. Buckingham: Society for Research into Higher Education and Open University Press.

Note-taking is an art, and there is no one best way of doing it, but it helps to be aware of the different purposes to which notes may be put. Look at the examples in Figure 2.1 which were all taken during the same lecture on accounting, and then suggest what the three different students were trying to accomplish with these.

We can identify at least three different purposes, then, for note-taking:

- to set down a brief record of the main points of the lecture,
- to help you map out the conceptual structure of the argument as the lecture proceeds, and/or
- to provide a stimulus for you later to work through the content of the lecture.

None of these is better or worse than the others. We cannot make that judgement until we know *what else* you may be doing to support and structure

Example 1

Budgeting – *Textbook* ch 6

Budget periods – tax periods, reporting timescales

Hierarchy of objectives – corporate – divisional – departmental – team

Draft budgets and consolidation

Control methods – standard costing, cash limits, activity limits, objectives

Example 2

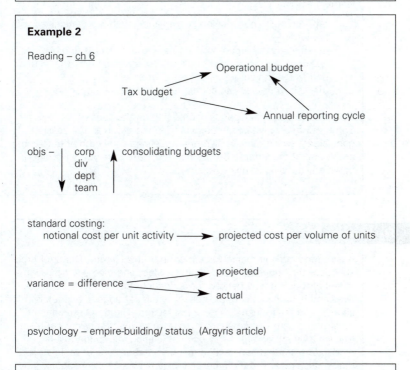

Example 3

Text ch 6

Tax/reporting periods
Consolidation
Control
Human aspects

Figure 2.1   Note-taking

Question

In what ways can students in a classroom or lecture situation take an active role?

Answer

There may be times when a tutor expects you to be active, such as when they ask for questions, or when an exercise is set to be completed in class. But even when classroom participation is not encouraged, there are ways in which you can be proactive in your learning within a classroom, such as:

- taking notes – not copying but engaging with the material as you are writing;
- questioning the argument – perhaps noting doubts and queries;
- seeking clarification of difficult points – perhaps with the lecturer, perhaps with your fellow students later; and
- offering examples and contributions, when the opportunity arises.

How you do this will depend in some part on the style of the lecturer. Some will freely invite contributions from the group as the session goes along, whilst others will prefer questions and comments to come at the end. If the latter, then you need to make sure you have jotted down any puzzling issues to raise later.

Response

It is not too difficult to see the structure of this lecture. The tutor probably gave the suggested reading at the start, and then went through a series of topics – time periods for budgeting, the hierarchy of objectives and how this affects the consolidation of budgets, budgetary control, and the human/psychological factors. The three students had most of the same information. It is clear that the first two were trying to have a brief map of the key points. Relating this to the SOLO model, one student approached this from a more uni- or multi-structural perspective, and the other (the pictorial) in a more relational way. The third, however, is less easy to link to SOLO – it looks more like simply a set of triggers. Key words have been put down but there is no evidence of any further thinking involved.

your learning. There are several things that one can do with notes after the lecture. For example, rewriting the main points from a different perspective. Sharing notes with others can be useful – seeing what you put down and omitted in comparison with others. Writing notes for others to explain one of the points teaches you a lot – inevitably you will write in greater detail, and spell out things which, if the notes were solely for you, you would probably write in your own shorthand. Or try cross-linking points to material from previous sessions, or to other modules.

Given that your ultimate aim is to move towards an abstracted understanding of the subject matter, you should try to indicate in your notes where a point is an opinion (of the tutor or someone else, or even your own thought as the lecture proceeded) as opposed to something that is presented as accepted orthodoxy. Of course, you should be able to challenge both.

We referred earlier to the plans and intentions that a tutor may have for a session. Clearly these may vary widely, depending on the nature of the subject, its place within the overall teaching scheme, the aims of the programme as a whole, the style of the teacher, and so on. The clearer you are about what the teacher is trying to achieve the more effectively you can learn from the process.

One central question that every teacher has to deal with is how much of a topic to cover in class and how much to leave for private study. This will be based on their teaching aims – if these are more on the information transmission side then they will deliver structured linear lectures where they run through all the key points. This will likely lead to uni- and multi-structural learning outcomes. If, however, they are aiming for conceptual change approach, then they may deliberately just cover some representative aspects in depth, and leave it to you to fill in the gaps with your own private study. This should lead to relational and extended abstract outcomes. In Masters level learning, you would expect more of the lecturing to be guiding your own private study, so just attending the lectures will not be enough. This may be different from some of your undergraduate experiences.

A second key question is whether the lecturer chooses to present the material following an orthodox framework, or decides to formulate their own intellectual structure for the subject matter. The latter is often tempting for a teacher when they are lecturing on a subject on which they have done a lot of research, especially where they have published books or articles in that area. It also can be particularly stimulating for students to know that they are dealing with new ideas drawn from up-to-date research.

So it is clear that your teachers will work in different ways – some focussing on the imparting of knowledge, others on the development of your understanding.

Remember that it is *your own* understanding, *your* own conceptual framework or mind map, that matters for your learning. At this level your personal constructs become as important, if not more so, than those of your teachers. You will also have to apply your learning in your professional life as a manager. So it is perfectly legitimate for you to devise your own structures and frameworks for subjects. In doing so you represent the material to yourself – re-present, that is, present over again, which is an active engagement with material rather than a passive one of swallowing whole what is provided for you. And this is the best way to achieve the extended abstract learning that is the essence of Masters level study.

Question

How can you get the best from each type of teaching?

Answer

You need to develop activities and approaches that will balance out whatever the tutor does in the classroom. Where there is a lot of in-depth discussion on a few topics, you need to read around the rest of the syllabus. Where there is a lot of information transmission, you will need to focus on the application of these ideas and concentrate on the conceptual changes.

In doing this, the more you can make private study *not* private but group-based, the more effective you can be. A small learning group, for example, can act as a seminar group exploring areas in greater depth, or can split up the process of collecting and structuring the detail for a range of topics.

It is an extremely valuable practice at all stages of the learning process to think through and at times write down the key questions that you would ask someone concerning a particular topic. This can help you focus your understanding. Questions can cover the full range of areas of learning, including the following:

- to bring out the basic elements of knowledge,
- to relate one area to others,
- to probe the depth of specific features of a topic,
- to put the topic into a broader context, and
- to evaluate the arguments for or against a particular idea or technique.

There are potential difficulties at each end of the continuum from information transmission to conceptual change. The conceptual change approach can often seem vague, especially to someone who is used to an information transmission model. Similarly, the transmission approach can look too directive, especially if someone thinks of their own learning in terms of conceptual change. It is a matter of getting an understanding of what a tutor is trying to do and then seeing how well you as an individual can make use of that approach and what additional work you may need to do to complement class-based activity.

Activity

Imagine the following comments had been made about teaching styles on a Business Masters course:

1 The lecturer planted an idea, but he never told us that we were supposed to go and fill out the subjects from our own reading. We were left not knowing what to do.
2 The sessions covered all the ground we needed.
3 The tutor went into too much detail.
4 The lecturer always helped us put the topic into the wider context so we knew where we were.

What expectations relating to the continuum of learning are reflected here (a) on the part of the lecturer (b) on the part of the student making the comment? And what should you, as a student do to compensate?

Response

1
Lecturer: expecting conceptual change.
Student: expecting information transmission.
Compensating activity: programme of reading, planned around (a) how many topics, (b) how much time and (c) what level of detail is required.

2
Lecturer: offering information transmission.
Student: expecting information transmission.
Compensating activity: seminars and group discussion to move towards relational and abstract understanding.

3
Lecturer: offering information transmission.
Student: expecting conceptual change.
Compensating activity: two responses. The lecturer is probably not going to cover the full range of topics, and the student might not engage in much conceptual change. So, programme of reading, planned around (a) how many topics, (b) how much time and (c) what level of detail is required, and seminars and group discussion to move towards relational and abstract understanding.

4
Lecturer: conceptual change.
Student: conceptual change.
Compensating activity: further reading, for both detail and intellectual enjoyment.

The main thing to learn from these examples of student feedback is how important it is to understand what your teacher is trying to do. *A great deal of ineffective learning in the classroom can be put down to tutors trying to accomplish one thing and students expecting something different.* The classroom involves two way dialogue to be fully successful, and this applies as much to the orientation to learning adopted by teacher and students as it does to other aspects of the delivery.

You should therefore approach classroom sessions *tactically*. You know what you want to get out of the session, you also should be able to identify the tutor's prime objectives. There are therefore several specific actions you can take that will help you derive the most benefit out of a lecture. Do remember, though, that the lecture is an event for all participants, and your individual needs might have to be modified in the light of what the class as a whole is looking for.

- Decide what you want to hear discussed in depth in the lesson, and make comments and ask questions that will help that happen.
- Offer examples for clarification, or to explore the limits of the idea under discussion.
- Never reject, out of hand, contributions from others in the class. Take separate notes on questions that other people ask – especially the ones that seem to you pointless, because they may have a very different conceptual basis from yours.
- Always ask the tutor to explain something if it seems important but is not clear to you – obviously if this is happening too often you may need to ask yourself if you are doing sufficient backup reading to follow the lectures, but if it is a relatively rare event, then something which is unclear to you may well be unclear to others; you may do everyone a favour by asking for clarification.

Activities to undertake after the class
There are several important things you can do to consolidate your learning. Of course these take time, but learning that is done well at this stage is much more easily recalled when writing assignments and more easily revised when preparing for examinations.

- Complete all activities that the teacher specifically directs you to do.
- Follow up the main references (usually for each lecture topic there will be two or three of these, but in practice if you look, at this stage, at one of these references then it will make it easier to grasp what the other key references are getting at when you read/revise them later).

- Write (make up) exam question(s) that you think are appropriate for this topic.
- Make time with colleagues in the class or syndicate to discuss a session to confirm understanding.
- Decide what was the tutor's overall aim – information transfer or conceptual change – and then identify for yourself the private learning activities that will *complement* this.

This is especially important for the study of Management – much more so than for many other subjects. For Management is a multi-disciplinary field. It draws on a wide range of disciplines, each with its own rules and paradigms – psychology, economics, sociology, information systems, game theory and many others. This requires the greatest flexibility on the part of teachers and learners. It also makes it far more difficult for a tutor to cover all the relevant approaches to a topic within the confines of even a three-hour learning session. And most problematic of all, there are no set rules for integrating individual items of knowledge into a whole, so you have to develop your own relational knowledge in many cases.

This might sound challenging – it is. But it has advantages. One is that not only is there no single right answer, there is no single *type* of right answer. So you can develop your own style of thinking. What matters then is to be able to give a coherent and justified account of your view. You can often, therefore, choose to approach an issue in a different manner from how the tutor presents it in class, but it does mean that you must be prepared to rigorously support your point of view.

> *To summarize the key points of this section*:
>
> - Begin by getting as clear as you can about what you hope to get out of a class, as well as what the tutor intends.
> - Start getting familiar with the field by reading an easy intro- ductory text.
> - Identify whether the tutor is nearer to a conceptual change approach or an information transmission one and adjust your behaviour in the classroom.
> - Use interventions (questions and comments) and note taking systematically to help you achieve what you want from the session.
> - Listen to all questions – the daftest sounding ones are usually not daft at all, but can be useful indicators of alter- native ways of approaching the topic.

● **Approaches to reading**

> When you have worked through this section, you should be able to:
>
> • identify the range of textual resources available to you;
> • use a range of approaches to reading to maximum effect; and
> • use references effectively.

Identifying the range of textual resources

If you were asked what is the range of textual material available to you that could support your Masters study, doubtless you would come up with a list including the following:

- Books
- Tutor handouts
- Journal articles
- Newspapers and magazines
- Podcasts
- Weblogs (blogs)
- Internet information pages
- Internet discussion groups

What is important, though is not simply the range, but (a) *how wide* the range is and (b) *what you do with it*. Of course you should focus your reading on the key texts that are prescribed on the course, but a really successful student (or academic) will often draw links between unlikely materials. Keeping a keen eye on the possible relevance of what (for you) might be casual reading, for example, will often help you to spot a useful and original fact, incident or idea. The daily paper is a perfect example – many people will read directly a small range of stories that directly interest them, and not pay too much attention to the rest. But if you are alert to the possibility that somewhere in its pages the paper may have something of value for your studies you are likely to do a much more focussed skim of all the main stories. Similarly, it is always useful to have a quick look at a wide range of internet discussion areas.

The way to make the most of this is to systematically capture material that might be useful which you accidentally come across: note down useful or potentially interesting references, keep a scrapbook or folder with articles from newspapers (or their references) that might come in useful, file reports and ephemeral material (grey literature). Open a folder on your computer for storing downloads, web pages and references. You may eventually choose not to follow this material up, but if you don't keep a record of it, you have nothing to work with.

Reading to maximum effect

Texts are often, mistakenly, treated as narratives to be followed through as one would a novel – start at the first page and read each page right through to the end. For an academic book or article, this is inappropriate. *Academic texts should be regarded as resources to be mined.* Here we shall indicate some of the ways in which you can extract what you need from a text quickly without getting bogged down.

A text is an argument; it moves from point to point. Sometimes these are in parallel, sometimes they build up to a conclusion, sometimes they may be for contrast or one point may illustrate a general idea. Whatever the points are meant to be doing, they will be expressed in paragraphs. For the sake of this discussion, *the paragraph is the key unit of writing.*

The best paragraphs express one main point, and the rest of the paragraph in one way or another is supporting that point. Often the key point is the first or last sentence in the paragraph, and after a few pages you will recognise the pattern the author is using. Occasionally it may be buried inside the paragraph, but then it is usually marked off with an inference word such as 'Therefore'. So you can extract the key content from a chapter of a book quite quickly simply by identifying the main point of each paragraph. This means that you can skim a paragraph and jot down its main point in maybe just fifteen seconds, rather than the couple of minutes that it might take to read the whole thing carefully and digest it. When you have to read three chapters of twenty pages each, and an average of three paragraphs per page, that means that you might get through these in maybe 45 minutes, as opposed to 6 hours. Time management indeed!

Reading can serve a variety of purposes. You may be trying to master a range of texts quickly, aiming to get a framework to develop a relational or extended abstract understanding – your own context, in other words, which you can use to help process fresh information rapidly. You might be trying to acquire knowledge of some factual material, but this is less important at this level than developing a structure into which you can place the information you access. That is why it is important to use every device the author has provided to help you develop your own structure of the subject. The context and the background matter more for your studies than the specific narrated facts. On the other hand, when a more factual multi-structural outcome is needed (e.g. with technical material) then your notes may need to cover

Activity

Take a chapter of one of your recommended textbooks and give your-self 15 minutes to summarize its main points and jot these down.

Response

How did you do? Did you go to a text that you knew had chapter summaries? This helps, though you are relying on the author to summarize all the really key issues in a way that suits you, even though they might well have a slightly different agenda from you. But still this can be a useful way to orient yourself – just don't use it as a substitute for the chapter itself.

Look now at the notes you made. If you summarized each paragraph as you worked your way through, you should have a brief, highly condensed but reasonably accurate summary of the chapter. This may be the right time to check your summary against the author's (if she has done one, that is). If you found you couldn't do this in the time allotted then maybe you picked too large a chapter or too dense a writer.

The point about summaries is an important clue, though, to how to approach effective reading. Every device which the author has used to make the text easier to read should be exploited by the reader. If there are section headings in each chapter, scan these first to get cues on what to expect. If each section is decimal numbered, look carefully at the numbering to identify the major paragraphs – it may be possible to skim through paragraphs 1, 2, 3, etc. to get the overall gist, and then come back to 1.1, 1.2, 1.3, etc. Then when you have done that you may find that you do not need to go to the next level at all (i.e. 1.1.1, 1.1.2, etc.).

more detail – but here also a relational model is helpful, because it can act as the trigger to help you recall distinct factual components.

Management theory uses a lot of diagrams illustrating qualitative models. Often these are the key focus of theoretical approaches, so working on a diagram can be the best way of summarising the main points of a writer. Bear in mind that whilst a picture tells a story better than a narrative, the picture on its own can easily lose its significance – do not forget then to reproduce the key terminology as well as the visual image, and your own questions about it (sometimes keeping a really good example for each category represented in the diagram is also very useful).

Build on the idea of keeping a record of items you come across in the course of other reading by noting ideas as they strike you. It is said that

Beethoven would often stop in the street and quickly jot down an idea that had occurred to him – it seemed to work in his case! Ideas are the currency of any Business Masters course, and are too valuable to waste.

When you develop methods of noting your ideas (both the material that you come across by accident, *and* the material you encounter as part of your more formal studying) you will find that you can stretch and extend the possibilities around each topic. You will be able to re-use material that otherwise might be forgotten or undervalued.

You will also be protecting yourself from any suggestion that you are falsely claiming material as your own and you will become more confident in putting forward argument within an academic community.

Using references effectively

References are a crucial part of the way in which you develop and expand your reading. As with other aspects of reading, the principle is that you should use whatever cues are available to you to decide which books and articles you should consult. The frequency of citation is a good clue as to the importance of a source. If a work is referred to often by other writers, then it is likely that it will be worth reading. Unfortunately, the reverse is not always the case – many very valuable works are not referred to because they have not received the appropriate exposure. An article on recruitment and selection in the *Harvard Business Review* gets read by a wide audience, and gets accessed by researchers frequently. One in *Selection Development and Review* (a journal on assessment and psychometrics produced by the British Psychological Society) may be read by fewer people, and therefore may be omitted by authors when they are researching for new material. But it may be of at least as high a quality and of as much value to you.

Citation can also be a good clue to the overall landscape of a topic area. Many articles will include a brief summary of key aspects of a subject, often as an introduction to their own original contribution. Secondary sources can therefore help you to scope both the field and your own necessary researches. We shall return to this in the next section.

It is by following up references that you can also build up a historical picture of the development of the topic or the main descent of a line of argument. Again, introductory books are extremely valuable as a start on this process – though you should not depend on these for anything more than that initial construction of the shape of the field.

Students often wonder *how many different texts* they should look at for an assignment and how much time they should spend reading. Our suggestion for the first question is that you should be seeking variety and difference. Two good texts with contrary or interestingly different positions are more valuable than four which present an orthodox opinion and therefore become repetitive. At Masters level it is more important to be able to argue using ideas than to find and present the 'right' answer. The question about time is particularly hard, as so many students on Masters programmes often have to balance major pressures from work and family against study. Using some of the ideas of effective reading in this chapter should enable you to make the best use of whatever time you have. Beware reading for perfection and completeness – if you start planning, thinking and writing soon after you start reading, you will quickly learn to manage your reading time effectively.

To summarize:

- Reading across a wide range of types of source is as important as reading recommended texts.
- Keep personal records of key material you draw from texts, ideas that occur to you, useful facts and examples you come across.
- Use every cue the text provides to help you form your own mental structure of the subject.
- References can be used to provide trails of the development of a subject and as a cue for identifying texts to be accessed.

Accessing and using sources

When you have completed this section, you should be able to use different strategies to access the relevant material from different sources effectively

In this section the focus is on access and development of a reserve of appropriate sources. So although we shall again be writing about reading and referencing, this time it is intended to support you in *looking for* texts, whereas the previous section was more to do with what you did with them once you'd *got* them.

As well as the list of books, articles, journals, periodicals, newspapers, magazines etc., that we identified at the start of the previous section, one might add other sources to the list – government documents for example (in many countries these are becoming available electronically, as well as being held in collections such as the National Library of Australia, the Bibliothèque

Nationale de France, or the British Library), or reports published by research institutes or consultancies.

One might add here what is sometimes called 'grey' literature – material that is in the public domain but may not yet been indexed because it has not been fully or formally published (for example, reports, draft papers placed on the web, consultation documents, working papers, conference reports, student theses and dissertations, etc.)

In this section we shall focus on two main areas – building up a bibliography, and using quick reference material. We shall also look at what you can do if you do not get all the information you want.

Firstly, then, building up a bibliography. Frequency of citation is a quick method. When you need to be more systematic (and on some occasions, such as when you complete your dissertation, you certainly will need to be) an alternative approach can be useful.

You know that in researching a field there is a degree of depth and a degree of breadth you would ideally like to achieve. At Masters level you need to have a fair idea about a wide range of the field, and a very good idea about a smaller proportion of the field.

Imagine your reading as defining a knowledge space in your understanding:

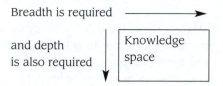

A common misconception is to feel that you should try to become a complete expert on a subject. We have seen that this is too demanding for this sort of course. What most of us need is sufficient broad understanding to help us extend this knowledge space laterally, and a certain amount of detailed knowledge to help us extend it in depth, so that it becomes genuinely a *space* rather than just a sequential *list* of ideas: this is especially important for more abstract learning. Immediately, then, we can see that when accessing academic literature, the material we read can fulfil two interrelated functions:

- it may help us to expand our understanding of the whole range of the subject,
- it may help us to deepen further our understanding of specific items within the field.

This image should help to confirm many of the points we have made earlier about using the full range of material open to you. Introductory books (such as the well-known 'For Dummies' series) help with breadth, though they are unlikely to help much with depth. The major research papers will usually help with depth but not necessarily with breadth.

The process of developing *both* your understanding *and* your bank of referable material from your reading comes from the fact that questions spawn more questions. We start off with a basic question: for example, *how far is marketing theory applicable to hospitals?* (Figure 2.2).

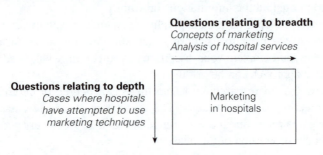

Figure 2.2   Developing the knowledge space, 1

Each of the directions shown in Figure 2.2 creates the same dynamic pressure, so there are issues about breadth and depth relating to the contextual analysis of hospital services, and there are questions of depth and breadth relating to the cases given as examples of marketing in hospitals. So the model becomes no longer a simple parallelogram but a series of branching boxes, as in Figure 2.3.

This process is driven not so much by the material that you collect, but by the *questions that it generates for you.* You look at further material in order to resolve questions that earlier reading has suggested. That is one of the reasons why we suggest you write questions on topics not only as a part of exam revision but also as a general way to advance your understanding.

How should one use reference books? These are the texts that are usually kept on reserve in a library, on the basis that they are too frequently used to be loaned out to people for even days at a time. Usually these are large encyclopaedias, yearbooks, dictionaries, abstracts of research (such as ANBAR), directories and indexes of other works.

Use these as part of your context setting. If you keep coming across a 'big name' – a management guru, for example – it may be useful to read up quickly a condensed version of his or her main views. Similarly, if a concept

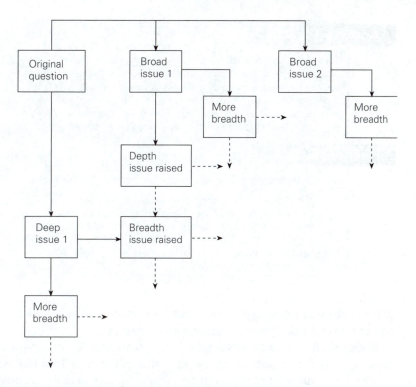

Figure 2.3 Developing the knowledge space, 2

Question

How do you draw the line? What stops this going on for ever?

Response

If you treat this as a static process where you study sufficiently to meet any possible question, then there IS no rational point at which to stop, for each new item expands the knowledge space. It would be rather like digging to get to the bottom of a hole – each fresh spadeful makes the hole deeper.

Essentially, at each step you need to refer back and ask how far this fresh issue will affect the main point. If you can see clearly that whichever way this issue is resolved will most likely produce the same effect on your discussion, then you don't need to read further on it. It is only where the issue makes a difference that it is important.

Activity

Take a subject or topic in one of your assignments. Set aside a couple of hours or so in a well-stocked library. See how far you can get, in terms of using the material available to you to identify questions that extend the breadth of your thinking on the issue and those which will extend the depth of your thinking. Evaluate at the end how far you progressed, and identify what problems you encountered.

Response

In the past students have reported two outcomes for this activity:

- the difficulty of knowing when and where to stop
- libraries often have a lot of generic reference books but rather fewer of the relevant key authored texts that you need.

We shall look at these as the final element of this section.

or technique keeps getting referred to but not explained, then a quick look at a definition of it helps you go forward with your study.

Students often invest considerable effort searching for one particular book, such as the original works by, say, Michael Porter or Fred Herzberg. Usually this is fruitless because (a) there are usually several quite reasonable sources for any major theory, and (b) often the primary text (the one written by the originator of the theory) is not as clearly expressed as the secondary explanations of the concept. Occasionally, however this is important where an original idea might have become corrupted by repetition of what the idea is assumed to be rather than what the author actually presented. Look for evidence in the secondary text that the author has consulted the originals.

Therefore the absence of one text should rarely be a major problem (though the absence of *any* book on a topic might be when you should start looking elsewhere). There are usually secondary sources. Additionally, you might benefit from using unexpected source material, or gain credit for having unearthed a less well-known text that presents ideas in an original way.

So the key strategies for dealing with a restricted range of textual material are:

- scale down your proof requirements;
- look at the diminishing returns on further study and decide whether going elsewhere to find that particular text is really worth the effort;

Question

What will you do if you cannot access all the material you feel you need?

Response

There are different ways of making the best of what one has. One of these is simply to require less evidence – simply saying in an assignment something like 'there is little evidence directly available on this matter, but on balance it suggests that . . .' may seem a bit obvious, but it is surprising how often people spend a disproportionate amount of time trying to resolve that one last 'little' issue. Remember the oft-misquoted Pareto principle:

> 80% of what we need to achieve can be done with 20% of our work but the other 20% of what we need will take up the other 80% that remains

That is, if you feel that a reference is convincing then you can stop a lot earlier than if you are going for the very best. Sometimes it is essential to go the 'extra mile' to resolve a question, and often that is where real progress is made. But you should do it knowing that it will take up a larger part of your time than much of what you have already achieved.

Remember: the purpose of much reading is not to supply answers to questions, but to set those questions in context and enable you to ask broader or more penetrating questions.

- check if the additional material you are looking for really makes any difference or not to your discussion (what is sometimes called having *parallel outcomes* of your research); and
- accept alternative theories if they can be used to similar effect.

To summarize:

- Use reading and citation of other references as a means of generating new *questions*, both to broaden and to deepen your understanding of the issue, not to provide conclusive *answers*.
- This process is indeterminate, but there are several potential bases for managing it – in general there is a law of diminishing returns on the value of the material you seek.

- Much of the time you will be working with limited source material. In such cases it is important to extract material from what is available to you – don't spend too much time looking for a specific text.
- Reference books are a particularly useful means of fixing your understanding of key terms and for summaries of the views of key writers.

● Online and other electronic sources

When you have worked through this section, you should be able to

- identify key sources of information available online;
- use a range of methods to get the most value from online sources of information and to use time most efficiently in online searching.

All the things we have said about the use of paper-based learning material apply to electronic ones as well. The following activity is intended to bring this out.

Consolidation activity

Try to recall (without looking back) what you would see as the four key things to bear in mind about getting the most out of learning materials.

Response

You might have different sense of priority, but in our view the four key things to bear in mind are that:

- Reading materials should be approached in terms of the key questions you need answering, not as a linear narrative to be followed from a to z.
- Every appropriate clue should be used to minimize the amount of time you use chasing sources.
- You should not get obsessed with reading a specific text – any source that deals with your question is appropriate.
- Reading for questions is not a matter of finding answers, but of generating fresh questions that will develop your understanding of the topic in terms of depth and/or breadth.

In terms of electronic sources, there are two fresh issues to add:

- What is the range of sources available?
- How does one extract the content one wants from them?

We shall mainly discuss the second of these, as searching is a generic skill that applies to whatever electronic source you access, whereas the question of what is available changes as the organization changes, as technology changes, and as fashions of communication change.

Identifying key sources of online information

Activity

Write down all the online sources of information that are available to you (so far as you know)

How many of them do you use: Daily? Weekly? For specific purposes? Not at all?

Response

You are likely to have your favourite search engine, as well as having specific access to databases or intranet sites related to your work. We shall consider search engines a bit later. There are some specific academic internet services that you should be aware of. The resources of most of these are only available through a university or college library.

In recent years the impact of Information Technology on academic libraries has been enormous. For the librarians it has been a very exciting time and in many respects they are at the forefront of this new information age. As a profession they are devoted to the idea that every student should be 'information literate'. They are helpful and skilful in supporting your studies, and wise students invest time in learning about the full range of resources and methods they have to offer. In some countries, resources which are paid for by subscription will normally need an authentication process called Athens, and when you register with your university or college you will generally get a password to use Athens when you join your library.

However, not all universities will subscribe for every service, for cost reasons. If you are able to, you are strongly encouraged to register with the libraries of more than one educational institution (this may be possible when, for example, you are studying a course that is jointly run by two colleges, or your institution is part of a federation such as the University of California, or you are studying at one institution but the Masters is accredited by another institution). Doing so will increase the range of online sources that are available to you.

One source for such services is the JISC collections (Joint Information Systems Committee, www.jisc.ac.uk). These are data sets for particular subjects, mainly bibliographic indexes and abstracts.

Many general research tools have become available in recent years – for example Questia and Pro Quest both help researchers and postgraduate students access relevant material in a wide range of subject areas.

A useful summary of business and management abstracts may be found on ANBAR, which contains the summary abstracts from articles in a wide range of business and management journals. The advantage here is that you can access and read summaries without having to spend too long on the whole texts of articles that you want to use for breadth and context.

A related, proprietary service is provided by a publishing house called MCB. They have put summaries of all their academic articles online on a database called Emerald, but note that this only covers their own publications.

Several newspapers provide archived services. *The Financial Times*, for example, has a comprehensive site that covers many journals. One such service, FT Profile, will allow you to search for articles in several 'quality' newspapers back for ten years or more. This can be especially useful if you are researching a particular company, for example, or an industry. Many newspapers now archive their recent issues online.

Additionally there are specialized data services, which are outside the Athens system, and mostly subscription based (and usually not cheap either) such as Bloomberg or Datastream. Many of these are highly commercially based and useful only if you are looking at blue chip companies. A free service that many UK libraries have (available via Athens) is an online directory of annual reports of UK companies – FAME (short for Financial Analysis Made Easy). It will access annual published financial reports, will list out balance sheets and profit and loss accounts, and in some cases do simple ratio analysis as well.

As with paper-based sources, it makes more sense to spend a bit of time looking around a library's electronic collection and access arrangements and see what they can offer you.

When it comes to the internet proper, remember that what is out there is essentially unregulated. You may access the work of a Nobel prize winner, the report of a ten-year research study, an online journal that operates like a paper-based one, a proud student's undergraduate essay or just some ideas that one individual wants to talk about and sticks up on the web – remember that not all personal weblogs ('blogs') are identified as such by the people who produce them.

The huge increase in access to resources brought by the internet has greatly improved the working lives of scholars and researchers around the world. However, the long-established processes for bringing new knowledge to the academic community (peer-reviewing and the making of editorial judgements in publishing) have been side-stepped by these new processes. You will have to apply the same sceptical questioning process for all sources, be they paper or electronic. Who wrote this? When? Why? Is it the complete text or has it been changed? Why is it being used by this organization or author? Who benefits from this and what might they exclude? What is not here that should be? Our advice is that you should be even more sceptical about electronic material where the source or provenance is not clear. Keep your wits about you and take nothing for granted.

As well as standard websites, there are very many discussion areas, also known as zones, rooms and groups, as well as blogs and downloadable podcasts.

Blogs represent a very personal view of a subject, and some reputable writers use them as a way of putting new ideas out to get a quick response from the community before developing them in detail. They do not currently have their own archiving or directories, and in general it is not easy in some cases to distinguish them from other web pages.

Podcasts (MP3 audio files of someone talking about a subject) may be individually based, like blogs, or organizationally generated (many universities around the world that teach by distance learning will have some material available on podcasts). Some podcasters run a regular commentary series, and signing up for this means that each week or month you will hear a fresh opinion. Podcasts and blogs tend to be accessed in the same way as other world-wide-web pages, and therefore how easy they are to access depends on your ingenuity with search techniques.

There are almost countless discussion rooms on just about any subject you care to think of. If you wanted to know about postmodernism in management, you might well find a number of discussion groups devoted solely to that topic. Such rooms or groups are often visited frequently by a small number of aficionados, who can from time to time appear to be conducting a private – and sometimes quite intense – discussion about their favourite subject. It would be unwise to set too much store by what you could discover from such discussions, but it is as well to know that they are available. Many of them are hosted by major internet service providers or search engines, and thus are often free access.

Getting the most out of online sources

The central phenomenon of the internet, however, is the web page, and the search engines that find them for you. Different search engines look for web sites in different ways: some search for pages on the basis of an indexing of key words in the text, coupled with how many links they have running into them (so if a site isn't well-known, it has few links going into it and stays not well-known), others search for key words in the title bar at the top of a page (which may be misleading) or in concealed 'metadata' devised by the creators of the site.

None of these is perfect, so while you may prefer to use one search engine most of the time, it does pay to occasionally check out how another engine might handle the same search. Each engine gives important guidance in their 'advanced searching' pages to the methods they use. Google in particular has taken this to a new level, with services such as 'Google Scholar' which will search abstracts and texts of articles and books across a vast range of subjects.

Many companies will also offer search engines if they have themselves complex websites. Governments in particular have quite elaborate websites, and their search functions tend to be less sophisticated than, say, Yahoo or Google. Perhaps the best device for finding an up-to-date list of search engines and the algorithms or processes which each uses is to enter 'search engines' into Wikipedia.

Avoiding time-wasters when searching online

Internet searching is almost entirely keyword-driven. You may have already had the experience of putting in a word and getting nothing at all, or at the other extreme, discover over a million pages that matched your search word.

The key skill here is to be able to vary terms so that you get a good but not unmanageable range of sites to access. Try to think of terms that are unique to what you are looking for (remember that putting phrases into quotation marks restricts the results to those words in that order). If this does not work, use reasonable alternative terms – for example substituting 'company' for 'business'.

Activity

Take a topic from one of your essay questions – or try this one: *Strategic management is not relevant for small businesses. Discuss.*

Spend an hour searching on the internet for pages that are relevant for this question, then review your progress:

How many did you get that were useful?

How many different engines did you use?

How many different searches did you do?

How many pages were identified by your search that you did not have any time to look at?

How many site were complete rubbish or of no value for your investigation?

Response

We would be very surprised if all went well. Brown and Duguid (2000) give an example of a search they did – out of 150 sites they accessed (which is too many to handle in one go) *just one* provided an original and useful source. The others were either irrelevant pages that happened to point to or have a link to that one useful one, or just plain errors in the way in which the engine searched.

As with all the sources you have available to you, search engines are there to be mined and plundered. They are not there as your best friend (although commercially that is what they want to be). They are there for you – and millions of other people with different questions and agendas – to extract what you need from them.

When you do finally access the site, and have assured yourself that it is of decent quality, we would strongly urge you to keep a record of the URL (i.e. the 'www . . .' address) and the date you accessed it. You will need to quote both in a reference. If you think that what you have accessed is really important, save it electronically or print it off, as the internet is generally treated as ephemeral, and people change their sites without warning or archiving.

In particular, look carefully at the links that the site has to other sites. Just as with paper-based texts it is not so much what answers you get but what fresh questions are suggested, so here it is less what one website tells you than what it does for your overall network of web resources. Building a 'web-ography' is first and foremost about creating a framework for breadth.

If you want to follow this up, perhaps the most useful web site to start with is the 'Managing Business' interactive tutorial which is one of 40 tutorials in the Virtual Training Suite of the JISC-funded site INTUTE. You will find it on www.vts.rdn.ac.uk and it will introduce you, amongst other things, to SOSIG (**S**ocial **S**cience **I**nformation **G**roup) which you are likely to find helpful on many future occasions.

To summarize:

- There is a range of electronic sources over and above the internet itself – many of these, though very useful potentially, are restricted access.
- Accessing websites is like getting hold of books – they are there to be mined.
- Sites are valuable less for the information they contain than for the links they indicate or suggest.
- Key word searches are an art – work on the assumption that you will need to spend a disproportionately long time finding what you want.

3 Examinations

● **Introduction**

The term 'examination' is used in slightly different ways in different countries, so to be clear we will use it to mean: *time controlled assessments, usually between one and three hours in length, where you will be required to respond to unseen questions by writing individual answers, usually in essay form.*

It is a requirement of accreditation bodies such as AMBA (the UK-based Association for MBAs) that a certain proportion of the assessment of an accredited MBA will be examination based, and many employers perceive an examination as conferring greater authenticity on a qualification. So you will almost certainly be required to take some examinations at some point in your course.

Exams should require people to consider the content of the module overall. You will be expected to react swiftly and appropriately to the task set. Although no one in the business world uses exams in their daily work, it is a commonplace requirement for managers and professionals to have to deal quickly and effectively with an intellectual challenge such as the unexpected contact from a major potential customer who then wishes to discuss a complex product with you, or a presentation to the Board at short notice that your boss can't make. Exams resemble these situations, in that they present you with questions that you have to deal with immediately, without the benefit of time and resources to research the issues in depth.

Exams place you in an *academic crisis*, but by well-planned preparation you can be effective in meeting this kind of crisis. In this chapter we will indicate how skills that you use in other situations can be brought to bear on the challenge of the examination.

To be successful in an examination, you need to do each of the following:

- Understand what is expected of you, in broad terms.
- Identify the key elements required for each question.
- Make the most of what you already know and consciously use it to construct an answer.

- Construct the answer so that you do your understanding full justice when the examiner comes to read it.

The five sections of this chapter will all help you with each of these areas:

1 **Unpicking a question**: identifying correctly just what each question is really asking.
2 **Generating ideas**: bringing out your knowledge so that it can be used in an answer, often taking account of questions that are asked in unexpected or unusual ways.
3 **Planning an answer**: organizing your thoughts and constructing an answer to the question as set.
4 **Avoiding pitfalls**: the most common hazards to avoid people make when sitting exams.
5 **Revision**: making sure you have sufficient knowledge.

Unpicking a question

When you have worked through this section, you should be able to identify quickly, and differentiate between, the different tasks implicit in the wordings of exam questions.

It is vital to understand exactly what a question is asking. Many students make the mistake of assuming that questions are about *topics*. In fact they are usually about what you can *do with* a topic.

Look at this question, taken from a past MBA economics paper:

'Whilst not without its weaknesses, the economist's market forces model applies to a wide variety of sectors, including public and voluntary.' Discuss

'What's it about?' is everyone's first question. Try to write in four words what you think it's about. Here is what two students wrote down in reply:

Johnnie: market forces model, weaknesses
Frankie: model, weaknesses, applications, sectors

It's not simply that Frankie gets more into her four-word summary than Johnnie; she approached it from a different angle. Rather than simply looking for one 'thing' – the topic – she started from the idea that the question was asking something specific, and her summary reflects this.

Johnnie's summary isn't bad – it would be worse if it just said 'market forces model.' But it may be harder for him to shift into a mindset that answers the question as it has been put. And it may be tempting for him to fall into a major trap of approaching an exam question as a challenge to show how much he knows about a topic. This is a very common mistake and should be avoided at all costs. Writing a long answer that includes everything someone knows on a topic demonstrates several shortcomings in their learning:

- they have not responded to a set brief (a key business skill)
- they have not shown the ability to sort out parts of a topic by their relevance (also a very important skill in business)
- they have approached the exam question in terms solely of basic knowledge (sub-Masters level study)
- they will probably have not structured the answer well (well ordered thinking being an essential in business practice as well as a key to achieving Masters level learning)

> A golden rule: exam answers are *not* the place to show all you know, but they *are* the place to show how you can **use** your knowledge

So use the following technique when approaching an exam question – *analyse the question.* How? You need to get inside the examiner's head. What is he or she looking for? What to do they want you to do? Why?

Remember what any assessment is – for you it may be an opportunity to pull together your knowledge and understanding, but for the tutors it is the primary means by which they measure your learning. So it is essential to have a clear idea of the *intended learning outcomes* that your tutors are using to make those measurements. You may recall this phrase from Chapter 2, but for reference these are: statements made in the clearest terms about what a student should be able to do as a result of completing the study, assignments and other essential learning activities relating to a topic. Learning outcomes are the bridge between study and assessment, and will generally be the basis on which your tutors will construct their marking schemes for exams.

At Masters level the intended learning outcomes will inevitably involve not just your ability to use established knowledge, but also your ability to make effective use of less firmly established ideas, to deal with weaknesses in established research, to critically evaluate material by exploring strengths and weaknesses and to demonstrate a balance between scepticism and the need to make decisions even when matters are not certain.

These outcomes may include the following (this list is adapted from the benchmarks for Masters awards in Business and Management formulated by the UK's Quality Assurance Agency) (http://www.qaa.ac.uk/academicinfra structure/benchmark/masters/MBAintro.asp):

- critical thinking and creativity
- problem-solving and decision-making
- managing information and knowledge
- skills in managing quantitative information
- effective use of computer and information technology
- personal communication
- self-awareness and self-management
- performance within a team
- leadership and managing the performance of others
- ethics and value management
- research skills
- learning through reflection on practice and experience

These are, of course, highly valuable qualities in business as well. Almost all management decisions are made with some degree of uncertainty. All business people have to deal with a large volume of information that comes across their desk daily, and often they have to judge on a very brief evaluation its professional value as well as how reliable it is.

Learning outcomes such as those above are increasingly used by tutors to structure exam questions and marking schemes, as well as coursework assignments. Tutors are guided and supported by such statements of standards for Business Masters courses that are used in many countries to help set the curriculum as well as specify skills and particular achievements that students should be able to attain by the completion of their studies.

Not all of the outcomes listed above will be directly tested out in an exam, but if you look at the totality of your assessments (i.e. coursework as well as exams) you should find that at some point each of these is addressed. In preparing for any exam, over and above the subject content of the module or course unit, you should think about how the examiners (your teachers) will look for evidence of these skills in your answers.

Exam questions will therefore range across many of the key forms of learning that a programme at this level requires, which come down to the following:

- having the key *knowledge*;
- comprehension – *understanding* knowledge elements in their broad context;
- being able to *apply* knowledge and understanding in practice
- being able to *analyse* and pick apart ideas;
- being able to put ideas together to *synthesize* your knowledge to develop effective solutions and plans;
- *evaluating* ideas, theories and situations.

An exam question will normally be looking for at least one and sometimes more of these. So over and above the topic, there is the question 'what aspects of learning am I meant to demonstrate?'

This is where the wording of an exam question is crucial. Getting clear what the examiner is looking for will help you provide the right material. Failing to do so means that you will provide something that is only partially relevant. Most important to bear in mind is that the wording of a question will usually be designed to test out several different areas of learning. Some about the topic itself, some about your general skills such as critical thinking, and in a Business Masters there will often be an element of general background knowledge – after all, in business and management the ability to make quick decisions based on one's latent overall general business knowledge is a central requirement that good professionals draw upon every day.

People often worry about misunderstanding the underlying requirements of an exam question. Of course there is always some risk of this, but if you analyse the question carefully you will almost certainly arrive at a plausible interpretation. In most cases, if this is not exactly what the examiner was looking for, but is a reasonable way to interpret the question, then it will be assessed on its merits. For this reason, it is generally useful to state in your introduction to an answer what your understanding of the question is. In the example discussed above, a student could usefully begin by saying something like *'In answer to the question as to the strengths and weaknesses of the market forces model when applied to the public and voluntary sectors, I will argue that . . .'* This way the examiner can see what you understood by the question, and then they will mark the answer on its own merits.

The *key verb* used in a question is the central aspect of this, and it is possible to categorize the instructions given in a question into the six areas we have listed in Table 3.1. So when you look at an exam question, look at the instruction or question word to get clear what the examiner wants. Is it knowledge? Is it your ability to design solutions to problems? In practice there will often be a combination of these elements.

If the question includes:	You are probably being asked to demonstrate:
define, identify, list, what is/are, state, arrange, order, name, relate, reproduce	Knowledge
classify, locate, describe, discuss, report, explain, restate, review, select, indicate, express	Comprehension
analyse, differentiate, appraise, discriminate, calculate, distinguish, categorize, examine, compare, experiment, contrast, question, criticize, test, critically evaluate	Analysis
apply, operate, choose, practice, demonstrate, schedule, dramatize, sketch, employ, solve, illustrate, use, interpret, how would you . . .	Application
arrange, formulate, assemble, compose, create, design, prepare a plan, develop a proposal, construct, devise, compose a solution	Synthesis
Critically discuss, assess, what are the strengths and weaknesses of . . . , compare and contrast, do you agree . . .	Evaluation

Table 3.1   Key verbs

Source: Adapted from the work of Alan Jenkins (Oxford Brookes University) and Dave Unwin (Birkbeck College) for the National Centre for Geographic Information and Analysis, accessed 5 November 2006 (http://www.ncgia.ucsb.edu/education/curricula/giscc/units/format/outcomes.html)

Another exam question – this time from a Marketing exam – will show how the difference in the wording could change the kind of answer you would provide:

> *Discuss the proposition that marketing management needs to develop a new philosophy to achieve success in the 21st century.*

Discuss is a fairly broad instruction, but essentially it requires you to demonstrate your <u>understanding</u> of the issue. Here are some brief notes that someone might have used in a plan for an answer to this question (please note that these are provided to illustrate the points about exam questions – they are NOT intended as model answers or model plans):

> definition of philosophy of marketing
>
>   20th and 21st century philosophy of m and its successes
>
>   changes in the marketplace since the late 90s -
>   globalisation
>   internet
>   demand for higher ethics
>   intensified competition and tighter margins
>
>   how far can current philosophy address these?
>
>   new approach more cost effective, more ethical, more responsive
>
>   use examples from financial and energy industries

The candidate has discussed the question, drawn out what he/she regards as the key issues and – note this – given examples that illustrate the argument.

Now suppose the question were only slightly changed, to become:

> *Marketing management needs to develop a new philosophy to achieve success in the 21st century' Do you agree with this statement?*

An element of *evaluation* has been introduced. Rather than illustrate and analyse the issue, we are challenged to provide an argument either for or against it.

Here is an illustration of how someone might have planned an answer to this second question:

> definition of 20th and 21st century philosophy of marketing
>
> changes already and in near future (use financial services and oil/gas examples) - e-commerce, ethics, trading blocs such as EU and NAFTA, global economy and 1st/3rd world relationships
>
> show how existing philosophy can accommodate all of these
>
> conclusion: disagree - different focus and context, but basic principles the same

Here we see some of the same content, but cast in a different way. The argument has become the centre of the answer. Notice again that examples are used, and also that even in the plan this candidate has explicitly said at the end what their conclusion is.

As a final example of how an answer could change significantly, imagine that the question was now:

> *Using examples from corporate or public service experience, illustrate how far you would agree with the statement that marketing management needs to develop a new philosophy to achieve success in the 21st century.*

Here there is still an element of argument, though not so much on an agree/disagree basis. More importantly, though, the emphasis on examples is explicit. The examiner wants you to demonstrate that you can apply ideas to concrete situations. This is how you might plan this answer:

> **a.** pre-C21st marketing mgt phil - define and identify key factors
> **b.** C21st - changes and new challenges
> **c.** my view - some changes some continuity
> **d.** example 1: public sector social housing markets – ageing populations
> **e.** example 2: retail clothing – competing with internet
> **f.** summary - depends on market and segmentation/position

So in these three examples even quite slight differences in wording would lead to quite different kinds of answer. In each case *the content* was identical. *What you had to do with it* changed, and this had a major impact on the kind of answer required. Incidentally, you will see that in this plan too there is an explicit indication at the end of what your overall answer to the question might be.

In the last example there was a third aspect of questions as well, namely a particular kind of context to the question. In the last version of this question you were able to choose which context – corporate or public sector, whilst in the earlier questions this was absent. Such contextualization is designed to test out application and synthesis, and is often a central feature of some questions – for example a question such as *'Discuss the expectancy theory of motivation with reference to the management of knowledge workers'* is much more explicit with the context. Questions such as these will normally require a response at the relational or extended abstract level on the Biggs 'SOLO' model that we encountered in Chapter 2.

Activity

Write a fourth exam question relating to the same content, and test this out on a colleague.

Finally in this section, here are two examples of exam questions – in each case they are given with two slightly different wordings – rather like the example we have discussed above. We will discuss these in terms of the differences in the task that the alternative wordings involve.

A1 *'According to John Burgoyne, what are the key features of a learning organization?'*

A2 *'Illustrate how the key features of learning organizations (according to Burgoyne) may be applied to your industry.'*

A1 is a classic knowledge question: you list out and explain each of the features the writer has identified. You may give brief examples of each to illustrate the explanation. But this is all about showing that you know the theory. However, at Masters level you should always presume that some critical evaluation and, where business and management are concerned, some practical application, are also expected.

A2 is about practice. Here you still need to know what Burgoyne has said about learning organizations, but now the question requires you to show how they would be used in your own industry – it would be open to you to argue that they did not, of course. Your examples here would be more extensively discussed.

Now consider this pair of questions:

B1 *'Discuss the idea that strategic management principles cannot be applied to small and medium sized organizations (SMEs).'*

B2 *'Compare and contrast the way in which strategic management principles might be adopted in large corporate businesses with how they might be used in the management of very small companies.'*

B1 looks at first sight like a straight understanding question, but be warned that the fact that the statement is in the negative suggests some degree of argument of the sort we saw earlier. You would clearly need to explain 'strategic management principles' and then explain those particular features of SMEs that might prevent strategic principles from being applied. A really good answer would probably also offer some positive conclusion, even if they agreed with the statement – you might offer a revision of strategic management principles so that they were applicable, or maybe you would qualify the statement to some extent ('agree but in certain cases they may apply to a limited extent' or a similar message).

B2 is clearer. This question calls for both application and evaluation. You define 'strategic management principles' and the differences between large corporate businesses and very small companies, then explain how these principles might be used in each kind of organization, and finally draw out where there are similarities and where differences. A good answer will try to give an underpinning explanation of why this might be the case, and maybe offer some forward looking view of the future for strategic management and SMEs.

> ### To summarize:
>
> - Exam answers are not opportunities to put down everything you know about a subject.
> - As well as attending to the content of exam questions, you need also to look carefully at the instruction of the question as well as its context in order to clarify what the examiner is looking for.

Two final points . . .

In the plans we looked at, people tended to include concrete examples to deepen and illustrate their points. Even when not explicitly asked for, examples tend to make abstract ideas MUCH clearer, so do take the opportunity to use an example whenever it is appropriate.

For the kinds of exam you would normally encounter on a Business or Management Masters, be aware that it is rarely simply a matter of showing knowledge – usually you will need to show some understanding, and some evaluation or critical application. *For Masters level you should also assume as a general rule that the examiner will be looking for some degree of relational or extended abstract thinking*.

● Generating ideas

> When you have worked through this section, you should be able to identify a variety of different methods of generating ideas for answers

In the previous section we looked at how best to work out what the question is after. Now, how to get the ideas to write your answers?

The first and most obvious point is in some ways the most crucial. You should PLAN the answer. This section is about the first part of that – bringing to the front of your mind what you know, in order to have some ideas about what to do. The following section will deal with planning the structure of the answer and actually writing it.

Knowing is not remembering. If we remembered even a small amount of what we know at any one time our conscious mind would be completely overloaded. We have many psychological defences that protect us from information overload. They keep knowledge away from our consciousness when we don't need it – unfortunately they sometimes do their job too well and keep it away when we *do* need it! So the important task in an exam is to have methods that bring knowledge to your conscious mind when you need it.

There are in turn two parts to the generation of ideas:

1   getting a rough beginning of an idea to start on – a 'hook' on which to hang some content; and
2   developing this 'hook' into a proper idea.

Let us start with the rough beginnings – the 'hooks'. Sometimes getting ideas is not a problem in an exam. You sit down read the question, work out what is required by the examiner and happily everything comes back just as you put it down in your notes. Not always though – the real value of a methodical approach comes when you find your mind is a blank. This can often happen with the first question you attempt: do remember it is very common, you are not alone!

There is one golden rule here: **There are no golden rules!**

Everyone is different. Some people find certain approaches helpful which others do not. It is always a case of trying out an approach and seeing how well it works for you. You can start the process by engaging with the question to find out what the examiner really requires. The process of analysing the question that we described in the previous section can often stimulate your mind to start producing ideas and patterns that can be the basis for a creative answer. If not, here are two main approaches which people find useful for making the ideas flow:

- text based – lists, brainstorms, associations of words;
- diagram based – mind-maps, rich pictures, fishbone or system diagrams.

Whichever you use, help your conscious mind relax to allow the material to become available.

> At first, aim for a flow of ideas

It is important to keep a flow of ideas in the initial stages, avoiding any interruptions to this flow. Criticism slows down your thought processes. It makes you focus on an idea when it appears, which means you spend time on one idea when at this early stage you need to get many ideas out. It also inhibits your imagination, because even before you consciously start the criticism your unconscious mind may have censored something out because 'its not good enough'. The more you practice generating ideas without immediately critiquing them, the more ready your mind is to do it on demand.

Activity

Right now, on a piece of paper, spend two minutes putting down as many ideas as you can suggested by the word 'control'.

Here is a list that one person generated in that time:

Conflict	Delegating
Authority	Responsibility
Holding	Communication
Discipline	Keeping in order
Tightness	Reporting and monitoring
Opposite of lax	Tether
Personalities	Systems

The thing is not how good these are in themselves, so much as whether they provide a starting point for more focused exploration. For that reason you should only use non-critical idea generating techniques as much as you need to. When planning an exam question, where you may have only five to ten minutes to do the plan, two or three minutes of this kind of work is usually sufficient to get you going.

Look again at the words in the box. Once we analyse and critique these, we can see that some of them go a bit away from the point. But some are relevant, and that's all you need to get moving on your question. From those words, you might choose reporting, communication, systems, delegating, and responsibility, for example (it would naturally depend on the specifics of the question).

Brainstorming is generally the most effective method for getting a hook started, when we turn to developing the idea, then brainstorming may be less useful and many diagrammatic methods come into their own. One of many such approaches is called the 'sunflower' diagram (Figure 3.1). The idea is to use the metaphor of the petals of a sunflower to develop secondary ideas that are suggested by the first few thoughts you have had. The approach works best with a larger space of paper, so in an exam you would use a whole side of an A4 answer book.

1. In the centre draw a circle – put the main term in the middle.
2. Having already generated a few ideas draw long petals for each of these coming out of the circle.
3. Write a key word at the tip of each petal and then add things to it as they occur to you.

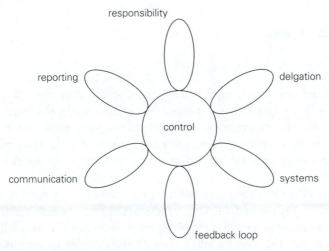

Figure 3.1 A 'sunflower' diagram

An alternative is to use a network diagram (Figure 3.2). Each main idea is placed in a circle, and these are then related by lines to indicate logical dependencies (one could even place one circle inside another, though the example below does not do this).

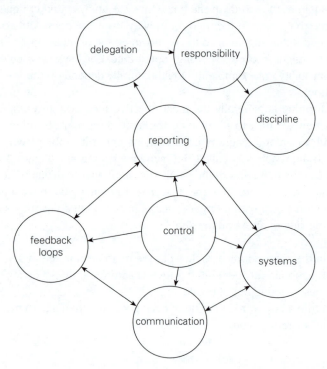

Figure 3.2   Example of a network diagram

Do not spend any time trying to make your diagram neat and tidy – it is a plan and will not generally get marked. More importantly, you may try out one diagrammatic arrangement and later change your mind. Use a whole side of your answer paper (write clearly at the top that it is a plan) and then sketch out a diagram in the top half in pencil. Remember that the eraser is a creative tool!

This has taken us a long way, but it is important to recognize it is not the end of your essay planning. Firstly, try to keep open to new thoughts up to the point where you have to commit yourself to an answer. Secondly, you have to translate the diagram into a planned sequence of paragraphs. If you have drawn a diagram with heavier and lighter arrows then that helps you to

Activity

Take one of the exam questions we have already discussed. Using one of the key terms involved, and using a combination of brainstorming and network diagrams, try to develop the idea.

The example below is for the question we discussed right at the start:

'Whilst not without its weaknesses, the economist's market forces model applies to a wide variety of markets, including public and voluntary.' Discuss

Again, we can detect some idea of how this diagram was built up – the main term was placed in the middle, the thicker lines indicate the next ideas to be generated, and then the final ideas were joined with thinner arrowed lines.

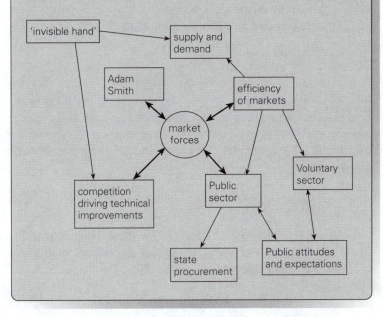

focus on which are the most important steps in your argument. If you assume that the central idea is visually in the central circle, then the boxes which are linked to it with heavier lines are the main points or steps in your argument. Those boxes that are linked to your main points with lighter lines are supplementary points, and should be collected under each of the main steps.

The diagram above might then be translated into a series of paragraphs as follows:

Theory:
Definition of market forces
   Origins with Adam Smith and idea of invisible hand
   Competition drives technical improvements
Supply and demand
Market efficiency
Summarize strengths and weaknesses

Application:
Public sector applications
   State procurement rules
Voluntary sector applications
Role of public attitudes for both sectors

Summary

This may not be the only or best way of making the translation, but it is coherent and would be the basis of a sound answer to the question. What has happened has been no more than collecting together the items that were depicted in a logical format in the diagram into an appropriate sequence of paragraphs.

> **To summarize:**
>
> In this section we have looked at the development of the key elements which you will put together to form an answer. The key points we have seen are:
>
> - generating ideas is about (a) getting started, and then (b) developing ideas;
> - to get started it is essential to stay open to new ideas; and
> - diagrammatic methods, such as mind maps or networks, can be useful to indicate logical relationships.

In the following section we will develop further the process of creating an essay out of these elements, focusing further on how an answer should be organized.

● Planning an answer

> When you have finished working through this section you
> should be able to:
>
> • identify the general criteria that examiners use when
>   marking exam papers;
> • organize ideas into well-planned answers.

In the previous section we saw some ways to get ideas and develop them. Ideally this will result in you having a number of points that you want to include within the answer. The next step is to turn this into an organized response that meets the examiner's requirements.

At this point we have to look back again at the question itself – what it specifically asks you to do – illustrate, analyse, discuss and so on. Your answer needs to manifestly do just that. There are two things that are important to bear in mind here:

- the need to provide a logical answer to the question; and
- the need to make quite clear to the examiner that you HAVE answered the question.

The second of these is included because it is all too easy in one's own writing, at any level, to presume that the reader is able to fill in the gaps where you have not stated something. In fact it rarely happens, and an examiner is specifically only meant to mark what they see in front of them, not guess what someone *might* be trying to say. So it is crucial to ensure that the reader (i.e. the examiner) knows exactly what your answer is. This is why summaries are important. Make quite sure that the structure of your answer is clear to the examiner. A useful way to do this is by using the language of the question to help structure your answer – if a question asks you to compare and contrast, then you could have headings named 'Comparisons' and 'Points of contrast' or similar. Not every question will lend itself so easily to this process but where it is possible this does help the examiner see what your answer to the question is.

It is important clearly to signpost different aspects of the answer. If the question asks you to 'Give examples . . .' the examiner is expecting to see at least two examples. Using headings marked 'Example 1 . . .' and 'Example 2 . . .' leaves the examiner in no doubt where to look in your answer for these. Discussing something generally without such headings could just, in the haste of writing, leave some doubt as where an example starts and where it finishes.

But the more important issue is how to produce a clear argument. Making sure that the structure of the answer follows a logical strand is extremely important. Even if you have a good understanding of the subject and all the right knowledge you can wreck an answer by not expressing your logic clearly.

Remember that at Masters level the examiner is expecting to see evidence of higher level thinking – relational and abstract, identifying connections between distinct concepts, acknowledging gaps and shortcomings in the theory or the research evidence. So the clearer you signpost these aspects of your argument the easier it is for the examiner to see that you have demonstrated this level of thinking.

Activity

Here are one-sentence summaries of eleven paragraphs that someone has generated as part of their plan of an answer to the exam question:

'Critically evaluate the idea that organisations must commit themselves to just one of Michael Porter's generic strategies to be successful, and that if they try to adopt more than one they will get 'stuck in the middle' and thus fail'

What order would you put these in? Explain why. There is a catch – three of them don't belong here.

Examples of organizations getting 'stuck in the middle'– and how they retrieved the situation (or not).

Porter's model of generic strategies – 1 cost leadership, 2 focus and 3 differentiation.

International businesses may have to modify their products to be saleable in different countries.

Conclusion: mainly agree, but ambiguities in the idea of 'cost leadership'.

Explain focus (targeted on a niche market) – use example of womens' magazines.

Factors leading to market leadership, e.g. for retail — bigger stores, more stores, internet presence.

Explain differentiation (higher priced 'high quality' goods) – use example of designer labels with clothing.

➜

Porter – each strategy appeals in a different way to the market, and to different segments; hence "all things to all men" falls between each market ('stuck in the middle') and satisfies no one.

Introduction: will use retail examples to argue that Porter's model is ambiguous.

Mobile phones changed from being an extension of the fixed telephone to developing features in its own right (e.g. text messaging).

Explain cost leadership (cheaper and more basic goods) using examples, but argue that 'cost' ambiguous between price the customer pays and costs the organization incurs.

One or two of these paragraphs are easily placed – introduction comes first and conclusion last.

Even if you don't know what Porter's theory is, you should be able to see that there is a paragraph introducing the three strategies, and then one paragraph for each of them, plus a further paragraph about being 'stuck in the middle'. There is also an example relating to getting 'stuck in the middle' which clearly links to the previous paragraph.

But it is harder to fit in the other three paragraphs. They all could potentially have some relevance, but it is not spelt out. Better to leave out than muddy the answer with potential irrelevancies. So our final essay structure is shown here:

Introduction: will use retail examples to argue that Porter's model is ambiguous.

Porter's model of generic strategies – 1 cost leadership, 2 focus and 3 differentiation.

Explain cost leadership (cheaper and more basic goods) using examples, but argue that 'cost' ambiguous between price the customer pays and costs the organization incurs.

Explain focus (targeted on a niche market) – use example of womens' magazines.

Explain differentiation (higher priced 'high quality' goods) – use example of designer labels with clothing.

Porter – each strategy appeals in a different way to the market, and to different segments; hence 'all things to all men' falls between each market ('stuck in the middle') and satisfies no one.

Examples of organizations getting 'stuck in the middle'– and how they retrieved the situation (or not).

Conclusion: mainly agree, but ambiguities in the idea of 'cost leadership'.

Here we can see a clear logical structure – an introduction, presentation of the theory, explanation of each part of the theory, a clear and recognizable example, and then finish off with the summary. Whether or not it's the best content, it will get credit for a demonstration of clear thinking.

Another side to planning your answer is to try to work out what is the examiner's marking scheme. Look at this question, which was in an Economics paper on an MBA programme:

> *Identify and appraise the key issues in the oscillation between*
> *Keynesian and market-led economic models in the twentieth century.*

Using the techniques we have been developing in this chapter, we can build up a picture of what the examiner is looking for. It should be clear enough that this is not simply about comparing the two models of economics, but about the see-sawing between them in the twentieth century. 'Identify' suggests we are going to need to set out in factual terms the transformation from one to the other and back again. 'Appraise' suggests we need to provide some degree of analysis and explanation of the causes of this process.

What kind of learning is this question testing? Clearly there is some relational thinking sought – links between the two different economic models. And in a question that involves an historical perspective the examiners are likely also to be looking for generalizations from this process, and also for candidates to challenge the account (where appropriate).

As there is no specific focus on a sector of the economy, or a type of industry, a range of examples should be used that come from different industries – this demonstrates good general background business knowledge.

So we can see the kind of structure that the examiner is looking for:

- something on each of the two models, classical market-led, and Keynesian;
- something explaining Keynesianism and why it replaced the classical model and was subsequently replaced by the classical model in turn;
- a demonstration within the argument of your general understanding of economic argument, theories and models.

We can see below that this is in effect what the actual marking scheme covers. A marking scheme sets out what the examiner is looking for, and thus what they will give marks for. Most tutors will mark with the marking scheme by their side, consulting it as they work through each answer, and giving credit where key points are made. In addition, of course, markers will be looking for clarity of thought, good argument structure, and so on.

- Classical model and its replacement by Keynesian economics in the 1930s. Historical and theoretical points.
- 1970s and the move away from Keynes back to market-led classical approach.
- Key issues – money supply, deficit finance, inflation, full employment.

What is not always expressed in an exam question is the weighting given to different sections. Where this is provided, then you should pay careful attention – for it is an important clue as to the most important priorities of the examiner. Weightings also a very useful clue as to the investment of your time – if a question has three equally weighted sections, then clearly you should make every effort to spend an equal time on each. If on the other hand one of the sections carries half the marks, and the other two only a quarter each it should be clear that you should endeavour to spend half of your time on the higher weighted section, and split the rest of your time equally. It is occasionally not as easy as this – when there is a lower weighted section that you have to get right in order to move on to the higher weighted parts (for example, carrying out statistical calculations before discussing what the results might mean). And in some exams the weightings might not be revealed to you. But where you can get an idea of which parts of a question are most important for the lecturer it is a very valuable indicator of what to focus on.

If we get to this point, then we are already more than half way to developing a coherent answer, because we already know which buttons we should be pressing to get the marks.

Activity

In the box below you will see there the start of an answer to an essay entitled *'Discuss the principal benefits of delegation.'*

Imagine you are the examiner – and mark this fragment. Remember this is not a matter of how much you currently know about content, but about recognising good structure.

One of the principal benefits of delegation is that staff are often well motivated by this process. For instance, an individual in my office had been stuck at the top of his grade for several years, with no chance of promotion. He had become, in a word, a time-server, doing what was necessary but always finishing dead on 5 p.m., and never considering going the 'extra mile' for the company. Then one day he was asked to take on the departmental budgets. It is clear that he was only waiting for something like this to happen, as since then he has been totally different in his approach, and is in line for an upgrade within the next few months.

One problem that Charles Handy has mentioned is that delegation needs training. If someone has a task delegated to them and they do not know how to do it then they will inevitably do it poorly, and this can be a cause of serious demotivation, quite the reverse of the intention. In 'The One Minute Manager' it is recommended that you should always consult with someone before delegating something to them, and only when they are fully trained can you delegate without preliminary training.

Delegation is a useful vehicle for enriching someone's job, and this can often bring about the kind of motivational benefits mentioned at the start of this essay. Herzberg suggested that this be used strategically as a method of enhancing motivation. However he also cautioned about not neglecting the 'hygiene' factors such as working conditions, which can cause people dissatisfaction before motivation proper can kick in.

What did you think of this? One thing to notice is that the author is not short on knowledge, referring appropriately in several places to well known management writers. But there are some very strong danger signs.

Firstly, to start without an introduction leaves your reader to work out what the structure really is, and if it's not clear then you run a risk of the examiner misunderstanding you. Secondly, the essay starts with a benefit, moves on to a problem, and then comes back to the first benefit again. The reader isn't clear if this all the development of one point or is meant to be several distinct points.

To summarize:

A key feature of your answer is to organize it into a logical response to the question. Make sure not only that it is logical but that you signpost this to the examiner. What is also important is to be clear what the examiner is looking for – be clear about where in your answer you are going to demonstrate Masters level attainment – relational or extended abstract thinking.

● Avoiding pitfalls

> When you have completed this section you should be able to:
>
> • identify the major reasons why people do not do themselves full justice in exams;
> • have strategies ready if things go wrong in an exam.

While some things may be genuinely out of your control – the heating in the exam room breaks down, or you are taken ill just as the session starts – focus on the aspects over which you have some control and do what you can within the limits of time and other commitments to maximize your chances.

Clearly a sufficient degree of knowledge and understanding is essential. But we have seen enough in the previous three sections to recognize that it is not at all simply a question of having the knowledge. It is a matter of using your knowledge and understanding effectively, having gained a clear idea of what is required in the exam.

In the exam room, there are three things that need to be kept in balance:

- the time available
- the number of words you can produce
- the value that your answer can deliver

Trouble usually stems from a failure to balance these three things . . .

Basically, you should allocate time in proportion to the marks available for a question. If you are sitting a two hour exam and have to answer three questions carrying equal marks, then you are strongly advised (after deducting 10 minutes for reading the paper and 5 minutes at the end to check your answers) to allocate one-third of the remaining time (35 minutes) to each question – and to stick to this ruthlessly.

Hazard no. 1   The temptation to think that good answers compensate bad ones

Students often believe that they can get a really good mark by carrying on with one question which will compensate for poor performance in another. This is mistaken for two reasons. Firstly, the marking scheme for a paper may require that you get a minimum on each question in order to pass overall. Secondly, you will pick up in absolute terms fewer marks for the excellent answer than if you cut this off and spend the appropriate time on another question. This is because exam performance suffers from its own law of diminishing returns. Suppose you are near to the end of your allocated time on a question and you have gained 12 marks out of a possible 20 – a performance level of 60 per cent is a good standard. To pick up a further 6 marks, for example, means that you would have to take about 75 per cent of the marks still available. You would need to significantly raise your game, as it were, to achieve this. In contrast, to pick up just 6 marks on another question that has not yet been attempted would require a much lower level of performance.

> Moral: when writing exam answers, the best can be the enemy of the good.

Hazard no. 2   The idea that 'I'll catch up later'

You get stuck into a question, and realize that you are over-running your original allocation of time. It is so tempting to think that you can catch up later, but where would this extra time come from? Only by taking it from a later answer.

An instructive exercise is to take a blank sheet of paper, and copy non-stop from a newspaper or book for five minutes. You can scale this up and calculate the maximum number of words you can produce if the questions were to be all so easy that you could start straight away and complete each question without losing any time for planning or thinking. It usually isn't all that much – the average half-hour exam answer is about 700 words, a couple of sides of double-spaced A4.

This also tells you something about how much material a good exam answer should contain. On each of these sides in an exam answer you might only have three major paragraphs. Given that one paragraph generally equates to one main point of the answer, you can see that the volume of material you need for an answer can be only about six or so main points.

Note well the consequences of missing your own deadlines. If you are completing five questions in three hours, and you overshoot your target timing on the first four questions by just four minutes each, then you will have only just over half the allotted time left for your last question – and some of that will inevitably be consumed by planning and thinking. Accumulating delays can be dangerous.

Hazard no. 3   Not answering the question

We have seen several reasons why this can happen. Failure to unpick the question properly is one of the most significant of these. Another is simply not following the basic instructions correctly. Make sure you are clear on what you have to do – how many questions in each section, how many parts to a question, whether the separate parts of a question are alternatives or all have to be completed. A very common hazard is to be too confident – you might recognise a topic you have worked hard on, and then take the question for granted.

And not to put too fine a point on it – 'give examples' requires several examples, 'give reasons for your view' is different from 'justify your view'

Hazard no. 4   Answering the wrong questions

It is important to read through the paper as a whole. You should give each question enough consideration to judge how much choice you have on the paper, and this will help you identify questions you feel confident you are prepared for. There may be some questions that look extremely difficult. Many people avoid unusually worded questions, but as we have seen the wording of *all* questions should be carefully attended to. If it is a subject that

> There are no easy questions, only ones whose difficulty you have not yet realized.

you feel you know, conduct a solid analysis of what the question is actually asking. If there are topics you know less about, use your analysis of the question to work your way into the answer

Above all NEVER go in desperation for a question because it looks vague and you could do some kind of waffle on it. These answers usually pick up hardly any marks at all.

Hazard no. 5   No overall exam plan

No one's timing is perfect. There are, however, ways that you can help your timing.

Question

You have read through the exam paper. You have to do four questions in three hours. You have identified six possibles. Of these you feel really confident you could answer one well straight away. Two are on topics you have revised thoroughly but are slightly oddly worded and you are unsure about them. Two involve topics that you have some knowledge about but are not an expert, and the tasks/requirements are not especially straightforward in any case. And the last is rather vague but you know you could make something of it.

What should you do now?

Answer

Plan your whole paper strategy, so that once you start writing you have sorted out what you are going to do for the next three hours. This relieves you of one burden later on in the exam, and once you have decided on a set of questions, ideas will start popping up as you answer your first question, and you will see connections that you can use later. Some people even suggest you do all your plans in one go – this can work if you have a strong sense of time.

The nearest to a golden rule here is – **do the hardest thing in the middle of the exam.** That is when you still have a fair amount of time, but you have already unloosened your mind in doing the first answer.

In the situation outlined earlier, you could start the question you feel very confident about, to get you going, or you might decide to save this until last so that if time is short you can write it quickly. If you saved it until later, then the best thing to do would be to take one of the questions you knew a lot about but felt unsure about the wording, carefully analyse the question so that you are clear what it wants – and then you should be away.

And the vague question that you think you could do an answer on? You should know the answer to this by now – *avoid it!*

Hazard no. 6   No contingency plan

Question

You are sitting a paper with three questions of equal marks to do in two hours. And you have got the timing wrong, so you have only 48 minutes left for both your second and third questions.

What should you do?

Answer

This is the time to re-plan – do not carry on regardless.

Split your time again equally, for the same reason as we saw before: it is easier to pick up a few marks in a few minutes on a new question than to spend longer on one question going for the high mark. Reduce your planning time – you will have less time to write, so you need fewer points, and so less of a plan is needed. However, structure and answering the question remain paramount – if anything has to go in this situation it is probably best to reduce the content.

And what if your timing has gone completely wrong, and you are left with eight minutes for your last question? There is one emergency approach that could help you pick up a few marks which may be sufficient to secure your pass mark on the whole paper. *This is to make your plan your answer.* Do this carefully – a section with 'plan' written above it may often not get looked at all.

Plan the answer as you normally would, but write more legibly and leave a space at the top as well as several lines between each main idea. If you generate a list of ideas set them out as bullet points. Then write at the top of the plan the introductory paragraph you intended to write. Add in at tactical points in your plan brief comments so that the examiner can follow the main lines of your argument. At the end write a brief summary of the argument. You probably will not get a magnificent mark for this – if you have mismanaged your time this badly you don't deserve to. But you will have got your points down and drawn the examiner's attention to your argument, and this will certainly get you a few marks at least. It also looks more in control and may create a better impression on the examiner than 'run out of time please refer to plan'.

To summarize:

- Exam failure is usually caused by a failure to balance (i) the amount of time you have (ii) the number of words you can produce and (iii) the value of the question. Keeping these closely linked in your mind and your exam performance is bound to strengthen your technique.
- Time planning is essential – allot time in proportion to the marks the question will attract. Keep to your allotted timing.
- Make sure you unpick the question, but also be sure you understand clearly the basic instruction of the paper (how long, how many questions, marks for each part etc.) Always bear in mind that the examiner will be looking for higher level thinking in a Masters exam.
- It is easier to pick up marks on a fresh question than to spend time trying to make a good question brilliant.
- Consider planning in one go which questions you will answer.(if you are confident about managing the time).
- There are no easy questions – avoid ones that look vague to you (they aren't really) because you will probably do them badly.
- Have a clear contingency plan – if all else fails, plan well and convert this into an emergency answer.

Revision

When you have completed this section you should be able to:

- identify which areas of the syllabus will be most time-effective to focus on;
- evaluate your own strengths and weaknesses in relation to a particular examination;
- design and execute an appropriate revision plan, using all the resources available to you.

The message of the preceding sections has been very much that knowledge is not enough, and the thinking that you put in to an exam is also crucial – whether this is in terms of unpicking a question, getting an idea of what the examiner is looking for, or planning and writing your answer. However, having said all that, knowledge and being ready to use it, is still a necessary condition of exam success. However good your technique may be, if you don't know about relationship marketing at all you can't answer a question on it.

Revision

The great deception that everyone has about revision is that it means going over the work you have already done. In practice this is rarely the case. Most students will have kept up with some parts of the subject and dropped back with others. You may have skipped something so that you could focus on something else. You may simply have not fully understood something at the time.

The difference between the time before revision and the time for revision is that in the earlier period you were still building up a framework of understanding. In revision time you are able to reorganize what you know, establish links between concepts, and build your own critical positions on topics (essential at Masters level). All study at this point becomes a revisiting not simply of knowledge but of interconnections – the more extensive these are the better.

> Revision is partly re-visiting old knowledge, and partly about creating new learning through building fresh interconnections between ideas.

As your revision time is limited, you will need to apply strict controls on its use. Try to work with texts that give you specifics – a book with long reams of uninterrupted prose may be extraordinarily insightful but it may take you a long while to get these insights. A book with easily assimilated material – using bullet points diagrams and so on – is likely to be more superficial (and one must always be on one's guard for that, especially with subjects such as Business Management) but you can absorb it quickly, which makes it time-efficient.

And do not disregard other principles of learning – write down important ideas to consolidate them. If it's important, try to think of application to examples (this is particularly useful because you will build up a stock of ideas for illustrating answers). Especially try to find linkages between one topic and others.

Revising the syllabus

One of the great uncertainties with any exam is how much you need to know in order to be able to answer the questions. The reality with a Masters course is that it is *partially intended* to develop your ability to cope with intellectual uncertainties.

Question

Where would you look to identify your revision priority topics for a particular subject? Jot these down on a pad now.

Reply

- the syllabus as written in the course handbook;
- a module or unit guide given to you at the start of the teaching of the unit;
- past exam papers;
- representative textbooks.

But like all documentary information, the real syllabus can silently drift away from what is written down (as we said in Chapter 2). Although all courses are regularly reviewed, a tutor can change, and the new one can give a different emphasis, external events can make one aspect more important than another, changes in general business practice may drip-feed through, and the syllabus is often large enough to allow for internal variation.

As well as the written documents you have received, look also at the balance of the teaching in workshops and in lectures. This may help you to 'second guess' the real order of priorities in the minds of the tutors and examiners. The only time this would not apply is when the teachers are not examining you – for example on professional qualifications such as the examinations for membership of the Chartered Institute of Marketing, which are centrally devised, though the courses are taught at local colleges.

Pay special attention to material that is introduced relatively late in the course, and to material covered in revision sessions. Of course tutors cannot reveal the subject matter of unseen exam questions in advance, but they will make reasonable attempts to ensure that candidates are familiar with all the material they need in order to pass.

Question

All this will give you a wealth of data on the course. And it is unlikely to all point in exactly the same way. So if there were discrepancies between, say, the syllabus and coverage of the leading textbooks on the one hand, and the way the course was taught by a new member of staff this year, what would you do?

Reply

It is probably best to rely on the written sources in this case. If, however, the tutor made particular mention of the differences and guided you away from a topic that had previously been emphasized then you could take that as a clear sign.

Always remember that even with an internally examined programme, a lot of people may have an input into the structure and content of the exam paper, over and above the tutor. The process of development of examination papers often works in this way:

- module leader prepares a draft of the paper, in consultation with the rest of the module team;
- programme leader comments and may propose changes;
- other internal lecturers may propose changes;
- external examiner is consulted, who may propose further changes.

So while the tutor may be the best indicator of what you should cover, he is not the full authority.

Trying to reduce the amount you need to cover involves a certain degree of risk. The theory of examinations is that they can draw from any part of the syllabus, so you would have no complaint if they did just that. The preceding paragraphs are based on the assumption that one can identify areas of greater or lesser likelihood. But as the investment adverts say: 'past performance is no sure indicator of future returns'. Remember too that signs can be misread and you may misinterpret a statement or the emphasis of a particular teaching session, drawing the wrong conclusions from it.

Perhaps you are thinking 'So exactly how much of the syllabus should we cover?'

Question

You are studying a subject that has ten major topics. The exam will require you to choose two questions from a selection of 5. How many topics do you need to revise in detail?

Reply

Although many students ask this, it is a misleading question! At Masters level much of what is sought at the higher end of learning is relational, as we have said before. Therefore, many questions will expect a response that links different topics, even when they do not explicitly state this. And the breadth of questions may well require a reasonable familiarity with several topics. If the module has a large amount of detail in it (which would be unusual at Masters level) then some degree of risk taking may be in order, but even here you should assume that questions will cross over subjects, so that however many topics you think you need, you should revise significantly more than this.

Using past papers and other indicators of exam questions

Needless to say, the best work you can do in the final time leading up to an exam is to focus on exam papers and questions themselves. Do be aware of the various ways in which you can do this. A key feature of this process is

What you need to test out	What you could do
Coverage of syllabus	Taking whole papers, selecting less attractive questions, preparing plans
Knowledge of specific topics	Writing your own questions and then planning answers
Speed of recall	Taking whole questions, selecting desired questions, planning answers
Ability to apply knowledge in different ways	Writing your own questions and then planning answers
Essay planning and writing	Taking individual questions, planning and writing up full answer
Overall exam performance	A full scale mock exam

Table 3.2   Practising exam answers

being aware of what is expected of you, as you have established through consultation with module guides, statements about intended learning outcomes, your general understanding of what it is to study at Masters level, ans so on. Table 3.2 illustrates some of these:

You will notice that we are suggesting not just doing questions and plans, but also designing your own questions. This is a particularly instructive exercise.

Activity

(a) Take one unit or module that you know you are to be examined on. A few weeks before the exam write a whole exam paper that you think is fair overall (not just fair to you). At this stage use the points made in earlier sections on the wording of exam questions, but do not consult past papers in advance.

(b) When you have written your paper, compare it with some of the most recent past papers. Look carefully at the gaps and try to evaluate them. Is this because exam question always have some element of randomness to them, or are they indicators of some gaps in your understanding, or are you clear about the intended learning outcomes for the course . . .?

(c) Now take some of the questions you have written and produce a marking plan for them (along the lines of the marking plan given in section 4).

By the way, this is an excellent exercise to do with one or two colleagues.

A very important additional element of doing practice papers, questions and plans is the review you give this activity later. Again this will vary depending on what you think you need most out of the activity.

If you are testing out your speed of recall, then maybe the best review is to compare the plan or answer you produce in the allotted time with your detailed study notes. If on the other hand, you are checking how well you understand an area then it may be useful to compare your plan/answer with course material and textbooks.

Where you are practicing essay structure, or seeing how well you unpicked a question, it is best to leave a fully written-out answer for a day or so and then read it through to see if it makes a coherent whole. For a plan, again leave it for a day or so and then look at it alongside the question – ask if you could summarize the answer in one sentence (this will help both with evaluating the coherence of your writing but also with whether you have unpicked questions satisfactorily).

An aspect of examinations is that you will often be asked to illustrate or give examples. In the exam room you have to try to recall a situation, think whether it fits, how to express it, and so on. It can be done quickly, but it still takes planning time. And all planning time is non-writing time (and therefore in itself is not mark-generating activity).

It can be useful to specifically prepare examples in advance. Not that you know exactly what use you will be making of them. But if you are in employment, look at your own organization, for example, and think through its information strategy, or how well does it appraise the performance of individuals (or whatever the content of the exam is likely to be). If you are studying full-time, perhaps you can find a placement for a short while. Or together with your course colleagues, try to visit companies, to build up a sense of how they solve the problems of management – all this will help provide you with a stock of examples that may be useful in different places.

As a result, (a) you have thought through a bit more on the topic which always helps, and (b) if you are asked to provide an example, this kind of case always carries credibility. As well as preparing examples from your own experience, keeping up to date with current events is always important, as it demonstrates that you have not merely learnt material but are also doing something with it.

Much of this you will do on your own, inevitably. But there is also a huge value in doing some revision in a group. We shall look at this below.

Revision in groups

Working with others can bring a wide range of benefits, including:

- independent appraisal of written answers,
- sharing ideas on difficult areas,
- dividing work up between you,
- forming a wider understanding by pulling everyone's ideas together.

Independent appraisal

The basic idea is that if you re-read your own writing you may be less able to evaluate it properly than someone else who is more distant from the work.

One way to do this is for each to do a question individually and then swap the answers with other people and see what each has chosen to emphasize, what has been left out, and so on.

Another is for everyone in the group to write an answer to a question, and then the group as a whole decides what would be the appropriate marking criteria for this question. When they have done that, they collectively use these criteria to evaluate each answer.

A more sophisticated way (which only really works when the group is getting on well together) is for one person to write an answer and then be questioned on it by the rest of the group. It helps to develop logic skills but also the skills of getting points written down succinctly, as often the questions are more for elucidation than debate.

Sharing ideas on difficult areas and forming a wider understanding

This is where groups can be especially effective, supporting each other and building up a joint understanding of what is involved in a particular subject.

- *Mini-lectures*. Members of the group prepare a short lecture explaining an idea and deliver this to the group, who then discuss the topic and devise possible examination questions.
- *Writing exam questions* jointly can be the most effective way to develop an instinct for what the questions are likely to bring out. One effective way is first for individuals to write their own questions, and then compare and discuss their wordings with other people. Whenever you write questions, also try to set down marking criteria. What would someone expect to see in this question, what is it looking for? Usually this will come to mind as you are writing the question. Groups can also analyse the questions to establish what is sought (using the list of different terms given earlier in this chapter).
- *Shared summaries*. People share their notes and a composite of these is drawn up on a flipchart
- *Group brainstorming*. Still one of the most effective ways of several people sharing thoughts (but always go beyond the brainstorm itself; some kind of summarizing or organizing of the brainstorm is essential otherwise it is just a list of words)
- *Planning and marking*. For a particularly difficult subject, split the group into two: one half writes a joint plan/answer to a question, the other half separately devises what they think are the appropriate marking criteria; the two groups come together and use the criteria to evaluate what has been written
- Various kinds of *debating exercises* also can work very well. For example, the group sub-divides into 'pro' and 'anti' camps, and then prepare a short debate on a 'Do you agree . . .' type question.

Dividing up the workload

Sharing the workload can be accomplished in a number of ways:

- Each member of a group takes a chapter of a textbook and writes a short précis of it. The group then has a number of texts that they can all benefit from.
- Each member of the group can take a separate topic and scan past exam papers to see where it comes up – when the group puts these together they will find how often questions are cross-topical, and come up on more than one person's list.
- Producing posters individually or in pairs that summarize books or articles.

Different kinds of examinations

As well as the traditional model of an examination being a written paper containing a number of unseen questions to be completed within 2 or 3 hours, two other kinds might be encountered in your studies: (a) case-study exams and (b) open-book examinations.

(a) **Case study examinations**

It is common with Business and Management Masters programmes for there to be one or more case study examinations as part of the assessment package. These differ from the more traditional examinations in that you are presented with a case study of an organization or industry, sometimes containing a large amount of detailed background information, sometimes also including a narrative of a series of events. Very often cases are distributed to candidates in advance of the exam, sometimes as much as a fortnight beforehand.

As with all exams, it is important to be as clear as you can about what the examiner is looking for. Case studies are especially suitable for Masters level assessment, as the real life element they bring to questions means that you have to consider the full context for the organization.

Group revision becomes even more important for case study exams, as part of the test is usually related to the analysis you have done prior to entering the exam room. Question analysis as a revision tool tends to be less important with this kind of exam than issue analysis – getting clear what the major issues are that the case presents. An important part of your preparation for a case study exam is therefore the use of analytical tools to make sense of the case study.

Remember that even though the case may be given to you as part of a Strategic Management course, or an HRM module, you will be expected to show a good relational understanding of the way one set of issues links with other subject areas. You should certainly establish clearly with your tutor if they expect you to do any further research on the company discussed in the case – some may require this, some may explicitly tell you not to: so check what your tutor wants.

A common mistake that is made with case-study answers is to spend time repeating back to the examiner the material of the case. What is needed is to *use* the case material – if the case provides figures on sales, for example, then rather than simply summarize these, you should in your answer go immediately to inferring from them. So rather than say *'Sales have declined by 16% over the last five years'* you should state *'The probable cause of the 16% decline in sales over the last five years is . . .'*

Another issue that can cause some difficulty is that case studies, as with real life, provide incomplete information. This is one of the things that make them a useful test at Masters level. Where there are gaps in the data then you have to make assumptions. These need to be realistic and demonstrate your grasp of the corporate environment.

(b) **Open-book examinations**

An open-book exam is sometimes encountered at Masters level. This involves unseen questions, but candidates are allowed to bring reference material in to the examination room. These exams are intended to reduce the focus on retrieval of facts, in favour of broader discussion focusing on deeper levels of learning. In some cases your tutor will specify what material may be brought in (e.g. a specific textbook, or a certain number of pages of your own notes).

Where you are in a position to choose what you bring in to the exam room, you are strongly advised to rely on your own notes. Experience suggests that when students take textbooks into an open book exam they are distracted by the apparent 'benefit' that this provides, and waste time going through books trying to find the appropriate item. Use of your own notes is advantageous for several reasons: as you have prepared them you will have a better idea where to locate content when you need it (so please ensure they are clearly sorted and labelled), they are also likely to be more condensed, and finally they have been prepared by you specifically to help with an exam – which is NOT the purpose of a textbook. Remember, the purpose of the exam is for you to construct answers and essays, not to find them – either in your notes or in books.

To summarize:

- Revision continues the process that operates throughout the course of revisiting old knowledge, incorporating new knowledge, filling in the gaps in your personal conceptual framework, and establishing fresh connections between ideas.
- Revision activities should be adopted in relation to specific learning targets, such as speedy recall, or coherent writing.
- It is prudent to go for as much coverage of a syllabus as you can find time for. At the very least, assume that more knowledge will be needed than you would normally expect.
- Try to estimate what the 'real' curriculum is, rather than simply the official one. Refer to module guides and discuss with colleagues and tutors what the intended learning outcomes really involve. Use your understanding of the real curriculum to set priorities for learning.
- Past exam papers and questions can be used for a variety of purposes, and are especially useful towards the end of your revision.
- Revision and learning in groups creates a vast range of further potential activities which you could not do so well on your own. Do try to have at least some collaborative revision activity.

And finally, five things to remember always with exams:

1   perfection is never there – you will waste a lot of time chasing it fruitlessly;
2   always balance the effort you are putting in with the value you are getting out;
3   do some revision in groups;
4   try to understand what the examiner wants and demonstrate this explicitly;
5   doing well in exams is about *what you do with the knowledge you have*, not just how much you've got.

4 Responding to Assignments

● **Introduction**

Your Masters will be awarded on the basis of your assessment results – assignments and exams. So in this chapter we will provide you with a number of tools and concepts to help you do yourself full justice in assignments.

Assignments should be evaluated on the basis of formal criteria for assessment. These specify the key elements which markers are looking for when they assess your work. Tactically the most effective method of succeeding in assignments is to work to ensure that your work demonstrably meets the stated criteria.

Commonly on Masters-level programmes, two levels of assessment criteria are used:

- generic criteria – these demonstrate your general intellectual skills in the field and will be constant across all assignments; and
- specific criteria – these constitute the particular elements of knowledge, skill and understanding that an assignment focuses on and therefore will be specific to each piece of work.

In this chapter we will focus on generic criteria. In many countries frameworks have been devised in recent years that define what is expected of Masters-level Business students. These tend to focus on areas such as communication, critical thinking, problem-solving, managing and interpreting information, research skills, leadership and personal development. Within the requirements of assessed coursework, many of these are captured by specific assessment criteria, but the communication and information handling related areas are generic issues that affect all assessments. Therefore each section of this chapter will deal with one of the commonly used generic assessment criteria:

1 **Structure:** appropriate structure and study framework.
2 **Argument**: the progression and quality of your argument.

3 **Research**: the scope of the appropriate research and reading.
4 **Presentation**: the quality of the communication and presentation of your ideas.
5 **Conclusions and recommendations**: strength of conclusions and /or policy recommendations.
6 **Originality and reflection**: what distinguishes your thinking – creativity, originality and how you can use reflection to learn from working on assignments.
7 **Managing time**: using time efficiently when completing assignments; avoiding timewasters, prioritizing and planning.

We suggest that you read through all this quickly on the first occasion, but return to and work carefully through it as you start work on each assignment.

These areas have been selected as they are used in many business schools and management departments. However, you should at the earliest opportunity try to establish what are the generic criteria that are used on your own programme – which you should be able to do by consulting programme outlines and module guides, and by asking your tutors.

In your module guide you should also be looking for a statement of the 'intended learning outcomes' of the module. This is the section of the guide in which the lecturer has aligned their module to the intended learning outcomes of the programme as a whole. In a well-designed module the outcomes will lead naturally to the assessment criteria. Studying the intended outcomes carefully will give you a good perspective on what the lecturer is really trying to achieve in the module, and will help you interpret the detail of the assessment criteria.

● **Structure**

When you have completed working through this section you should be able to:

- relate questions of structure to the different kinds of learning outcome sought from an assignment;
- describe different structural shapes that can be applied to essay-based assignments, and evaluate their appropriateness to different types of assignment task.

Here are three essay titles:

1   *Describe the principle causes of group dysfunction.*
2   *How far does the theory of group dysfunction apply to managing professional staff?*
3   *'Group dysfunction is directly related to the quality of the group's leader.' Discuss.*

The subject matter of these three assignments is very similar – they are all about group dysfunction (a topic you will encounter when looking at organizational behaviour). But what they are asking you to do with this topic is very different. You could not provide the same 'off-the-peg' answer for all three and expect to do well each time. This is a key issue which underpins the correct approach to assignments.

Different key words in a question indicate that the assessment is seeking a demonstration of different types of skill, knowledge or understanding.

We can tell what the direction an assignment should take by reference to these key words – usually the instruction or the main verb of the question: 'discuss, compare and contrast, identify' and so on. These tell us the level and depth to which the assignment should aim. One way of categorizing the degree of depth that is required in an assignment can be found in work done by John Biggs, in his Structure of Observed Learning Outcomes (SOLO) taxonomy which we discussed in Chapter 2 (a five-stage scale – pre-structural, uni-structural, multi-structural, relational, extended abstract).

What has this scale of learning outcomes got to do with structure? Well, the main point is that *different structures fit different kinds of purpose.* A uni- or multi-structural assignment question will often require a simpler and more linear answer than a relational or extended abstract one. At Masters level the balance will shift from uni- or multi-structural thinking to relational and abstract thinking, and your tutors will look to the way your written work provides evidence of organized thinking as a major indicator of your achievement of learning outcomes. This mirrors the criteria that are applied to academic contributions, which are as often judged in terms of clarity and illumination as they are by originality or proof.

Activity

Look back at the essay titles. Firstly, try to identify which of these five types of outcome is being sought (referring back to the SOLO model detailed in Ch. 2). Then, outline very briefly the kind of structure you would envisage for each question, and compare with our suggestions below. Don't be deflected by claiming how little you know about group theory – you probably know a lot. Otherwise take a subject you know well, try to compose equivalent questions and then compare these with the examples you have just read.

Suggested replies

Question 1 ('*Describe the principal causes of group dysfunction*') could easily be seen as uni-structural or multi-structural (depending on how many different causes you have been able to describe – some replies might be merely elaborations of the one principle cause). It is unlikely that a whole Masters-level assignment would look for simply knowledge of these factors. But it could be an initial part of an answer. A reasonable structure for question 1 might be:

Definition of group dysfunction.
A short paragraph explaining each cause.
A brief discussion, maybe of an example.
Summary.

Question 2 ('*How far does the theory of group dysfunction apply to managing professional staff?*') is clearly at a significantly deeper level. It requires someone not only to know about group dysfunction but also to apply it to the features of a specific workforce, and then use this to feed back to provide some evaluation of the theory itself. It is therefore at the relational level and is close to the extended abstract level.

An answer to this question might involve something like this structure:

Definition and key features of group dysfunction.
Nature of professions:

qualifications and training,
professional cultures dominated by fee-earners,
multidisciplinary teams in professional firms,
conflicts between different professional groups.

Comparison of group theory and professional service organizations; identification of differences as well as similarities, with examples. Summary of extent to which theory applies, challenges to existing theory and/or possible recommendations for professional service organizations.

The most obvious thing to notice here is that the structure is more complex. It is no longer a case of a linear approach, but of something coming up in one place that recurs elsewhere. Also here there is more discretion for the writer in terms of what should come where – examples are sometimes put at the end of a discussion of this kind and sometimes woven into the fabric of the argument.

Question 3 (*'Group dysfunction is directly related to the quality of the group's leader. Discuss'*) explicitly requires some attention to the theory but as it links with another concept, that of leadership. It is not simply about how far does the theory apply, but of what does the theory really mean when put together with a separate concept. It would not be sufficient to list a series of examples of successes and failures – they would have to be given in the contexts of group and leadership theory. An acceptable assignment would have to be relational, but a better response moves into the extended abstract category as it may develop an appropriate synthesis of different theoretical positions from which the examples can be re-analysed.

So an answer might look like this:

- Definition of group dysfunction and key features.
- Explanation of leadership via a recognized model.
- Comparison of common elements, causal relationships between the two areas.
- Identification and explanation of areas where there is incongruity or a lack of fit.
- Examples from actual life.
- Evaluative summary of the link between the two concepts, perhaps development of a new position.

Whilst the structure itself here is more linear than in the second example, the kind of depth each component will go into is far beyond that of the first example.

So different kinds of assessment activity involve different intellectual levels. And whilst the lower ones might have some role in some parts of an assignment, at this level you should presume that somewhere in your essay a relational or extended abstract response will be needed. As we have stated several times in this text, Masters level implies the ability to deal at a high level of abstraction with multiple and sometimes messy theoretical complexity, so you should aim to demonstrate your ability to manage these as a matter of course.

Since it became possible to use the internet easily to search for materials, references and information to support academic writing, a form of assignment has appeared which is known as 'patch construction' – the putting together of blocks of text from many different sources, assembled up into a text, partially related to the question which has been asked. There are many reasons for avoiding this approach – not least because each lifted text should be referenced properly. But is completely inappropriate for the sort of Masters-level work we are describing in this chapter, where the structure, shape and voice should be individually related to the specific task.

Related to the issue of structure is the metaphor of *shape*. Each different type of question implies different shapes of answers. A task that required you to explain whether you agreed or not with a particular statement would have a linear form. On the other hand, a task where you are asked to compare and contrast two items (such as two different approaches to investment appraisal) is likely to have a two-tracked conceptual structure rather like that shown in Figure 4.1.

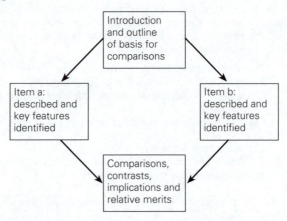

Figure 4.1   Question and answer structure, example 1

On the other hand, a question that asked you to identify and discuss the four elements of the marketing mix, say, would have a flatter form as shown in Figure 4.2.

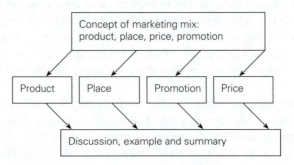

Figure 4.2   Question and answer structure, example 2

When writing your assignment it is important to make sure that the reader knows where they are in your discussion. If you are on step three of a list of four, make sure this is clearly flagged up, or *signposted*, to the reader – use numbered headings, or very clearly say things like '*Thirdly* . . .' Similarly, if you are moving from comparisons to contrasts, then say so: '*Having discussed the comparisons between x and y, we shall now look at the contrasts.*' Clarity of the structure of your logic is one of the most important aspects of assignments – as it is of most writing.

Finally in this section we think about the kinds of writing you will do for assignments. And in particular, the difference between reports, essays and other kinds of assignments.

A report is a formal presentation of facts and evaluations. It may contain the same content as an essay but it will lay out the material in a clearly sign-posted and logical sequence, and with a more objective basis for evaluation.

A report should not only set out an initial purpose (e.g. 'to evaluate the effectiveness of group working in professional organizations'), but it should end with a *conclusion* (what has been discovered as a result of this report) and a set of *recommendations* (i.e. proposals for action in the light of the conclusions). These two components of the end of a report are easily confused and should always be kept quite separate. We shall revisit this aspect in a later section.

The word 'essay' for academic work developed in the seventeenth century from the word to test or try out (we still use 'assay' when testing gold and silver). Then it described writing which was the first draft, trying out an idea, testing a theory, exploring a notion – today, what we call 'the back of the envelope'. The academic was aiming to write a treatise (today, a book or a paper) and the essays were steps on the way. Once Montaigne had published his elegant essays, the literary style was expected to be refined even if the ideas were tentative. So now academics use essays as training for profes-sional academic life.

Therefore an essay is a freer discussion than a report. It is acknowledged within essay writing that the author may be presenting their own perspective, and not covering every different point of view with equal focus. You are, of course, still expected to cover the main points of view represented in a debate and to evaluate them fairly, aiming for good quality in your argument. Also the requirements of academic writing mean that it is always essential to make clear what is your own work and what comes from other sources – whether these be books and articles or data someone else has collected from the field – so full referencing is just as necessary here as it is in any other writing.

Whether writing a report, an essay or some other form of assignment, the language you use should always be direct and clear. In an essay entitled

'Why I Write', the English author George Orwell wrote: 'Good prose is like a window pane', an idea which many authors try to follow. You can use the following as a checklist of your use of language:

- Is the language straightforward?
- Are all technical terms explained?
- Are there any vague terms?
- Are all generalizations clearly justified?
- Is there a basis for each evaluative statement?
- Is there any unnecessarily flowery language?
- Is there any unnecessarily rhetorical language?
- Are bullet points (if used) expressed clearly?
- Are sentences too long?

In many universities in recent years there has been a growth in the units which help students develop their writing skills. These may be called Academic Writing units, or have names with the words Student Support, Study Skills and Student Guidance in their title. While there are many helpful texts on the topic of learning to write academic English, many universities have also published guidance notes on their internal web pages. Giving good guidance on academic writing deserves a book on its own – in this text, we are aiming to help you understand how to create the structure of your work.

> *To summarize*:
>
> The main point you should draw from this section is that there are different kinds of task that a tutor may set you, and your structure will vary accordingly. Issues relating to structure will also recur in this chapter, significantly so in the next section.

● Argument

> When you have worked through this section, you should be able to:
>
> - identify the key differences between academic writing and other forms;
> - evaluate the validity of arguments within essays and assignments; and
> - identify the key benefits of referencing.

By 'argument' here we mean: the use of a set of statements as evidence or justification for another statement. The latter of these is a *conclusion* and is said to be inferred from, or implied by, the former set of statements, which are generally called the *premises* of the argument. Arguments often work in hierarchies, so that the conclusion of one argument may then go on to be used as a premise in another argument.

The nature of academic writing

The most important aspect of any assignment is that it is an academic piece of writing. This has several implications:

- The work should clearly set out an argument.
- The writer should indicate how their argument links with previous work.
- Other people's work should be critiqued fairly – with strengths as well as weaknesses acknowledged.
- The writer should not try to overly persuade the reader, but let the argument stand on its own merits.

Different kinds of assignment task may require different kinds of argument. As with learning outcomes and assessment criteria, you should make sure you are clear about what is expected on your course. If you are following an executive MBA you may find that arguments and points need to involve a close focus on application of ideas to real life managerial contexts. If you are on a full time MSc courses you may place greater reliance on theory. As always, the golden rule is to use all available evidence (documents, statements by tutors, examples of past work) to get clear what kind of argument is expected of you.

There are several pitfalls which can easily mislead individuals. One is to adopt a 'journalistic' style. Journalists may report factual material, but the underlying intention is quite different from the academic. Academic writing should set out both sides of a position and then soberly weigh them up. Journalistic writing avoids this as being too dry. The aim of a journalist is to catch people's interest, so they will usually try to present material in a dramatic form that will attract the browsing reader. For that reason, journalism, even very good journalism, tends to be one-sided, and often glosses over the difficult bits that complicate an issue. You may encounter the occasional management writer who successfully manages to capture a journalistic feel whilst retaining an academic standpoint, but this is rare, and very difficult to emulate!

Another potential trap is to adopt too pressuring a tone. Whilst you will want your work to be persuasive, too 'hard sell' an approach in an academic context will have the opposite effect. You must be sufficiently detached from the work for it to be independently read and evaluated by someone – in fact, it is an academic obligation to take account of opposing ideas. This is why too personal a tone is misplaced. If the reader is continually being reminded that 'I think that . . .' then they may well feel that what they are being asked to consider and evaluate is not an argument but a person.

Beware of other dangers such as using too superior a tone of voice in your text or using far more references than are necessary to justify a point. The main thing is to bear in mind that you are trying to demonstrate to the reader (i.e the marker) that you have attained the key intended learning outcomes associated with the assessment. The main question about argument is then whether it does enough to demonstrate this or not.

The use of 'I'

Opinions vary over whether 'I' is ever allowed at all. In some contexts, such as a discussion of the economic environment, you would be better to leave it out. In others, where there might be a more personal connection, such as the ethics of business, it may be appropriate to a very limited degree, but still it should be used very sparingly.

So what exactly *is* an argument? It is a process of reasoning involving a connected series of statements intended to establish a position and ultimately to stand as proof of that position – the presentation of a number of items from which a conclusion is drawn. This may seem very basic, but it is surprising how easy it is to lose sight of this when one is writing. Look at this sample paragraph:

Organizational objectives are rarely clear, and even when they are, are not often clearly understood. Moreover, as Argyris has pointed out (Argyris, 1992, chs 2*ff*) those who set the objectives are themselves often guilty of over-optimism as to how well the objective setting process has been followed - they want to believe that everyone is in agreement with the values and plans of the business. This incomprehension and self-deception surrounding the process distracts people from the really key issues, which are whether the objectives are achievable and will add value to the organization. It can sometimes look more as if we plan as a ritual than as a strategic device.

What's the argument here? There are two argument steps. The first two sentences support the claim that *there is incomprehension and self-deception surrounding the process of setting objectives*. Then from this is drawn a further inference that *this phenomenon distracts people from 'the really key issues'*. And the last sentence is not much more than a rhetorical flourish, even though it might look like the main conclusion of the paragraph.

This example illustrates two important principles:

- It is better for each paragraph to present a single argument.
- It must be made abundantly clear to the reader what is the conclusion – or key statement – of each paragraph and what are the supporting reasons.

On these two grounds the paragraph given as an example above, though flowing well enough, could be misleading. One isn't quite sure how important the last sentence is for the writer's overall argument, and this can cause problems when reading later paragraphs, as one is unsure whether they follow on from the statement about ritual or the statement about distraction from the key issues. The question of what is conclusion and what are reasons is less problematic, though the fact that the main statement appears to come as the penultimate sentence does not help focus the reader's attention strongly enough.

A simple device which most of us use instinctively when writing or speaking but which would help tremendously in the example paragraph is the use of an inference word or phrase: *so*, *therefore*, *because of this*, *consequently*, and so on. Simply by inserting 'so' at the start of the penultimate sentence, the writer would have erased these doubts once and for all.

Validity and covert assumptions

The ideal argument would contain a series of statements – premises – acceptance of which would mean that someone could not deny your conclusion. But we are not often able to argue so clearly.

Much academic discussion at Masters level is tentative in one way or another, so it is about *challenge*. You should not take any major statement at face value simply as the truth, but be cautious about it, and be ready to ask *how* true it is. There are several different kinds of questions that might be used as challenges to a statement, including:

- Is the statement universally true or are there exceptions?
- Does the statement actually only apply to a specific category?
- Is the support or evidence for the statement justified?
- Does this statement conflict with other established ideas?
- How confident can you be about the statement: is it *certainly* true, *probably* true, *on balance* true, *indeterminable* but as good as any other statement?

Make sure that the degree of confidence you have in your statements is accurately reflected in the way you express these: if you are very sure, then it is in order to state 'There is a high probability that . . .' or something similar; if your view is only on balance, then use that phrase itself to show this.

Another aspect to be sure about is just what are your reasons for stating something. Are they direct factual claims? Are they opinions drawn from other writers? Are they ideas you have brought together from your own

Activity

Look through this passage and identify all the terms that are overtly or covertly evaluative. Are they well-placed or do they make unwarranted assumptions?

> At the start of the industrial revolution, employment was regarded as almost entirely an exploitative affair: people were there simply to provide labour power, and often endured extremely harsh conditions because employers were unwilling to forego any of their profits to improve conditions. This approach became progressively less and less effective, due partly to the growing assertiveness of the working population, but also because other market economies were beginning to catch up on the UK's flying start, and were finding that more enlightened approaches were garnering greater returns. Additionally, some Victorian philanthropists had highlighted the oppressiveness of the standard factory environment. The mill, long seen as the symbol of ruthless capitalism, began to appear more of an embarrassment than as a standard bearer of the new economy.

We identified the following evaluative or quasi-evaluative terms in the passage:

> Exploitative, harsh, effective, enlightened, oppressiveness, ruthless, embarrassment

It is difficult to be sure whether these are well-placed in this context. Certainly those which carry an implied criticism of Victorian mill and factory owners appear as if this is completely undisputed fact. This is an area of particular risk – where there is a commonly held opinion it is very easy to fall in line with it and simply accept it without question: in this case, that Victorian entrepreneurs were in general exploitative, ruthless, etc. The best researchers, however, will always look a little bit further, and show the limits of this kind of view, the extent or lack of the evidence, how many weren't like this etc. This is as true of factual areas where there is little strong evidence as it is where there are evaluative judgements made about behaviour, though the judgmental area is perhaps the more problematic.

thinking about the issue? Each of these has a role, but they should not be confused. Special care should be taken with evaluative statements – these should all be clearly based on some criteria. Avoid simply stating that something is ethically or socially wrong.

Referencing

The last main aspect in this section is your treatment of the work of others. First and foremost, as a matter of sheer prudence you should always acknowledge all source material. That way, at its most minimal, you protect yourself from any allegation that you are trying to cheat by passing off someone else's work as your own.

Your course guide is very likely to have a section about 'plagiarism, collusion and cheating'. Your university will probably have written a policy on these subjects – they are sometimes called 'academic misconduct' policies. Many of the students who get into difficulties here are not trying to cheat, but they have not understood the rules. We strongly advise you to discuss the texts about misconduct both with other students and with your tutors. A very common problem is that a student assembles an essay by selecting pieces from text books and other sources, puts it together as an argument, and presents it for assessment. In the student's mind they have used their intelligence to select the best sections and to create a well-structured argument – in the tutor's mind, they have copied sections of other people's work without acknowledgement. The solution, of course, is to reference all your work.

There are, though, stronger and more positive reasons for referencing and acknowledgement.

One of these is that by writing an assignment on a course you are participating in the academic community. The whole idea of academic writing is to present ideas for open debate and discussion, on the basis that this is the best way for knowledge to grow. Truth which emerges from open challenge is deemed more reliable than truth derived from authorities such as a divinity, nature, 'common sense' or personal feeling. So it is important, if debate is to thrive, that all participants reveal what they have drawn from other sources and what they have added themselves.

Acknowledging other people's work helps others to track your thinking, so it is easier to see what contribution you have made to the argument. Indeed, at times, it is not easy to fully appreciate what someone is trying to say unless you know what books, articles and research studies they have based their work on.

Treat other writers' work as objectively as you can. You may not agree with what someone has written – if so then you should express this via a well-constructed argument, giving clear reasons for your views. If you cannot, then maybe you should reconsider what you disagree with. Bear in mind, too, that sometimes irrelevant aspects of someone's work may distract from the key points of their argument. If you read a piece that strongly conflicts with your own personal values then it is always very difficult to put those to one side and treat the argument dispassionately. There is a lesson there for all of us in terms of reading as well as writing.

The most useful starting point for discussing someone else's work in your essay is to assume that there is some degree of validity in what they say but that it is unlikely to be totally correct. That puts you in the appropriate mindset of looking for the strengths and weaknesses of the work, rather than simply making a summary judgement that you agree or disagree.

> *To summarize*:
>
> - Each paragraph should consist of a key statement, whilst the other sentences should provide the evidential and justificatory support.
> - Evaluative and/or emotive material should be carefully distinguished from factual, and should be based clearly on criteria.
> - Discussion of material from other sources should be balanced and take account of strengths as well as weaknesses.
> - Sources of material – ideas and data – should be celebrated not concealed.

Research

> When you have completed this section you should be able to:
>
> - make effective use of different strategies for getting material from books, websites and articles; and
> - use textual material effectively with assignments.

There is a common fallacy that assignments follow a straight line process, where you start by doing a lot of reading and then when you have done enough, you stop and write your piece of work.

In practice this happens extremely rarely, and even when it does, it is not usually the best strategy. As we read, we learn more, we develop a greater understanding. We then try to put this down on paper, and find that in re-presenting our knowledge we see more issues and angles on the material we are working with. As a result of that we start asking more and deeper questions, which suggests that we need to do more reading, and that starts off the cycle again. Presenting drafts of work to others for comment, and reading and commenting on theirs in turn, is also a valuable step in developing understanding and formulating fresh questions.

Essentially, although this makes the whole process of reading for an assignment more complicated, it does reflect a healthy move beyond uni- or multi-structural thinking toward the relational and abstract investigation that is characteristic of Masters study. This requires you to treat knowledge tentatively, accepting that answers are often provisional, and are rarely completely established. Thus we make progress by the continued formulation of questions.

There are two related further fallacies that follow on from this:

- the fallacy that everything you have read and noted must be used; and
- the fallacy that you have to explore every avenue in order to resolve the issue.

The first of these can often lead to an overly 'inclusive' style of writing – unfortunately not restricted to students but also to some academics as well – where every single piece of work the author has accessed is referenced. Whilst in one sense this is laudable, it can mean that references are made artificially to ensure that a piece of work gets a mention in an essay. The text in such writing is often peppered by footnotes or parentheses giving names and publication dates. If you have not used the text then mentioning it adds nothing to your discussion. Use it or lose it!

The second fallacy is simply unworkable. As you read more and develop further insights the different branches of your thinking can grow at an exponential rate. Mind maps, for example, can often turn into thick bushes of boxes and lines as more and more ideas are identified and more and more linkages are established. At some point you have to bring each journey to a halt, indicating that this is as far as you will allow your research to go.

How to decide when and where to stop? The ideal point would be where you can see what are called 'parallel outcomes' so that whichever way an issue resolves itself, the impact on your overall analysis is essentially the same. In some cases even this would involve more reading and discussion than you have space for. In which case, the important thing is not to undermine the framework of your overall discussion. You may halt the investigation and simply allude to what you have passed over in a footnote, such as 'There are a number of different methods of appraising investments, but for reasons of simplicity we shall adopt the payback method here.' This demonstrates to the reader (i.e. the marker) that you are aware that there is a range of concepts even though you have only selected one of these.

Having established that reading must be used judiciously and to develop new and insightful questions rather than simply provide answers, we should look at the process of reading itself.

How do you read? This very simple question is central to the effectiveness of your studies. There are several key principles in reading for greatest effect.

- Read with a clear purpose.
- Do not feel you have to read textbooks like stories. You do not have to start at the beginning and read through to the end.
- Use chapter headings, summaries, and other cues to help you cut down the amount of text you actually have to engage with.
- Skim every text before deciding whether to read any of it carefully.
- Use notes both to consolidate what you have read and also to function as your brief reference point at a later date.

Underlying these principles is the basic fact that there is far too much to read on a Masters programme. So it is essential to find ways that you can get the information you need without going over every single sentence.

Which texts to access? Though it sounds simple, the first choices are those which your tutors recommend. This is for three reasons:

- if the tutor suggests the book, it is likely to cover the main areas;
- it is probable that the tutor has taken the content and presentation of this into account when designing the course; and
- the tutor themselves is likely to be particularly familiar with it, so it is easier for them to assess your use of material where it is drawn from the suggested text.

You will get more out of a textbook if you see it as a resource from which to extract content when needed than as a narrative to be taken all in one reading.

Deciding what else to consult is another source of false steps and potentially wasted time. It is a useful principle to consult texts that have been referred to in more than one source, as these are likely to be more authoritative or influential. At Masters level it is expected that people will look beyond the frame-

Activity

Go back over notes you have already made from a textbook. Then compare these notes with the text. What did you include? What did you leave out? Why? What do your replies tell you about the ways in which your note-taking could become more efficient?

Getting the most out of a textbook is directly linked to how clear is your reason for looking for information there. If you want 'general background' you are in danger of reading aimlessly and not knowing what to focus on and what to skim, at least on the first pass through. If you have in mind a specific objective – which may be to answer a specific question, to find out exactly what so-and-so said, or to be able to describe clearly the elements of a particular model – then you will know what to look for and will very quickly get it .

work provided by their tuition. The tutor may not be familiar with the material, so you will need to explain it clearly, and you may need to be more specific about why the theory or model is relevant to your subject. This is a necessary step if you are to achieve the originality of thought that is implicit in Masters-level study.

The internet is of course a major reference tool, with its huge potential benefits and some well attested ways in which one can waste a lot of time for little return. In academic terms, the main advantage of the world wide web is that it is a *source of sources*. In other words, it puts you into contact, via search engines, with sites that either themselves provide content or direct you to further sites with relevant content.

It is important to recognise that material taken from texts or websites can be used in different ways, and that these may be more or less appropriate.

Another issue is whether to *quote* writers or not. Consider what you demonstrate when you use a direct quote – you prove that you have accessed the text and decided the quote was relevant in a certain context. This is useful when you want to confirm that this is what the writer really said (often helpful in historical or philosophical subjects, where it might be questioned whether someone said what is attributed to them). It can certainly add authenticity. It also shows the marker how far you understand whether a certain idea fits a certain type of discussion. But avoid using quotes or any references solely as *decoration* – references are only required when you have used a source.

Activity

1. Bartlett and Ghoshall argue that for a company to operate successfully in a global context, it needs to have an effective communications infrastructure linking the central headquarters with regional ones.
2. As Bartlett and Ghoshall might say 'Managing across borders requires structural solutions – especially the communications links between global and regional HQs.'
3. International management requires structural as well as marketing solutions, such as good communication links between the global and regional HQs – a point echoed by Bartlett and Ghoshall.

To which of the five levels on the Biggs model do each of these three sentences, taken from the same source, best correlate?

Response

The second of these is clearly at a uni- or multi-structural level, where it is the presentation of a point that matters. The third of these looks to be operating at a relational level – bringing ideas together, and then finding some textual authority to support this. The first sentence, though, seems to be more concerned with the theory of the writers themselves, and so might be moving more into an extended abstract approach.

The key point is that each of these might be suitable at a different point in your essay. If you are aiming at demonstrating basic knowledge, then the quote may be sufficient. If on the other hand you are trying to demonstrate a deeper level of understanding then you may want to use one of the other two statements.

Consider what you demonstrate if, instead of quoting, you paraphrase. Here you may not prove for certain that so and so really said 'x' (though you could easily refer readers to the original text to prove this). But you do prove that you *understand* what is being said. And by rewriting it in your own words the idea gets put into the kind of language in which you characteristically express yourself. So it starts to become absorbed and integrated into your own thinking. Last but by no means least, this process of rewriting and summarising, as well as consolidating existing learning, continues the process of raising new questions which may lead to fresh researches or fresh insights.

To summarize:

- Reading is not a case of just looking at the text; it is a matter of engaging with a textbook to get what you need from it.
- It is both impossible and inappropriate to try to read textbooks all the way through; think of them as resources from which you extract content from time to time for a specific purpose.
- Skimming techniques are essential tools to glean material quickly from a text.
- Writing, especially summary and paraphrase, are important tools in reading.
- The use of material from other writers should be tactically aligned with the purpose for which it is used: at higher levels quotation becomes less important than paraphrase.
- Always start with a set or recommended text, and then work outwards for wider understanding.

Presentation

When you have worked through this section, you should be able to:

- evaluate your own and others' writing in terms of how well it communicates with the audience
- use a range of strategies to enhance the impact of your writing
- appraise your own style and use methods to develop your own writing style.

Activity

How effective is the following as a piece of writing? Working with a colleague, evaluate it and identify ways in which it might be improved:

> The most important aspect of crisis management is to identify the primary risks fast. A manager who focuses quickly on key issues is most likely to limit the damage brought about by the critical events. You can't, though, hold a committee →

meeting whilst the ship goes down. Decisions have to be made quickly and all involved should accept the manager's authority.

The extent to which the manager can exercise effective leadership and authority in a crisis depends to some degree on the level of shared value, for the urgency of a crisis means that there is no time to consult the rulebooks. People work on gut instincts – if these are sound, fine. If not, then the results may be disastrous. Many disasters happen partially because no one took responsibility – no one's gut instincts kicked in.

Some have argued that crisis management is always a symptom of management failure, for good management involves foreseeing all potential risks and hazards. But this is too demanding of the manager's role. If you are operating with faulty equipment that you inherited from your predecessor, then there is always a chance that it will go pear-shaped. And you can't have the resources there to be prepared against every eventuality. Good management is about being ready for crises and having a strategy to deal with them. It is not about being able to instantly avert every possible accident.

Management is central to good crisis handling. The consequences of not doing so can be enormous. In the famous nuclear accident at Chernobyl, there was intense devastation. Many fire fighters lost their lives trying to prevent the fire going out of control. The Soviet government took a great deal of time before they openly admitted what exactly had happened. And even today there is a large tract of land that is a 'no go' area. So it is essential that managers get this crucial part of their work right first time.

Response

While this sample makes some interesting points, as a piece of writing it shows several flaws, most of which come down to a failure to correctly pitch the style of writing.

Voice – The writer shifts from a formal style to a more idiomatic style at times. The most obvious symptom of this is the use of contractions such as 'can't'.

Addressee – Related to this is ambivalence between referring to the reader directly by using 'you' and 'the manager'.

Shared knowledge – Every writer has to make assumptions about what their audience knows. But here, this creates further ambiguity. The reference to 'many disasters' suggests that the readership will be familiar with disasters, when they happen and why. The other examples, however, are explained more clearly, suggesting a lower level of shared knowledge. Either might be acceptable

→

depending on the audience of the writing, but together they are inconsistent in terms of how much knowledge is being assumed.

Argument – The key statements of each paragraph are clear enough (first sentence in paragraphs one and two, second sentence in paragraph three). But the supporting reasons are varied and their own basis is not always clear. Both statements that 'you can't . . . (do something)' are ambiguous. They seem to suggest that it would not be sound managerial practice to do so, but there is no justification for such statements. The reader, therefore, might well regard these as personal opinions of the writer without any further foundation. Simple verbal devices can forestall this. For example, if the writer starts either of these statements with an allusion to evidence, such as 'It is generally accepted practice that . . .' or 'The Institute of Management's advice on crisis management is that . . .' then the reader has a better idea where these claims are coming from.

Similarly, statements such as 'People work on gut instincts . . .' or 'Good management is about . . .' look forceful, but on what are they based? It is not difficult to add some justification, such as 'Several studies have emphasized that people work on instinct in a crisis . . .' and give one or two references for this [note that the metaphorical word 'gut' is dropped; it is a journalistic flourish and adds nothing to the discussion – all instincts are 'gut'].

Claims that 'good management is this or that' leave the writer open to even greater questions. Any marker will come back to the writer and simply ask 'according to whom?' If you believe this then say it is your view. If it is based on someone else's work then acknowledge this. Generalized statements that look like iconic universals should always be regarded with suspicion. (And how suspicious are you of this last sentence?)

And what of the final paragraph? It is not especially persuasive, and shows some signs of trying to impress by emotive references. But above all it is not a very sound argument. Several points are made about the severity of the nuclear accident. But the main ambiguity lies in deciding what is the key statement of the paragraph. Is it that crisis handling is a key management responsibility, or is it that the consequences can be enormous? If the latter, then the argument seems valid. But if the former, then this is not proven in the text – it does not demonstrate that there is a necessary connection between the severity of the consequences of poor crisis handling and the idea that this is a responsibility of managers. The argument does not prove, for example, that this severity of consequence could not be someone else's responsibility. The crucial test for this kind of issue is 'Could I accept the reasons offered and still reasonably question the conclusion?' If the answer is yes, then the argument is not valid.

Behind the flaw mentioned above lies another one, which often appears in many forms: the idea that describing something is the same as analysing and explaining it.

There is a phrase worth remembering, summarized by the acronym DINA:

> **D**escription
> **I**s
> **N**ot
> **A**nalysis

Sheer repetition of the facts of a situation is not in itself an argument. You always need to bring out more. This may be sometimes by means of putting two or more aspects together and then drawing out something that each shares. Or it might be by contrasting certain elements. Or it may be by comparing a factual element with the prediction of a particular theory.

You will need to grow a repertoire of different 'voices' in your writing that you can use to suit each different audience for whom you produce written material. This is a long-term task, and no one, short of the great novelists, can say they have completed the job. It helps greatly to envisage a particular audience (basically comprising those who will be reading your work), and imagine reading the work aloud to them. What do they know about the subject? What kind of language is suitable for them? Are they generally likely to have specific expectations and pre-formed beliefs about the issue? Are they likely to have strong feelings about the issue? And so on. Do not fall into the trap of assuming that a good academic style is *all* that you need. A Business Masters course is intended to develop your professional skills, so some of your assessment may well require a more professionally directed approach – for example you may be asked to write a report suitable for senior managers. This would clearly require a quite different style of expression ('voice') than a theoretical essay.

Sometimes it helps just to read the work out loud – this is where working occasionally in a group can be extremely useful. But even if you only read the assignment to yourself, some things will jump out at you. For example, you can often easily detect whether your sentences are too long (very easy to write but much harder to read, because you simply run out of breath), how easy it is to identify the main clause in the sentence, how easy to spot the key statement for each paragraph. It is also a useful method of improving your punctuation.

As well as those who mark your work, you should encourage colleagues, both on the course and in your work, to look at what you produce, if time and practicality allows. So there are at least three groups (four, if members of your family get their hands on it!). Developing a voice for material to be read by your study or work colleagues might conflict with the voice you have established for your tutors. The voice for the tutors is likely to be dominant one, as they will be assessing your work.

There are three key aspects to take into account regarding the audience that will be involved in assessing your work (tutors primarily, but in some cases other professionals may be included as well, for example external managers who may give an industry perspective on the content of the assignment):

Context – They will be reading several (at least!) of these and therefore will be prone to eyestrain and reading fatigue. Their attention might drift away at times. Make it easy for them. Make the work visually easy to engage with by clear layout and simple design principles over headings and sub-headings. But beware – presentation that is too decorative is often as bad as under-presented work. Make sure that the reader is given lots of signposts to help them see where your argument has got to and where it is going. Signposting is one of the most important aspects, and you should work on the basis that if you, as the writer, have any thought that maybe a signpost is needed then it *will* be needed!

Assessment – The assessors are looking for specific things, so give them those. Do not clutter up your work with material that 'would be nice to include.' For example, many people on MBA and related courses, when discussing a specific organization, feel that they need to include as an appendix the last annual report. But if you do not discuss this or refer to it, what is it doing there? If it is not essential to your discussion, and in fact could distract the reader from what really matters, it can (and should) be harmlessly discarded. If there is something in the annual report that is important, include just that page.

Redrafting – Another important aspect of refining your style is the various ways in which you might re-draft your work, which is something that should be done for all assignments.

When producing a first draft, whilst it always helps to adopt a planned approach, there can also be a benefit in just getting something written down. Countless writers, as well as other people who rely on intellectual production, such as musical composers and designers, testify to the role of 'first drafting' in their work. It is important, especially when affected by any kind of writer's block, to have some material physically there on which you can work. For many writers it is the process of enhancement of an original draft that marks the difference between adequate and great work – this is just what the musician Johannes Brahms meant when he said 'Genius is 1% inspiration and 99% perspiration.'

Before redrafting, it is important to evaluate the first draft. As with all writing, you should adopt an attitude of deconstruction – separating out and acknowledging strengths as well as weaknesses. This is often much more successful if done with a group of colleagues. The criteria you should use (at this stage but also for the finished product) to evaluate the *writing* include:

- coherence of structure;
- ease of comprehension on a paragraph by paragraph basis;
- simplicity of argument;
- factual accuracy; and
- duplication or omission.

Each of these can then be the basis for revisions of the text. In addition, before finally submitting your work you should try to 'mark' the later drafts as if you were the tutor, in which case the key issue is whether the specific assessment requirements have been met. Again, this can be done very effectively on a joint basis with others on your course.

One very handy device with longer pieces of writing is the explicit use of signposting. We recommend you consider ensuring that every section over about 750 words or so should have an introduction and a summary so that the reader can ascertain where they are in the overall argument of the essay. In a large piece, such as a dissertation, signposting might well be required regularly to ensure that the reader is still following the drift of the argument.

Additionally, do not neglect the visual impact of the piece. While too gaudy or flashy a presentation may distract from the content, do make sure that separate sections are headed with appropriate titles so that the reader could, if they wished, skim through the piece quickly once at first to get an overall idea of the structure of the argument (just as we have suggested that you do with books and articles). Bear in mind that even the conscientious reader has a limited period of time when they can maintain full concentration. So breaking up extended passages of text with diagrams and tables – or even illustrations – provides a degree of relief to the reader. Also a well chosen and tastefully presented image, be it a graph, a diagram or a picture, might convey the significance of a point far more forcefully than the same point expressed in words.

To summarize:

- The ability to develop a clear 'voice' that takes appropriate account of the beliefs and knowledge of a specific audience is an important part of gaining credibility as a writer.
- Description is not analysis!
- Careful appraisal of the validity of arguments is always required – the key test is: 'Can I accept the premises and not the conclusion?'
- Redrafting is essential – it is better to start by getting something down on paper to work with than to aim for perfection immediately.
- Always use signposts for sections longer than 750 words or so.
- Don't neglect the visual impact of your work – let its shape emerge from the meaning and the points you are trying to get across.

● Conclusions and recommendations

When you have worked through this section, you should be able to:

- state the difference between conclusions and recommendations, and their respective roles in written reports; and
- construct sound examples of both, and link them effectively.

Activity

Classify these statements and identify what needs to be done with them.

Conclusions and recommendations

1   The organization lacks a BARS (Behaviourally Anchored Rating Scale) basis for their performance appraisal system.
2   There are several departments that do not conduct performance appraisals.
3   Resources are needed to support the development of trained performance assessors.
4   Comparisons with several other organizations suggests that appraisal works cost effectively when linked to training or to reward, but not both.   →

5   Senior management commitment is needed for any changes.
6   The purposes of the performance appraisal system have not been communicated effectively to all staff.
7   The existing system can be used to address reward and training issues if necessary.
8   Further research into this area is required before a final strategy is adopted.

Response

Firstly there is no distinction made here between conclusions and recommendations, which is a very common but serious flaw in any argument.

- *Conclusions are what you have found out about the current position*
- *Recommendations are proposals for action*

Ideally these should be separated out into different sections; assessors will certainly treat them as distinct types of statement. At the very least the conclusions should be listed together as a group. The mixture of statements in the example will suggest to the reader that the author is not really clear about this part of their work.

A way to present these two sets of statements is to try to match them one-to-one, so that for each finding (conclusion) there is a proposal (recommendation).

Secondly, some of the conclusions look rather like evaluative statements dressed up. For example, to say that the organization does not have something is a roundabout way of saying that it should have one; that is, it is a proposal masquerading as a conclusion. A telltale sign of this kind of move is when the conclusion states that the organization does not have something and the associated recommendation simply states that the organization should get it.

Often recommendations can be weak because of poorly constructed conclusions. Recommendations that 'further research is needed' should be considered carefully. Where the investigation has uncovered new questions that there has not been the space to deal with then it is legitimate. Where it is an admission that the present investigation has not resolved the issue then they should not be included.

Many recommendations can look impressive but when one asks what do they really add to the discussion it can turn out that they are fatuous. For example, take 'senior management commitment is needed'. When would such commitment *not* be needed? It is a vague hybrid between a conclusion and a recommendation that would be better rephrased in terms of what *kind* of commitment, or how it is proposed to *secure* such commitment. Similarly statements about the general communication systems of an organisation, or about managing change, all too easily degenerate into worthy expressions that have no real organizational impact.

This discussion brings out many of the most important aspects of the concluding parts of a report or policy-related assignment. Above all, the writing needs to be specific and tightly focused. The test of a sound recommendation is if it is clear how it could be implemented. Indeed, for a report it would be important to have a section following the recommendations indicating how they would be put into practice. In some cases this involves identifying who is responsible for actioning the proposal, how much it might cost, what results are anticipated and what contingency plans would be needed. It is essential that the reader should come away confident that your proposals are practicable.

The ultimate issues, however, are:

- whether your conclusions have some degree of *validity*; and
- whether your recommendations have some practical *value*.

Something that is a *valid argument* is the best we can do with the evidence available to us. It may not conclusively prove your points, but it will provide the strongest possible support for them.

A piece of written work may have *practical value* in a number of different ways, such as:

- developing a new technique,
- applying an existing idea of technique in a new context, or to a different kind of organization,
- collecting a strong body of information or data relating to a particular topic, and/or
- presenting a striking perspective on an issue.

These two factors can often work against each other, unfortunately. The greater the efforts you make to ensure that the argument is unassailable – for example, by employing elaborate statistical methods to analyse the results of a large survey – the less easy it might be for the professional reader to see what the work is saying about day-to-day managerial practice.

Many studies attest to the great pressures on the time of the average manager, so they are rarely able to stop working and spend time just thinking, however useful this might be. A managerial audience is always going to want to know how an idea or theoretical discussion helps them with their practical problems. On the other hand, the academic reader may be less concerned with immediate practical application and more with long-term application and theoretical interest. These groups therefore pull in opposite directions.

There is no simple resolution for this. The main thing to do is to keep a clear sense of the needs and expectations of your audience, and work to satisfy these. This is likely to guide your decisions about how much evidence to discuss in detail and how much to summarize. One useful and easy test is simply to ask, 'If this came across my desk one busy Monday morning, would I bother reading it, and would it be worth it when I had read it?'

In contrast to a report, an essay is not intended to lead to action. Therefore you are unlikely to include substantial recommendations, and so it would be inappropriate to go into details about implementation. However, the essay is an argument – it will lead to some conclusions. You should still have a final section that draws together the main conclusions of the work. Do not include a 'final word' or some similar section that adds anything new to the essay – the final section should simply remind the reader of the key points they have already encountered.

To summarize:

- Conclusions are what you have discovered; recommendations are how you propose to address what you have discovered; the two things must be clearly distinguished.
- 'The clearer the better' applies to both recommendations and conclusions.
- Practical application and validity are both important criteria, even though they work in opposite directions..
- Some conclusions are really covert recommendations – this should be avoided.
- It should be clear how to implement your recommendations – in some cases an implementation plan would be useful.

● Originality and reflection

When you have finished working through this section you should be able to:

- identify what is really necessary in the way of originality at Masters level; and
- use several techniques for learning through reflection on practice and on your own assessed work.

Activity

What does 'originality' mean to you? Try sorting out your thoughts onto paper.

Response

For some people, this conjures up creativity in the strong sense of wild imaginative visions that someone dreams up and then turns into a completely innovative product. For others it suggests coming up with a fresh twist on an old theme. These are useful, and when developed in an appropriate manner would certainly gain credit if someone produces work of this kind within a Masters assignment.

But for your course work, those senses of originality are not the most important aspects. On a Masters programme, originality is measured in terms of how far you approach issues with an independent mind. It is not so much whether you produce thoughts that are manifestly different from anything that anyone has thought before, but whether you approach ideas, experiences and techniques independently, and are ready to rigorously evaluate them. This sense of originality is based on the idea that if you adopt an independent mind for your study and assessed work, then it is very likely that you will produce material which will devise fresh solutions to problems, and will re-present existing material in a fresh and different way.

One can produce original material in many ways, including the following:

- applying an idea to a fresh context;
- testing out a theory in real life and producing an evaluation based on this;
- asking new questions;
- giving new and different answers to familiar questions;
- relating two or more ideas or theories together that have not been related before;
- bringing out latent implications of familiar ideas;
- exposing assumptions implicit in familiar ideas;
- querying what is generally accepted;
- bringing one's own experience to a argument.

These are all different kinds of originality that someone may bring to their work. But you will notice that they are all compatible with solid study; none of them requires you to be visionary or a mould breaker. What they do require of you is that you approach each issue on its own merits.

Activity

Identify one of those unquestioned beliefs that are completely standard and accepted by all on your course or in an organization that you may have worked in. Now think of what the statement of those beliefs really rests on. How many ways could you (sensibly) question it? How many alternatives could you think of?

No response is necessary for this activity. All and any answers have their value in terms of taking people 'out of the box' – beyond the normal confines of working assumptions.

Closely linked with this idea of originality as independence is the process of *reflection*, and what it can contribute to your learning.

By reflection we mean the process of reviewing experiences and assessed work as a basis for further learning and development. 'Reflection' sounds like a solitary activity. In fact, while you can do it that way, it is much more effective in pairs, threes or fours.

Reflection is not just about thinking over what you have done. It is about thinking and doing as a basis for learning. The best-known model is that of David Kolb (who has acknowledged his debt regarding this model to Kurt Lewin, the great-grandfather of occupational psychology), as depicted in Figure 4.3.

The idea behind this model is that learning via experience is not a matter of being thrown in at the deep end of a pool, and having to sink or swim. It is about making the most of every experience we have. It assumes that in each case, there are four elements. For example, once we have the experi-

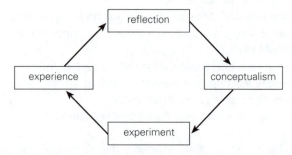

Figure 4.3   The Kolb model of experiential learning

Source: Adapted from Kolb, D. A. (1984) *Experiential Learning*, Englewood Cliffs, NJ: Prentice-Hall.

ence, we should reflect on it – ideally discuss it with a colleague or mentor. Then when we feel we have talked it through and analysed it sufficiently, we should take an overall view of situation of that type, and later experiment to see if our general concept works. It is a process which you can enter at any point – it does not have to start with the experience. Some think it is better described as a spiral, as you move on to new situations rather than imagining yourself locked onto one cycle.

This was originally proposed as a theory of how we learn at work. But it is clear that it can also apply straightforwardly to learning via any experience, including study. Crucial to it is the way in which we reflect. The optimum is to be with a colleague in whom you have confidence. Then we should talk through the key features of the experience – in our terms. We may identify aspects that went well and others that did not, but at this point it is not appropriate for either to come to final summary judgements. It is more appropriate to examine the experience from a variety of different perspectives, such as those of key stakeholders (the tutors, for example), whether it meets certain stated objectives, whether you felt comfortable with the sequence of events, and so on. The list can be long. The important thing is to identify a wide range of these possibilities. Only at the later stage of conceptualization should you decide which main factor you will focus on, and that this should be treated in a certain kind of way (the conceptualization stage).

Once you have done this, then you can try out your idea in different contexts, which then can lead to new experience, about which you may wish to reflect. Learning in this way can become a virtuous circle of thinking and doing.

To summarize:

- Originality in Masters written work does not have to be about vision or imagination; it can be about looking at every situation or theory independently, and taking each on its own merits.
- There is a wide range of different kinds of originality that may be relevant to the production of assessed work.
- Reflection – based around a cycle of learning from experience – is an important tool for development; it is best done with a supportive colleague.

● Managing time

> When you have read this section, you should be able to iden-
> tify key steps that will help you make most efficient use of your
> time when completing assignments.

As your Masters programme progresses, you will have a significant amount
of reading and writing to do within a relatively short time. You will certainly
get to a stage, often approaching the end of a semester or year, where you
will have several assignments to complete at about the same time, and in
this situation your techniques of managing time become particularly important.

An important aspect of your development as a professional is that you
demonstrate the ability to deal with complex issues, sometimes involving
significant levels of uncertainty, in a compressed amount of time. Looking
back again at the very idea of Masters level learning, part of this is the ability
to integrate different kinds of information and interpret these appropriately.
The more skilful you are in assimilating and interpreting diverse collections
of material the more quickly you will cope with the uncertainties and
complexities of high level professional responsibility.

So in this final section we are going to revisit the issue of time management, as a complement to the discussion in the introductory chapter. When
you have worked through it, you should be able to identify and use further
approaches to manage your time effectively

We saw in the Introduction that there are activities that can waste time,
and we also looked at the well-known 'urgent-important' grid to help decide
what to do. That leaves a question – what *is* important, as opposed to merely
urgent? It's not as simple as you deciding on your own what to place value
on; sometimes your priorities are set for you. A superior in the organization,
for example, may well insist on a different set of priorities from yours, and
due to their position in the hierarchy you have to comply. Sometimes other
people can force their personal importance on you by escalation – for
example members of a learning group threatening greater levels of conflict
unless you comply with their requirements. However, there will also be times
where the choice of priorities is up to you.

There are two areas that you can focus on that can help to resolve questions of priorities:

- refer everything back to the overall objective
- evaluate every issue in terms of the potential damage it might

cause and the probability that this will happen – the so-called risk-return matrix.

Referring back to the overall objective

In one sense this is simple – the objectives for you on the course are to pass it and to learn from it. Therefore you can evaluate the importance of objectives in terms of how far they contribute to this. It can become more complicated than this because: (a) the course is not the only thing you are committed to, so what is important in course terms may not be so important for work or your personal life, and (b) as well as the official objectives of the course itself, you may well have a further objective for doing the course – perhaps to move on from your present post, or to improve your effectiveness, or some other reason.

So your first test of how important something may be is *How far is this helping me pass the course (and support, or at least not interfere, with my other objectives)?*

The other issue is the matter of balancing how damaging an issue could be as against how likely it is to happen. Look at the following box:

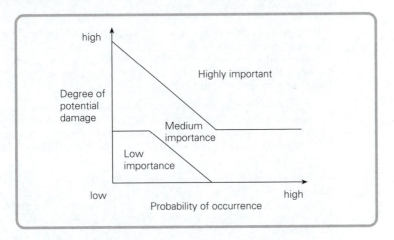

This graph is generally used defensively, to identify areas where something might happen that would have a damaging impact on your situation. It is possible to locate events on this graph in terms of (a) how likely they might be to occur, and (b) how damaging they might be.

For example, if you spend a great deal of time on the first of a series of assignments, then how likely is it that you will run out of time and not be able to do the last one properly? Maybe you assess this as a 50–50 chance. How damaging is this? If you have to pass every assessment in order to pass the whole course the potential damage is quite high (but you may have the opportunity of resubmitting a piece of work, to at least earn the minimum pass mark.) So this is on the border crossing over from medium to high importance.

Agreeing to take on a major project outside of the course that must be completed a week before the exams <u>will</u> have a larger impact (failing most the exams because you do not have time to revise properly?). Hence that certainly goes into the high importance field.

Activity

List out five different activities that you might become involved in that would have an impact on your work on the course, relate each of these to the graph, above.

Which of them are likely to have the most importance?

Response

Here is an example of five such activities that might be provided by a member of an MBA programme:

Going on a much needed fortnight's holiday a month before three assignments are due.
(High risk that you will run out of time and not pass all three assignments; if the holiday is not taken now there is a smaller risk that you will not perform well due to fatigue.)

Spending two weeks on reading one textbook very thoroughly as preparation to complete one out of five essays in that semester.
(High risk that you will run out of time for the last essay of the semester; reasonable chance however that you will score quite well on this first piece of work.)

Missing just one day's lectures on account of pressures outside of the course.
(Small risk that you will miss some crucial material that you cannot get later on; medium chance that you will resolve a pressing non-course problem.)

Postponing fulfilling a major responsibility until after finishing assignments.
(Good chance that you will do reasonably well on the assignments; potential for serious trouble if you miss the deadline for the other responsibility.)

Working without a break on assignments the whole of my spare time for a couple of weeks.
(High risk that you will become tired, lose inspiration and not do yourself justice on assignments.)

The examples above are not profound in themselves, but they do illustrate the range of factors that you will have to juggle, and they illustrate several key issues that you need to consider:

- Keep a continual eye on balancing up different requirements.
- Do not pursue one need exhaustively.
- Keep yourself in good condition to be able to continue to work under pressure for an extended period of time – eat sensibly, try to sleep well, and don't neglect your leisure and exercise.
- You will undoubtedly need to cut some corners with the course as well as with other priorities.
- When you are immersed in work you can easily lose perspective – step back occasionally and re-plan your available time.
- Keep a sense of distance from your learning – you will learn better, and you will maintain your composure.

Another important issue is who else has some call on your time. It makes sense to divide your time up into discretionary and non-discretionary time for this purpose. If you are employed at the same time as you are studying, then a fair amount of work commitment is non-discretionary: you have to be there and focus on your responsibilities for most of the time whilst you are at work. One of the most difficult aspects for part-time Masters students is having to cope when unexpected and heavy demands at work coincide with deadlines for assignments and examinations. So the most valuable thing such students can do is to keep their employer closely informed about the progress and timetable of the course, to support what can sometimes become difficult negotiations.

For employed students, then, the time they can allocate for themselves is personal time. Full-time students may find that they have more time at their disposal, though they generally have to complete their Masters in a shorter time (typically a year or so compared with a part-time Masters which could take more than two years). Whether full or part-time, you will find that your time divides into that committed elsewhere and personal time over which you have discretion. But this can be subject to a surprisingly wide range of different demands.

The point is that each of these needs to be negotiated. As soon as you make your commitment to the course you should be making space from those on this list that can be influenced. Sometimes getting some easing of pressure from the 'high importance difficult to influence' group is also necessary.

Activity

Identify the range of people who have a call on your personal time, and how much influence and importance they may have.

Response

Here is an example produced by one MBA student:

Spouse	(important but can be influenced)
Children (3 all under 10)	(important and not easy to influence)
Parents (both over 80)	(fairly important, not easy to influence)
Parents-in-law	(similar)
Close friends	(moderately important; can be influenced)
Own need for exercise	(moderately important but own discretion)
Hobby (playing bridge)	(basically same)
Own need for other forms of relaxation	(same)
Brothers and sister	(low importance; difficult to influence)
Sister-in-law	(similar)
Social activities related to work	(low importance; easy to decline)
Social activities related to course	(same)

Coping with the potential assignment overload will involve a significant degree of juggling of these calls on your time. It is important to break tasks down onto manageable chunks. To think of something as 'three assignments to complete by Christmas' is daunting. But it is perfectly possible to break each of these down into a range of tasks, with the result that instead of trying to sequence these as three extended periods of time they may be interleaved. Three assignments can then be progressed together.

In planning assignments and even more in planning dissertations people tend to think mainly of reading, researching and writing. But there are two important activities subsequent to these processes. The first of these is that there really ought to be sufficient period of time between the completion of a first draft and the submission date to allow you to reflect on the work, re-read it with a relatively less involved mind and make enhancements to it.

The more time you have, the more you can take advantage of your learning group and compare notes on how you have all tackled the task.

The second activity is trivial but no less important – namely the need for contingency planning. For example, the production of a piece of work in the form required by your tutors can often take more time than you expect. You need to keep an eye on basic logistical issues – print cartridges, print paper, differences between screen layout and printed version – these and other issues can often delay the submission of an assignment, and are all especially acute with a large-scale piece such as the dissertation (for this you may also need time for binding the work). So it is important to build in margins for error or delay to your assignment schedule as well as to other planned activities.

Once you have broken down assignments into separate tasks then it is useful to plot these on some kind of time-based chart, such as a Gantt chart or a critical path analysis, or even just a calendar. Some people find it easier not to write the tasks directly on their chart but to write each of them on a small 'Post-it' – which means that they can move these around as priorities change and time becomes free or unexpectedly taken up. Some students use wipe-clean white boards, while others use flexible 'to-do' software (such as EverNote).

This is not only good for time management, but also for other aspects of your learning. As we have emphasized in the Introduction, management is not a set of separated responsibilities. Each area is directly linked with the others. The reading you do for one assignment will help you to put into context the issue raised in other ones, and equally the choices you make about your priorities will affect the whole juxtaposition of other choices you have made – never assume that you can make 'just one change' with a major project such as a programme of study.

> ### To summarize:
>
> In this section we have looked at several aspects of the management of time. We have seen that there are different kinds of priority, as indicated by the risk–probability grid, and that there are different parties that may have a call on your time. Lastly we have looked briefly at some aspects of planning as an approach to time management.

Example of assignment

In the Appendix (pp. 220–40) you will find an actual submission of an assignment on a Masters programme, along with the assessment criteria used. Following these we provide an explanation of how the grading this received relates to the stated assessment criteria. You may find it useful to decide for yourself beforehand what kind of grading they gained and why.

5 Learning in Groups

● **Introduction**

A key feature of many Business-related Masters programme is that you will find yourself working in groups or syndicates. (Note: on MBA and other programmes, tutors usually call a number of students working together either a group or a syndicate – in this chapter we shall use the term 'group'.) There are good reasons for this: the world of work involves operating in groups and teams, and as a highly qualified professional you will normally be expected to work in such teams and also at times to take a leading role in them, whether or not you are officially designated as a manager. Groups can be highly effective platforms for learning. And the subtleties and shifting dynamics and interrelationships that are inherent in groups are precisely the kinds of uncertain environment that will bring out the best of your Masters-level learning, which is above all a preparation for working in intellectually insecure situations.

In this chapter we will not only work through the issues about maintaining a cohesive group ethos, but more importantly how the group can be an effective learning resource for its members. One important element we shall see is that the incidental aspects of working in a group are often as important as the deliberate purposes. The chapter is structured as follows:

- section 1 **understanding groups**: the purposes of group work, the key distinction between task and learning groups;
- section 2 **group effectiveness**: managing the dynamics and composition of a group, how to ensure that a group works effectively as a cohesive whole, and the need to avoid preconceptions of how different individuals might interact within the group;
- section 3 **when a group encounters difficulties**: the different strategies that you can adopt when a group goes wrong or encounters difficulties – as most do from time to time; and
- section 4 **electronic resources available to groups**: the use of electronic resources for learning groups.

● Understanding groups

When you have read this section you will be able to differentiate between task groups and learning groups.

Groups can be set up in several different contexts:

- as part of a formal assessed activity;
- as a classroom or electronic learning activity;
- as the basis for a set piece of work to complete outside the classroom;
- as a voluntary opportunity to work together on assignments or revise for examinations.

Groups may also have different durations: they may be intended to last for a large portion of your programme – a semester or even a full year – or they may be of relatively short duration, say for the period of time necessary to complete a particular piece of assessed work. The important thing is to ensure that you make the most of group work: *working in groups is a major learning opportunity that if approached in the right way can bring significant and lasting benefits to your learning.*

The important thing is to be able to distinguish clearly between *task* groups and *learning* groups:

Task groups are set up in order to help you achieve a given outcome effectively. Their success is therefore measured solely in terms of whether the group achieved the best outcome. Not everyone need be involved, nor need everyone even agree about what is the best way to achieve the task.

Learning groups are set up specifically for you to learn from the experience. Their success is measured in terms of the development of each member. The process that the group goes through is at least as important as any specific tasks or outcomes that the group might achieve. How each member is involved and participates is a crucial feature of this process, and time needs to be allocated for individual and collective reflection and evaluation on what is being learnt.

This distinction will recur as a theme throughout this chapter. One significant issue relating to group activity is that you may encounter quite different philosophies of groups not only amongst your course colleagues but also amongst your tutors on your Masters course, with some of these using groups on a task basis and others seeing them in more learning-based, process-oriented, terms.

Even amongst the latter, there can be variations. Some tutors may only emphasise groups because their perception is that it is an effective means of learning, whilst others may feel that this is a key feature of business experience and that therefore students should be trained to work in groups. In terms of Masters-level learning, however, you should look to how such training can equip you to work with and manage the uncertainties of group work. You should also learn to resist the adoption of techniques that make group domination or manipulation easier.

Whatever basis you may be working in a group, there are some common challenges that you will need to address – individually and collectively – if the group is going be effective. One crucial issue is simply to be clear whether the group is a task group or a learning group. Our view is that you should always try to aim for the latter, even if your tutors have not set up the group in these terms.

The nature of the work can sometimes have a key influence on how the group works. Do note that it is essential for a learning group that the possibility of failure in a task is accepted as a potentially positive experience: in other words your group could fail to achieve a set task and still be a success in terms of gaining a great deal of valuable learning from the experience.

And if your tutors have only designed group activities in task terms (i.e. with no attention to the processes that the group goes through to complete tasks) – *even then* our advice about group working will help you get better results from group assessments.

This chapter will also cover some issues relating to the use of your time. Time management is an important aspect of group work, as well as being an extremely important resource available to you in your studies.

Group effectiveness

When you have completed this section, you should be able to:

- identify the key challenges that face any working or learning group;
- identify and evaluate the influence of key elements of the group process; and
- use specific strategies to enhance group effectiveness.

Question

What do you think are the main potential problems a learning group might encounter?

Reply

Some of the problems are similar to those you might face in many group situations, such as those set up in a working environment. These may include:

- domination of the group by one individual,
- one or more individuals opting out of the group,
- group fails to set ground-rules,
- different individuals may have different prior experiences which can lead to different preconceptions of what the group can achieve,
- groupthink (more of this later), and
- many international students, working in English as their learnt, second language, report that sometimes native English speakers can exclude them from making a full contribution to groups by talking too fast or by using acronyms, jargon and slang.

Other problems, however, are specific to the nature of a group set up as part of a Masters programme, such as:

- tasks are completed but the group does not learn from these,
- the pressure to achieve a good grade for an assessment can easily elevate the importance of the product or outcome over that of the process,
- learning is evaluated in terms of the group's perception of their success, excluding or minimizing consideration of the process,
- learning is evaluated in terms of the degree to which the group felt comfortable with each other, rather than in terms of achievement of objectives,
- learning about group processes is reduced to a series of formulae or 'golden rules' that do not provide the opportunity to take account of the specific circumstances of each group situation that may be encountered, and
- some students may resist the idea that they can learn from other students.

In the following sections we will help you develop an understanding of the underlying causes of these issues, so that you can more effectively manage them.

Question

Look at these views of the members (A–F) of a group and try to evaluate the group processes:

A: 'We never really got on right from the start. Some people were quite competitive, and there was one individual who seemed to take the view that he should be in charge no matter what. He wasn't even the most senior person there, though for a group like ours that shouldn't have made any difference. No one sat down and thought through what we were supposed to do, or how we should work together as a group.'

B: 'The group tried to elect a leader, but it was clear that one or two people were not interested. As a result the individual chosen was continually undermined. To make matters worse, we had a sudden change of personnel, when one of our group dropped out after just a week or so, and we were given someone fresh who joined the class late.'

C: 'Initially there was chaos. A couple of the others didn't seem to realise what we needed to do to complete the project, and seemed to just sit there waiting. When I tried to take the initiative this was not well-received. A late entrant to the group proved difficult, as they did not fit in at all well for quite some time.'

D: 'I joined the group a couple of weeks after the others, so I always felt slightly at a disadvantage, principally because there were clearly already several different agendas that were going on, and something had obviously happened before I appeared on the scene – I was never really clear about why the other person left. I was surprised that people had not sorted out a modus operandi, given that the task itself was quite clear. We did eventually produce quite a good project, but not without a lot of conflict.'

E: 'The group did well. We got the best result of all. Of course there is always some conflict when you have a number of people working together, but that is to be expected. One person came late, and he was very demanding in the early stages.'

F: 'I learnt nothing from the experience. I was not happy after x left in the first month, although he claimed that he was OK about going to another group. When y came in his place, she was a completely different person and at first it was hard to get used to this. True we got a good project done, but only because at the end everyone realised that they had to pull together in order to get any kind of result at all. It was obvious that we could have done a great deal better. At the end, we got told the result, everyone cheered, and then we went our separate ways.'

Response

It should be clear (a) that they achieved their main **task** objective, (b) there were strongly divergent views about how cohesive the group had been and (c) there is some doubt whether each member has learned anything from the experience.

A range of symptoms can be identified, though it is not so clear exactly which is the key determining factor. These symptoms include:

- a failure by the group as a whole to resolve issues of power and authority,
- the group did not seem to have reflected on their experience or their progress,
- a lack of agreed ground-rules,
- a failure to manage the group using the ground-rules,
- a divergence of views about the acceptable level of conflict,
- a failure to manage the late inclusion of another member of the group, and
- a failure to acknowledge or explore the reasons why an earlier member left.

Each of these is really a symptom of a deeper problem, namely that the group did not take responsibility for its own development. There was clearly a sense on the part of some members that the task needed to be gotten on with, but there is also a very clear indication that at least some members needed to consider the process by which the group achieved its goals.

The issue of the inclusion of another member of the group at a later stage is particularly telling in this respect. Any change in the membership of a working or learning group creates a whole new range of social dynamics. For a group to work effectively it is important to treat each change in membership as a change in the group as a whole, and to regard the introduction of a new member into the group as an opportunity to reflect on and learn more about group processes. The benefit of this is that where problems have been encountered – such as whatever had led to a group member leaving in the example considered above – then the group, having identified issues to address, can take steps which will not only help the group function more effectively but also thereby achieve whatever task is required.

A key lesson to learn from this, then, is that *for learning groups to work effectively it is necessary that there is a conscious effort by the group as a whole to manage its composition and development.*

The composition and development of a group

There are several models of the ideal membership of a group and the kind of progress that a group might go through; you will encounter these when you come to study Organizational Behaviour. When applied to a learning group, there is a temptation for these to become self-fulfilling prophecies. Some people often make the mistake of thinking that if they have judged members of their group as being of a certain type, then that means that group members must be like this forever, no matter what. And similarly some people, once they have identified their own role in terms of one model or another, may well regard themselves as essentially that type and never any other.

In practice, groups change, people change, and no model, however well structured or well researched, can predict the behaviour of individuals very well. It is always best to regard models such as the Belbin typology of team roles as guides or suggestions of the kinds of issue that you could be on the lookout for – on this basis they can be extremely useful.

One of Meredith Belbin's (1982) oft-quoted sayings is a good place to start: 'Nobody's perfect, but a team can be.' Much as we respect Belbin, we take a different view. It is rare to find a team that is perfect, and most of the time something is wrong. It may be a clash of personalities (rarer than people think), a failure to clarify and agree roles and objectives (much more frequent than people think) or a task that is not feasible within the time and resources allotted (at least as frequent as people think). How effective a team is comes down to how the group deals with the shortcomings it faces and gets over them. So maybe we would paraphrase Belbin – 'No team is perfect, but the way you manage it might be.'

John Adair (1973) has, over the last thirty years, used to great effect a model that enables groups to evaluate their progress effectively. It depicts a group or team as having to deal with three interrelated sets of needs:

- task
- team
- individual

Adair's purpose in depicting groups in these terms is to focus people's attention on the potential conflicts that can arise from incompatibilities and incongruities between these three elements. So it is clear that whilst the example group managed well enough with the *task*, they did not confront the needs of individuals sufficiently. Partially as a *result* of this and probably also partly as a *cause*, they did not consider the team as a whole, as a dynamic entity needing to be established, nurtured in its own right and maintained.

In the light of this, we can see that a group needs to consciously manage a range of elements:

- the range of *resources* that the group can call upon to complete their tasks;
- the extent to which the group follows some kind of rational process when completing tasks – is there a *methodology*?
- the degree of *creativity* and originality in the work done by the group;
- the *balance* between the creative, dynamic, aspects of the task and the basic 'bread and butter' elements that just have to be carried out;
- the manner in which all members of the group are *involved* in the task and in the process;
- the levels of *conflict* that arise as individuals attempt to resolve differences;
- the way in which the group *develops* or changes as tasks progress towards completion;
- the degree of *realism* necessary to be successful in completing the task; and
- the levels of *motivation* and enthusiasm for the task.

This is quite an extensive set of issues to manage. One of the merits of the Belbin approach is that he acknowledges that no one can easily deal with all of these at any one time – indeed few people are temperamentally adjusted to dealing with more than two or three. The main thing that a group needs to understand is that there **is** such a range of issues, and that at different times people may be dealing with some and not others. In the example discussed, another weakness was that there was little direct awareness of the strategies that could have been taken to resolve conflicts or manage the group as a collective unit.

We suggest that there are three main strategies that can be used to help a group work successfully:

- reflection on its performance as a collective,
- the use of feedback, and
- the use of ground-rules.

These three strategies work best when integrated.

Reflection

Reflection is, essentially, the asking of the question '*How well have we done?*' when this question is inwardly directed to, and answered by, the group itself.

Note – the group. Not specific individuals within it. The question *'How well have we done?'* is something that must be explicitly addressed by the group as a whole, and the views of all members taken into account, for reflection to take place appropriately.

Equally, it must be the group that comes to such a view, rather than the views of some external observer who passes commentary. During your Masters programme, you may well be expected to work together in groups, sometimes making presentations, sometimes completing group responses to exercises. The views of your tutor on how well your group has done are important, but they are not the final answer as to how well the group did, for the tutor was not present when the group worked together. The observations of a tutor, whilst extremely useful as they are based on an extensive experience of such work, are an *input* to your deliberations, not the *final output* from them.

Because reflection is an activity that includes the views of all members of a group, it is important that the group does this in a suitable manner. It works most effectively when it is built into group routines – for example, at the end of each session a certain amount of time is set aside for the group to evaluate what has happened and, where appropriate, identify any learning points. One advantage about this is that the giving and receiving of feedback is then seen as a natural part of what goes on. When it is not a standard activity then people can often misinterpret the reasons why someone has raised an issue at a particular point.

People sometimes think of reflection as a private affair where individuals go over issues in their own mind, but really it is a process of dialogue: the metaphor is about bouncing ideas off other people. Group members should be encouraged to express their views and then to defend them against scrutiny as part of that dialogue – what is your evidence for saying we succeeded in this or that respect? What kinds of alternative strategies could we have used to deal with this or that kind of issue? Ultimately, some reflection is personal – it is legitimate for the individual to say 'I felt this.' But for a group as a whole to be successful, it is important that there be a shared view of what has happened and about what should happen next – since in effect group working is about a set of individuals forming a collective consciousness and understanding.

Feedback

Feedback is one of the key mechanisms of influencing group dynamics; its purpose is to help people to change the way they behave in the future. Successful feedback occurs when people want to develop and change their actions, and creatively use their colleagues to achieve this. It can be done well or badly.

Feedback should be approached on a mutual basis. It is just as important for the individual who receives the feedback to adopt an appropriate attitude as it is for the individual giving it. For the person giving feedback, it is important to recognize that every individual, however resilient, has the potential to react defensively when their errors or faults are pointed out. One golden rule when giving feedback is the following:

Feedback should be about behaviour, not about the individual.

Whether the feedback refers to a success or a failure, it is not appropriate to phrase it in terms of the type of person who produced it. Far better to put it in terms of the behaviour being evaluated. Thus *'You're a very creative individual'* is misleading compared with *'You dealt with that situation very creatively.'* What you as an observer have seen is how someone has dealt with certain situations – the person who is very creative in certain contexts may be quite different in others. With members of the same group you may find that some members behave in different ways in their study work to their normal behaviour in their professional or personal lives. So it is going beyond your evidence to say *what the individual really is*. In any case, it is usually much easier for all parties to discuss issues when they are about a public piece of behaviour than about someone's character.

People sometimes feel that this approach is a good one when giving 'bad news' (such as suggesting that someone has been defensive in a certain situation) but it is acceptable to make more personal statements when it is 'good' news. The difficulties with this approach is that we can't be sure exactly how any individual make regard any particular evaluation, and even when someone does regard an evaluation as positive, it is not appropriate for them to be encouraged to make generalizations about themselves on this basis.

The safest course, therefore, is to approach every evaluation as being about a particular act in a particular set of circumstances, and avoid making our own judgement about what will be perceived as good or bad news by the recipient of the feedback – offering every statement sensitively and supportively.

Just as important is how someone *accepts* the news. If feedback is given appropriately (i.e. focused on what someone has done and could do in the future rather than on what kind of person they are) then it is incumbent on the recipient to deal with it appropriately. This means:

- accepting the feedback in the terms it is given;

- trying to ensure that they have a clear understanding of what the comments really mean; and
- identifying actions that they can take to deal with the phenomena commented on (which, depending on the nature of the feedback, may be about consolidating behaviour or changing it).

The focus on this guidance is how to use feedback to enhance the operation of the group, not on how improve other people's underlying personality. If individuals try to reject the feedback, or if they are unable to make use of what is told them, or if they simply try to explain away deficiencies in performance, it may indicate that you are shifting the focus of the feedback towards the personal.

But feedback given by team members is not necessarily the ultimate truth – so it is important for the recipient of the feedback to clarify what is really meant, and that may mean interpreting and putting into context what is said. This is why feedback should be a *dialogue*, not merely a comment from one person to another.

Ground-rules

The approach that a group takes to the setting of ground-rules is usually a determining factor in its progress and development. Ground-rules are the principles which a group needs to establish before it can get to work on the task it faces. This process is particularly appropriate for Masters-level Business programmes: it requires good communication skills, a sensitivity to the interpretation of what others say, an ability to come to a working basis for going forward even when there may remain some areas of uncertainty – key ingredients, in fact, of this level of learning.

Some individuals and some groups fail to see the need for explicitly agreeing ground-rules, and try to operate without bothering with such apparently time-wasting activities. Generally, these groups tend to perform the task, but fail to learn anything from it. For a learning group an overriding focus on task is a waste of an opportunity, and indeed defeats the purpose of group work – for often it can be easier to work on something on your own rather than have to explain and defend your ideas to several others, who may want to amend or even replace them. So the group without ground-rules is setting itself up to fail in learning terms, even when they might be successful in terms of achieving the task they were set. Sometimes they do not even do that – some groups which ignore ground-rules find that the implicit and unregulated differences in approach between the members lead to unmanageable conflicts, and they disintegrate.

Other groups go to the opposite extreme. Ground-rules are set at the start and become fixed ideas for how the group will proceed at every step from then on. These also set themselves up to fail in learning terms, for often the only real learning in a group is when it starts to get difficult. The difficulty may manifest itself in conflict – but not always. Sometimes the difficulty is more subtle – such as when the group loses a sense of critique and thinks that everything it does will be correct. This is the phenomenon referred to earlier as 'groupthink'.

In several cases where large corporations have been involved in major scandals – such as the collapse of the Bank of Credit and Commerce international (BCCI) or the Enron affair, the prime decisions had been made by a group of people with reputations as extremely high performers in their field. When the judges came to ask how this could have happened, it became clear that some individuals within these teams had had reservations, but had concealed them because the perception was that that if everyone within so high performing group as this was expressing confidence that this was the right thing to do, then it MUST be so.

When a group starts to lose its sense of self-criticism, it often loses its sense of danger. The practice of asking questions, then – of *each other* as much as of texts and study materials – becomes a central tool in the group learning how to progress, and ground-rules are a very effective means of building this sense of critique into the group's workings.

Ground-rules are effective when

- each individual accepts them sufficiently to be prepared to use them as the guide for how the group behaves;
- each individual is clear about what they imply for their behaviour and for that of others;
- people explicitly use them to evaluate their own and others' behaviour; and
- they are reviewed from time to time as a mechanism for the group to develop.

Note that we do not suggest here that there should be total acceptance from all members of the group. It may be impossible for even as few as four people to completely agree about ground-rules – the point is that there should be sufficient agreement that each individual can say to themselves: 'I can go with that'. One can also go too far with aiming for consensus: we know of one group planning to be together for a week for a group therapy course which had still not agreed about smoking after two days! Clearly, chasing the ideal is going to delay getting down to the business of learning and completing set activities.

So we need to adopt a realistic approach – sufficient agreement for the group to proceed, and ground-rules that guide and are used regularly without becoming overly mechanical.

If you are working with a new set of colleagues (such as at the start of your Masters programme), then the ideal process for establishing ground-rules is as follows:

1   Set aside a significant amount of time. Consider allocating a maximum of 10% of your total time together for setting up ground-rules and reflecting on progress. So for a project that will take up about thirty hours to complete, you might allocate an hour to set them up, revisit them for half an hour a couple of times during the project to ensure that they are actually helping, and spend an hour at the end considering what you have learnt and reviewing the exercise. In longer projects the actual time spent may be longer but the proportion may be less.

2   Each individual identifies those issues which are important to them, about how they hope the group will work – at this stage these may not yet be specifically in the form of rules, but just expressions of interest or concern.

3   All members of the group share all of these issues – sometimes this may need to be facilitated using a flipchart.

4   Each idea is discussed and the group agrees a provisional rule relating to this.

5   When all ideas have been discussed and provisional rules agreed, the group should consider the ground-rules as a whole and each individual should make an explicit commitment to them – it is essential at this stage that if someone has a reservation they should express it, even if ultimately they agree to the rule; the group should be ready to re-consider any or all of the ground-rules if there is disquiet at this point.

6   The group should finally agree on how these will be evaluated and when – it can also be a useful 'locking in' process to agree that group members will explicitly refer to these when discussing the way they will approach the tasks they are set.

You will get better at setting ground-rules each time you form a new group and as the course progresses you will get through this formal procedure more efficiently, so you can allocate less time. Some people on MBA and similar programmes, when seeing this process specified so explicitly, have wondered whether it is all worth it, and whether it is all rather too 'touchy-feely'. In practice the experience of tutors running such programmes is that where there are groups that work together for several months on several different substantial tasks, then the biggest single risk both to their learning and to their performance in assessments, is the failure to manage group processes. It is a far bigger cause of group failure than any ability to complete the task. Hence the need for an explicit procedure.

At Masters level your aim should be to develop to a situation where the need for tightly specified rules and procedures drops away as you progress through the programme.

Question

What areas do you think should be covered by ground-rules?

Response

Although this is specific to all involved in the group, and consequently it will vary greatly from individual to individual and from group to group, many groups try to agree on issues such as:

- when, where and how frequently they will meet;
- how they will support the group with electronic communication, such as use of any available VLE (virtual learning environment), e-mail discussion list, group website, shared files;
- how meetings will be conducted – e.g. who will chair, control or facilitate meetings, and whether these responsibilities should be temporary or permanent;
- how decisions will be made – for example, some groups may agree that all decisions must be unanimous;
- how records might be kept, and who might see them (i.e. the tutor may want proof of meetings, etc.);
- how members will treat each other – listening, respect, honesty etc.;
- that members take responsibility for their own participation;
- how the group will explain its actions and work externally – e.g. closed ranks, or confidentiality;
- how the group will use the expertise of its members – getting people to play to their strengths may be a good way to get a good task result but does little for the development of individual skills;
- how the group will balance learning and task completion – for example, where and when the group will reflect together on what has happened, or ensuring that every individual's contribution is taken on its own merits, rather than summarily judged and accepted or rejected; and
- how the group will manage any peer assessment process.

Remember that ultimately the test of how well a group has functioned on your Masters programme is whether it has learnt effectively and done itself full justice in its assessments. It is not measured in terms of how much fun they all had, or if they ended up as good friends at the end – this can be nice when it happens but if it does not, this does not defeat the purpose of working in groups.

What happens when people in a group stop following the ground-rules? This is the crucial test. If the group is to flourish, it is essential that breaches in ground-rules are explicitly discussed and there is a collective agreed resolution of the issue. This is not the same as someone being criticized or reprimanded for not following them: the assumption is that people adopt adult behaviour when working in a group and therefore do things for a good reason. More important is that the group understands why the ground-rule has not been followed and either reviews it or re-affirms their commitment to it.

> *To summarize*:
>
> - Certain models of group formation and development, such as those of Adair or Belbin, can be useful, but probably only as pointers towards the kinds of issues that group members should address.
> - Reflection is a central strategy for group progress.
> - Feedback should be a two-way process, rather than merely a comment from one person given to another. It should be about behaviour rather than a judgment of the individual, and should be accepted and explored by the recipient rather than explained away.
> - Ground-rules need to be agreed and then used with a small degree of flexibility.

When a group encounters difficulties

It is inevitable that a group will encounter difficulties at some point or another. It is not a mark of failure of a group that this happens. What IS a mark of failure is if the group does not manage these effectively.

> When you have completed this section, you should be able to:
>
> - identify the main difficulties that a learning group may encounter; and
> - use appropriate strategies to resolve these.

Question

We discussed earlier some of the problems that groups can encounter – try to write down what you can recall of that below.

Response

- cliques and outsiders;
- lazy or 'passenger' students who ensure the other students do all the work, but ensure they themselves gain marks in the assessment;
- high levels of conflict;
- low levels of productivity or creativity.

Feedback from students on Masters courses suggests that getting acceptable involvement from *all* individuals in the group is the issue which causes the most problems.

Question

Think back on a group you have been involved in recently – it need not be a learning group – a task group will do.

How far did all members of the group put in a relatively equal contribution?

What helped this happen?

What hindered it?

Response

Some of the factors that could help this to happen are:

- clear objectives and clear roles of each member,
- the task is equally valuable for all members,
- the members of the group share the same perception of what is involved in the task, and
- there is an explicit method of resolving differences (rather than extinguishing them).

Some of the factors that could hinder this are:

- individuals do not disclose their differences or disagreements,
- the task matters less to some individuals than to others,
- a student may fall ill and be unable to contribute,

- there is a lack of shared understanding of the requirements of the task,
- an individual wishes to be seen to shine compared with their peers, or has some other undisclosed competitive agenda,
- an international student may be finding it difficult to adjust, and appear to be shy and withdrawn,
- the leader of the group is not sufficiently skilled to address differences and conflicts effectively,
- the members of the group are approaching the task in radically conflicting ways, and/or
- students from different countries, with different cultural backgrounds, might not share the same assumptions about group work.

As indicated earlier, the key mechanisms for dealing with group difficulty are ground-rules, feedback, and an open attitude towards reflection (explicit, verbal reflection, not simply thinking to oneself).

Dominance of the group by an individual may result from several factors, a method for dealing with this should consider the various possibilities:

- *The individual does not realize his/her dominance.* In this case the strategy is to explicitly measure contributions (e.g. by one member observing and writing down how often each individual contributes, in discussion and in work done).
- *The individual does not grasp the learning objectives of the group.* Here the appropriate strategy is to use these to evaluate how the group behaves when together.
- *The individual does not share the learning objectives of the group.* The strategy for this is to review the objectives communally, and attempt to reach a consensus regarding these (note: a majority vote with this individual on the losing side would probably achieve nothing).
- *The individual believes that he or she has all the knowledge and expertise necessary to complete the task.* The appropriate strategy is to reaffirm the nature of the group as being for *learning* rather than just to get good marks.

These are behavioural matters. Clearly, some people may be overly dominant for more deep-seated personality reasons – anxiety for example. In those cases these stratagems may have only a limited success, but they are still the most appropriate responses: a group that stays together for a few months to do some joint assignments is not the place for making far-reaching personality changes, but you still can modify people's *behaviour* by means of structured approaches to agreeing and monitoring their actions.

Groups should be particularly cautious about forming early and fixed conceptions about their participants. Someone who takes the lead to get the group set up might not be the only potential leader. Someone who is quiet at the beginning might have much to say. Often international students are slower to contribute, because they are translating their thoughts. But often individuals become trapped in early assumptions. Successful groups give participants a chance to vary their positions and offer new (and sometime surprising) talents and skills

Individuals may be marginalized by the rest of the group. This can happen if they are perceived as socially different – the only man, the only woman, the only person aged over 50, the only black person and so on. Or it can happen if they are perceived as a less valuable contributor than the others – for example being seen as the one with the least experience, or the youngest person in the group.

Marginalized individuals often make limited contributions, and so the group has knowingly or unknowingly deprived itself of a resource. The group's responsibility is to work against any drift by individuals to the margins, whether this is occurring for personal or social reasons.

Sometimes an individual has an unjustified negative view of themselves – what is sometimes called a 'limiting self-belief.' Whilst it is beyond the group's role to try to effect personality changes in an individual, the fact that someone has such a belief should still not be regarded as an excuse for other members of the group to acquiesce in them.

The less experienced person, for example, may well have a different perspective from the rest of the group, and therefore raise questions that do not occur to the rest. Many people who are slower to raise ideas are so because they are more thoughtful than others, and therefore will have valuable points to make. Students who speak English as a second language often find themselves excluded by rapid talk, by too much slang, jargon or anecdote, by ungrammatical or idiomatic speech, or by forms of communication which share too many implicit assumptions (even teasing and laughter can work like this). Some people are often written off as less bright simply because they speak more slowly, or do not intervene as assertively as others in a discussion. Silence does not mean absence of ideas, any more than speech means an abundance of them.

The point is, hopefully, fairly clear: a high-performing group is one that values and makes effective use of the contributions of *all* members. This does not exclude critique and discussion – it certainly does not mean that every contribution from every individual is accepted without any further consideration. It means that every contribution is taken on its own merits, and if a point is not clear there is an effort made to see if there is something of value there.

When this does not happen, the remedy is relatively straightforward – to establish a ground-rule that everybody is consulted regarding decisions, and that each member is assigned a role to play in each task. Behind this are two values (a) that the learning group is there primarily to promote learning, not to complete tasks, and (b) that individual contributions should be accepted and used as a resource to the group's learning, and therefore all need to be considered before being acted upon.

An individual can opt out during the course of a conflict. That is clear and visible, and can be dealt with as an issue. It is more difficult when an individual opts out by drifting away. Usually this happens in a series of stages. Perhaps someone may begin by not turning up to a meeting, and then they find it harder to get to the next. Or perhaps they have not fulfilled a commitment and feel embarrassed by this and hence do not want to explain it. It is important to identify this process as it begins to build up and try to deal with the issues before someone converts their drift away into a complete loss of commitment.

The remedies for opting out also need to be implemented in a way that reflects the possible reasons why it is happening. Where there is misunderstanding of the task, or a failure to accept the objectives of the group, then adopt strategies to re-emphasize the objectives, and to review collectively the ground-rules that have been agreed, with a view to gaining a further, and greater, level of agreement. It is more difficult if there is a motivational issue. In some cases, this may be a matter of the work not having the same importance for that individual as for the others. Or it may be the subtler problem that the individual is opting out because they are uncomfortable with the situation – maybe the behaviour of other group members is unacceptable to them, for example. In this kind of case, the remedy may again lie in review of the ground-rules of the group as a whole.

So, the appropriate approach to managing the person who is opting out is via the review process, giving feedback without it becoming personal, encouraging dialogue to understand why someone is not participating. This may include the following:

- determine whether there is a question of agreement to objectives;
- review ground-rules and gain a consensus to them;
- agree specific targets with the individual in question; and
- review progress against these targets.

At times, none of these may work! That is the time when it is appropriate to refer this to tutorial staff. Just as in a professional context you would be expected to manage a poor performer, and exhaust the reasonable alternatives before going to the next level, so you are expected to do this with group members. But if you do adopt the solutions suggested above, then a group will not often go badly wrong.

> ***To summarize:***
>
> There are three main problems that a group can encounter with participation – over-dominance, exclusion of one member by the rest of the group, and individuals opting out voluntarily. In all three cases, the primary remedy is to review the agreed ground-rules, and re-establish these.

● Electronic resources available to groups

> When you have read through this section, you should be able to identify ways to avoid the main pitfalls when using electronic communications and learning resources as part of your group work.

We looked at electronic resources in relation to study and research earlier, it is important to recognize that there is a wide range of electronic resources and facilities that groups can make use of in communicating with one another. These include:

- Email
- Instant messaging and chat rooms
- University virtual learning environments
- Discussion groups on the World Wide Web
- Video conferencing
- Podcasts and videocasts
- Blogs
- Wiki pages

In their respective ways, each of these forms of communication gives group members opportunities to share a wide range of information and opinion. There are many benefits to sharing information, including:

- Cross-checking becomes easier.
- The group will have a wider pool of potential links, analogies, examples and supplementary material.
- The group will inevitably critique the shared material.
- Material and ideas can be developed taking account of several perspectives and viewpoints.

One of the most useful features of electronic sharing or material is that one can see how an idea has built up when progressive contributions have been made by group members. This can occur if electronic files are amended using a 'track changes' option. Another is the use of 'wiki' style software (available on many VLEs nowadays) where the history of development of a document, including each person's contribution, is archived and available for consideration (it should be noted that increasingly tutors assessing group produced documents are asking for evidence of how each member contributed, so a document history of this form is useful for that purpose also).

Each form of electronic information sharing also has potential to create great confusion if not managed appropriately. For example, an instant messaging facility can easily run out of control if people do not know when they can contribute and when they should sit back and let others do so. Similarly, a 'round robin' series of emails can quickly swamp people's inboxes if each email is sent as a reply to the previous one.

By now you should already have the idea that ground-rules are the means to manage these issues, by setting up protocols for how communications should be sent, stored, and responded to. Ground-rules, and the protocols that can thereby be set up, can help regulate the flow of information, can ensure that misunderstandings are avoided, and can make the process of information transfer convenient and effective for all group members.

Regulating information flow

Protocols are necessary to ensure that information is circulated in a standard format by all members. For example, ensuring that all members use the same file format and style attributes – there is nothing more annoying than changing a whole series of headings from one format to another. It should be clearly established what software and hardware capabilities are to be assumed for each member, what levels of skill are expected, and how incompatibilities (e.g. Mac to Windows file conversions) are to be resolved. File naming should follow a regular system, and each author should re-name a common file with their version number, so that others know which file they in turn should work on. Large projects sometimes use librarians as information managers – this task may be allocated to a member of the group.

Avoiding misunderstandings

It is easier to misunderstand the intention behind textual communication than where someone speaks to you face to face – the loss of non-verbal cues represents a serious loss of a category of information. Graphic techniques have been evolved to try to overcome this loss – for example, conventions about use of capitals and emoticons (little diagrammatic faces expressing simplified emotions, generated by specific combinations of keystrokes). Nevertheless the use of these needs to be explicitly agreed, and it should be borne in mind that a conventional 'smiley face' emoticon can itself easily be misunderstood.

Another key issue that can cause difficulty is how far group deliberations are to be public (e.g. accessible via a website or open discussion space) and if they are, how confidential material is to be handled. This is potentially an explosive issue – once an item has been transmitted to someone else then it is out of your control, so you need to be confident that it will not be disclosed in a way you would not have wished. E-mail discussions in which each new contribution is added to the top and returned are particularly hazardous when they are forwarded to someone outside the group. You may have written something incautious knowing it would be understood between friends, and suddenly it is out in the open for all to see! The best rule is to assume all e-mails will eventually be read by the wrong person . . .

Convenience

It is also important simply to make sure that information sharing is done so in a convenient manner. Issues such as the cut-off time for making mobile phone calls, or expected response times for replying to emails, and a system for acknowledging that a communication has been received (as well as a system for tracking if one has not arrived) need to be agreed. You also to be clear about how much participation is expected, from whom and how long to wait for others to contribute.

As indicated above, long threads of discussions can lose the reader, as can excessively long web addresses (the 'tiny URL' facility is one way to make transmission of web addresses much simpler)

> ### To summarize:
>
> Ground-rules, setting up protocols for how electronic information sharing is to be carried out, are essential for this aspect of group work to be effective. They cover fairly mundane issues, but ones that have a great potential for misunderstanding and difficulty if not regulated.

6 The Dissertation

Introduction

In this chapter we will look at the nature of a dissertation, its likely structure, and the various processes that you will need to go through in order to successfully complete it. In the subsequent chapter, we will explore the methods that you will need to use to conduct the investigation.

The dissertation is the most important mechanism both to help you develop your understanding and professional ability, but also to demonstrate clearly that you have reached the Masters level of learning and understanding. As we have stated several times in this book, this involves the ability to deal with uncertainties, handle gaps in knowledge, define problems in an unfocused field, and yet still be able to make sensible decisions.

In the Business and Management area this implies that you will be able to clarify a significant organizational or managerial question or issue, collect and process the available information, come to a reasoned and justifiable conclusion about the issue, and also make realistic proposals of what to do about the situation identified in your conclusion. You will be able to do this even though the information available may be in short supply, or be limited in scope, or may not all point in the same way. This is a very common experience for business managers – made more acute by the indeterminate way in which different subjects (such as strategy or ethics) connect in business.

This piece of work, then, is an opportunity for you to synthesize and integrate the various subjects that you have studied on your Business Masters. It involves you addressing a problem that will be of potential value to researchers or to professionals in the field. In dealing with this kind of issue, you will find that although at first it looks specific to one subject, once you start exploring it you are likely to be ranging across the whole of the curriculum of your programme.

The sections in this chapter will cover the following:

1   **what a dissertation is**: distinguishing different kinds of dissertation, and the stages of working on a dissertation;

2   **the scope of a dissertation**: research questions and adopting a problem focus for the work;

3   **clarifying the subject**: scoping the subject; setting clear and measurable objectives;

4   **progressing the investigation**: some of the practical issues relating to the process;

5   **concluding the investigation**: making sure the argument all ties up; reality-checking results; differentiating conclusions from recommendations; writing up and presenting the dissertation;

6   **getting the work finished**: some practicalities of dissertation production;

7   **what gets good marks in dissertations**: learning outcomes and assessment criteria for dissertations;

8   **working with your supervisor**.

● What is a dissertation?

When you have read this section, you should be able to:

- identify the differences between practice-focused and research-focused pieces of work;
- differentiate a dissertation from other large scale pieces of work; and
- identify the stages of producing a dissertation.

On most Business Masters courses you are required to produce a dissertation, a written account of an extended investigation into a question relevant and interesting to managers, business professionals, and/or business researchers. One essential aspect is that in some way it should aim to develop *some kind of new knowledge*. This is a broad aim, and can include, amongst other things, any of the following:

- a new question has been raised,
- a new concept has been developed,
- fresh evidence has been collected that tests out an idea in a new way,
- existing evidence is re-interpreted,
- existing concepts and ideas have been applied in novel contexts, and
- existing concepts and ideas have been critiqued.

The main point is that each of these is generalizable – these outcomes are applicable universally, to any relevant business context. True, sometimes research outcomes may be narrowly defined, but they still apply to anything within the defined category.

The most important distinction, in respect of the kind of dissertation that you might be expected to produce, is the difference between a *research-based* piece of work and a *practice-focused* piece. As these phrases suggest, each places emphasis on a different element in your work. However, it would be misleading to think that a practice-focused dissertation entirely ignores theory and research, or that a research-based dissertation omits any reference to practice (with Management, it is very difficult to imagine the latter at all). It is a case of how much emphasis is placed on each of these, and how this emphasis affects the nature of the questions you ask, the progress of the investigation and its outcomes.

Essentially the difference between research-based and practice-based dissertations can be explained in terms of the communities to which the work is addressed.

A research-based dissertation approaches an issue from the perspective of the research community. It deals with a question in terms of how it relates to existing knowledge and theories, and collects evidence and/or analyses material in order to address concerns expressed within the existing tradition of research and dialogue. It also takes the argument wherever it may lead, irrespective of the value or use of the outcomes for the professional management community. You are more likely to produce a research-based dissertation if you are following a specialised Business-related MSc or MA.

Although the main reason why somebody would produce a dissertation of this kind dealing with a management subject is ultimately to help managers operate more effectively, with a research-based dissertation the relationship between theory and practice is indirect. The outcomes deal with business, but they address issues that are of most concern to the research community. So a dissertation of this kind could be complete without any specific recommendations. Its primary rationale is to produce or critique theory.

In contrast, a practice-based piece of work will be focused on a problem, the subject matter of which would be directly relevant to the interests of working professionals. The question should represent an issue of application or implementation of ideas or theoretical concepts in an organization or industry, which in some way is seen as problematic or in need of enquiry. The outcomes should still contribute towards new generalizable knowledge, but this might be about how far organizations of a certain kind approach x or y, or how a certain issue affects a given industry.

This kind of dissertation is therefore intended to go beyond simply a resolution of the task; it should generate new learning, new approaches, new perceptions and perspectives that could be transferred to other contexts. But these will be *professional* contexts, and there should be recommendations for action that are realistic for the relevant professionals. Many MBA programmes will require you to produce a practice-focused dissertation.

Occasionally you may encounter the term *thesis*, in the context of the major piece of work completed on a Masters. This term is ambiguous. It can sometimes refer to a theoretical position, hypothesis or desired conclusion, along with its supporting arguments (we talk of someone 'advancing the thesis that . . .'), or it can refer to a large-scale work that puts together the arguments and evidence for such a position. As such it is in effect another term for what we have described above as a research-based dissertation.

Another ambiguous phrase is *management report.* This term is often encountered in professional life, where it is generally concerned with fulfilling a task, such as resolving a question for a particular organization – it is not normally expected to generate new knowledge, such as a fresh perspective, a critique of existing management theory, or to provide evidence in favour of or against a particular hypothesis. It is normally a *localized investigation* into an issue as it affects a particular organization or a department – sometimes these can be extensive, but they do not necessarily say anything generalizable about the concepts themselves or their application. Sometimes on an MBA or on a professional diploma course the major piece of work is called a management report, though in most cases what is intended is what we are here calling a practice-focused dissertation.

In this guide we shall refer to 'research-based' and 'practice-focused' dissertations distinctly where there are differences. If we write 'dissertation' on its own then the point applies to either kind. Each kind of dissertation has its own benefits and advantages. For example, the practice-focused will often result in technological innovations, whilst the research-based piece of work is more likely to produce effective interdisciplinary insights, and can often be a better vehicle to *play* with ideas.

Above all, discover what options are available to you on your own programme. Study the course documentation, talk to the course leader or the leader of any research methods course, and if at all possible get a look at previous pieces of work, to establish the parameters of what is allowed and encouraged.

The stages of producing a dissertation

There are three phases in the production of a dissertation, each of which comprises sub-stages:

- *Firstly, deciding what to do.* You need to identify a potential question or issue. In the case of a practice-focused piece of work you will need to establish via discussion with others that the question or problem you intend to address is of interest and acceptable to any key decision-makers, then you will need to estimate the potential scale and scope of the study, and clarify in more specific terms what is required. For a research-based piece of work the question and its scope is normally established via your reading of the relevant literature and, if possible, discussion with people currently researching in the area. We shall deal with these elements in the next section.

- *Secondly, conducting the investigation.* This needs to be appropriately planned – a methodology needs to be developed, which will give a rationale for the investigation to come. You will probably have further consultations with other parties at several points: for example, with a practice-based piece to ensure that there is the appropriate level of organizational support and to begin the process of gathering the information, whilst for a research-based piece you might want to maintain dialogue with others researching in the field, in order to help frame your questions.

  You then need to develop an appropriate conceptual framework, which will involve a substantial review of the relevant literature, and finally you will need to identify the questions that you need to have resolved. Not all questions will be resolved by collecting field data, though many will. Much of the time taken during this phase is in collecting data and analysing it. Most of this stage will be dealt with in the next chapter.

- *Thirdly, concluding your investigation.* You will need to make a decision as to whether you have collected enough evidence and carried out enough analysis/discussion to respond to the question or problem you have set yourself. Then the work needs to be written up and produced and disseminated to the relevant parties. This part is often overshadowed by the extensive work you may have done in the second stage, and it is often skimped. Many students do not do themselves full justice in their dissertation, because they leave themselves too little time for this stage, and see it as 'just' finishing off.

To summarize:

In this section we have defined what a dissertation is, differentiated two different kinds of dissertation (research-based and practice-focused) and identified the key stages of producing a dissertation. The next three sections will deal with these stages in turn.

The scope of a dissertation

When you have completed this section, you will be able to evaluate the suitability of different choices of subject for a dissertation.

Although a dissertation should be *focused* on a problem or a question, it is quite possible to successfully complete one *without answering the question or solving the problem*. The question/problem provides the key subject matter of the piece of work, but there can be valuable outcomes of the work even when it has not been finally settled (indeed by this stage of the course you should have an instinct that little at this level is completely 'settled' anyway). So what kinds of question or problem are suitable for your dissertation?

For consideration

Below you will find some topics which have been chosen by people in the past as dissertation subjects on Business Masters programmes. Decide which of these you think is suitable as a dissertation subject, which kind of dissertation (research-based or practice-focused) they would be suitable for, and clarify your reasons for your choices.

A review of the purchasing process for a Department.

An evaluation of the concept of cross-cultural management.

The design of a new IT system for an establishment.

The recruitment of a senior manager.

Internet security in the developing world – the next decade.

Financial projections for an independent cost centre.

Response

While any of these subjects *might* be suitable as the basis of one or other kind of dissertation, a lot would depend on exactly the form in which the objectives of the study were phrased. In each case one of the key tasks is to turn this 'topic' into a question or statement of a problem that can then be resolved by the investigation.

Taking the first example, reviewing the purchasing process is a standard managerial task, as it involves the use of resources and consideration of the impact this one process has upon the overall strategy of the organization. The kind of question that would be appropriate here would be such as *'Is the purchasing process adopted by this department cost effective?'* or similar – something that makes clear the professional value of the study. So it could be a sound practice-based dissertation, though it would not be likely to be of much value as a research-based one, unless it critiqued a current theory or model of procurement.

Evaluating a concept, such as cross-cultural management, looks to be more suitable for a research-based dissertation. However, if the work were related to the specifics of one particular organization – for example, how far its operations and strategy were affected by this concept – then it could be the basis for a practice-based study. One risk with this type of research-based dissertation subject is that it could easily be expressed too vaguely: it is generally useful in this kind of work to tie the study directly to an academic *question* – in this case it might be something such as *'How far does the idea of cross-cultural management help resolve problems of control with international organizations?'*

A discussion of internet security in the developing world could easily turn into a broad exploration of concepts relating to international relations and politics without having to focus on the professional responsibilities of managers. It would be a suitable subject for a research-based dissertation, so long as the objectives of the study bring out the professional relevance of the discussion (even with research-based dissertations, *some* kind of professional relevance should always be evident). So the question could be something such as *'How will business in developing countries be affected by changes in internet security systems over the next decade.'* This is broad and therefore of most interest to the research community, but it is also clear that the outcomes have a value for professionals as well.

Subjects such as the design of a new IT system, or financial projections for a department or cost centre, often straddle the difficult distinction between technical subjects and managerial ones. You could resolve this issue by reference to the objectives of the dissertation. Ultimately, a dissertation which dealt with detailed specifications and the functionality of computing systems, →

or which had a substantial proportion of its argument related to tables of figures or financial calculations, balance sheets or profit and loss accounts, is on the technical side rather than the managerial, and is therefore not of the right scope for a business dissertation of either research or practice. A piece of work that looked at the strategic implications of financial projections, on the other hand, or looked at the organizational impact of a new information system, would most likely be sufficiently managerial in scope to provide the basis for a practice-focused dissertation.

What of the example of recruiting a senior manager? This is probably too low level for a Masters-level dissertation. It is operational in focus, and unless there are severely complex problems relating to the recruitment of that particular manager, which raise general issues concerning the ability of the organization to provide adequate human resources to meet its strategic challenges, the problem is too simple. This might be a suitable subject at first-degree level, or for a professional diploma course, but it does not provide the appropriate level of complexity that is necessary to demonstrate mastery of the subject of management.

We can see from this discussion that *the subject matter of the dissertation is often less important than the way in which it is expressed as a question or problem*. A managerial treatment of the subject should relate to the broadest questions of how this problem impacts upon the ability of organizations to achieve their overall purpose, the efficiency with which they use existing resources, or the effectiveness with which specific areas such as HR or marketing contribute to the organization's or industry's overall purposes.

On an MBA or another strategic management programme, the subject matter of a Masters dissertation would usually also need to have a *strategic* element – relating to the ability of the organization to meet its ultimate aims within the context of its existing resource base. In other programmes this element may not be so evident, though in practice dealing with a significant issue often will have some strategic relevance.

There is often conflict between what is *useful* in managerial terms and what can be *well-supported* by available evidence – this will form a major theme in the next chapter. Often these two demands go in opposite directions. For example, a theory of motivation that took account of all the relevant factors would be far too complex for us to make use of on a day-to-day basis when managing teams of staff: the range of factors would be too wide, and the probabilities of different kinds of behaviours would consequently be too difficult to measure with any degree of accuracy.

So, professionally, managers often work with 'models' that in many cases are little more than traditional notions without evidence to support them. These work, we know how far to take them, and what they can and can't do for us. Validity, then, whilst important for any dissertation, is most important for the research-based piece of work, where the intellectual contribution is to the fore. For a practice-focused dissertation validity may be less important than utility of results.

In some Masters courses the dissertation questions may be organized around the supervisors. They will have prepared a list of topics which interest them and relate to their research work, and the students will be expected to select a topic, and therefore a supervisor, from that list. This presents various difficulties for students – for example, they may be interested in a specific area, but they may have formed a good relationship with a tutor who does not supervise in that subject. Because a significant part of the intellectual benefit of the dissertation lies in your learning how to frame and re-frame the topic as the research develops, it is important to establish early on with your supervisor just how much freedom you will have in that developing process.

> *To summarize*:
>
> For both research-based and practice-focused dissertations, the subject matter is less important than the questions or problems it raises.

Clarifying the subject

> When you have completed this section, you should be able to:
>
> - use a range of relevant criteria to decide on the subject matter of your dissertation; and
> - construct effective objectives for your dissertation.

Before doing anything else, you should start by opening a diary of the research process. This should be a record of *all* your ideas, however fleeting, as well as any material gained from discussions with others. It will develop into a chronicle of the process of investigation you followed and how you have learned during the work. This has many potential advantages, including:

- Writing things down reinforces them so there is less chance that a bright idea will get lost, especially those which at the time seem so completely obvious they don't need to be recorded.
- Written records are useful in the case of any future disputes (e.g. an interviewee who says 'I never said that').
- Reviewing the diary will remind you where you originally intended to go – and thus help you decide whether that is still the right goal or should be amended.
- Reviewing the diary will help you understand how far you have travelled.

The diary will be invaluable to help you identify and then clarify your dissertation subject.

How do you decide what subject to pick for your dissertation? There is no simple formula, as everybody's situation is different, but nevertheless there are pitfalls to be avoided.

For consideration

Look at the reasons that some people have given for why they selected a particular topic. *Which of these do you think are suitable? Which do you think are inappropriate? Why?*

(a) I have always been very interested in this subject.
(b) I think it's disgraceful that this area has been neglected for so long by many companies and I want to shake things up a bit.
(c) This has been a problem for our Department for several years, and we've always said 'if only someone had the time to look at it . . .'
(d) My boss suggested I should do this, and has even told me the kind of solution he wants to see at the end.
(e) I think this will be useful when I want to make a career move as it will make a good addition to my CV.

Response

You should always pick a subject that you are interested in. You are going to have to work with the subject for several months and if you feel at the beginning that the subject is dull, you will not be motivated to work on it for very long.

If you are already employed, then it is a very useful benefit to your organization to get some kind of return on the investment they have placed in you by sending you on the Masters course.

It is, additionally, a legitimate aim to have a personal reason for wanting to investigate a particular subject, so long as that personal reason is appropriate within the context.

For these reasons, it should be clear that:

(a) Interest in a subject is an acceptable reason.
(b) To want to shake things up a bit *may* be legitimate but – it may be difficult to manage your levels of bias when carrying this study out, and – you may not improve your career prospects by doing so!
(c) To want to resolve a long-standing strategic problem is acceptable and can provide something of value to organizations – a bonus if you work for them and a possible route of entry if you want to.
(d) To want to solve a problem that your boss is keen on may be acceptable, but to be expected simply to follow their suggestions, and to be told the kind of solution to reach, is not acceptable.
(e) To want to develop your own personal skills as part of your career plan is acceptable.

There are other aspects that you need to consider carefully before embarking on your investigation:

- Whether you can satisfactorily complete the investigation within the appropriate time and with the resources available to you.
- Whether the subject would yield generalizable results that will be valuable to the research or practice community.
- Whether you will be given the appropriate support within any organization that collaborates with the research, to be able to access the really key information and to ensure that that the investigation will not get blocked or undermined on account of political sensitivities. (You may think if you already work there that you can handle some of these 'political' considerations, but still need to think this through and plan carefully.)

These are difficult questions but you can move towards resolving them by early discussion with whoever you think might be a key stakeholder in this subject – anyone with an interest in, influence over, or exposure to the effects of your subject is a stakeholder of your investigation. In the case of a practice-focused dissertation, you might want to discuss the issue you wish to investigate with those who are directly responsible for it in an organization, or with those who benefit from the process you are considering – such as internal customers or suppliers.

With a research-based dissertation you will need to talk to others researching in the field, face to face, by email or perhaps by joining electronic academic discussion forums. But here too it would be useful to get the views of some professionals as to how far the academic question you are interested in relates to their day-to-day responsibilities.

The more people you speak to, the better will be your idea about the subject you want investigate. You will get valuable hints and tips about conducting the investigation and be able to form an overall context for the problem. In particular, you may well be given the extremely useful advice not to investigate a subject because it is too politically sensitive. For a practice-based dissertation, especially if it is conducted in the organization that employs you, this is essential information.

This process of raising the subject with as wide a range of stakeholders as possible will also help you to understand the scale of the problem, and therefore how much work needs to be done to collect the appropriate amount of information in the field. It may well be that a subject that initially you thought was quite feasible turns out to be much larger than you first believed. *Most dissertation subjects have a tendency to expand in scope*, so it is important to try to keep a tight control from the outset.

Once you have decided upon a subject for your dissertation you need to formulate the targets as specifically as possible. On the basis of this you will be able to develop your understanding of the scope and scale of the investigation to the point where you have defined the range of management subjects you will need to study and the range of field information you will need to collect. This kind of scoping process is often done implicitly, but there is a great value in writing it all down in the diary we referred to earlier, even if it does not feature in the finished dissertation – reference to this statement of scope will help you as you progress through the work, and help you to prevent the dissertation running out of control.

Formulating targets specifically is probably the single most important task that you will complete when doing your dissertation.

> The experience on Business and Management Masters courses is that the vast majority of poor dissertations have been weak because they were hampered by weak objectives.

Objectives are statements of intended outcomes – what management consultancies might call 'deliverables'. They set out the criteria that someone would use to evaluate whether the dissertation had been successful or not –

if these are vague this cannot be done and it is also difficult for you to have any check on what you are doing during the work. The Masters dissertation has a life of its own. As your investigation progresses, you will learn more and more about the subject and more and more about the organizational context. Your understanding will naturally develop and grow, as will the number of new and interesting questions you should tackle, and so will the scale of your dissertation. You will need to have some very clear basis of evaluating your progress, to counteract this inflationary tendency. *Clear, measurable objectives will do this for you.*

For consideration

Here is a set of objectives that have been formulated for a dissertation that deals with human resource management in large legal firms:

- to examine the management styles of office managers;
- to evaluate the needs of qualified lawyers and legal clerks;
- to compare workloads between different offices;
- to make appropriate comparisons with other organizations;
- to review relevant literature; and
- to draw appropriate conclusions and recommendations.

How satisfactory are these as objectives – i.e. as statements of intended outcomes?

Response

None of these is entirely satisfactory. Some of them are weak because they do not really specify *outcomes* at all but only indicate *activities* that support the investigation. For example 'to examine' and 'to review' are activities not outcomes. It would not be difficult, however, to turn them round, for example, 'to produce a categorization of the styles of office managers' or 'to report on the comparative workloads of different offices'. Both of these now specify what the reader could expect to see when they turn to that part of the dissertation.

As well as turning activity words, such as 'examine', 'review', 'compare', into outcome words such as 'report on', 'evaluate', or 'identify', well-written objectives will make *specific* what the reader can expect to see. So, instead of 'drawing appropriate conclusions' a more suitable objective might say 'to draw conclusions relating to the human resource strategy of the department'. Equally, instead of just referring to recommendations, a well-written objective might be 'to recommend an action plan to enhance the management of human resources'.

These differences are not purely verbal. They represent a mindset. Instead of focusing on what the researcher will do, they focus on *what the reader will receive*. A useful acronym to help people check that they have well-formed objectives is SMART:

S specific
M measurable
A achievable, accountable
R realistic, resources taken account of
T timescale specified

The more specific your objectives, the more likely it is that you will meet them satisfactorily and complete the dissertation. The more imprecise and unspecific your objectives, the more likely you will lose your way, either during the investigation or during the writing up.

But objectives do not always stay the same. Sometimes you find things out along the way that means that you really should change them, although this is a serious decision which you should make carefully. For example, you may discover during your research that the issue you are looking at is an offshoot of another question which is really much more important. Or you might find that as you have mis-stated the issue, and revising your objectives will make collecting information easier. This is realistic practice, given that all research is an enquiry into what is not known. It is better to amend your project midstream rather than to carry on with the wrong question and produce work that the examiners will feel is a missed opportunity.

What helps here is, as well as having a set of objectives, is to have a single more broadly based statement of what you are looking at – a statement of **aim**. This need not be SMART, because it is not there to set the precise direction you want to travel in, but to help you monitor in broad terms whether the course you have set is the right one. Often this will be simply a sentence summarizing your chosen topic, such as 'to review the HR needs of office staff', clearly this is compatible with several different sets of objectives. The objectives turn the vague aim into something operational, in effect. You should be ready to amend objectives if circumstances seem to require this but changing your aim is in effect deciding to stop doing one dissertation and start doing another. It is therefore not to be recommended once you have passed the early stage of scoping and setting objectives for yourself – it is rather like deciding to stop doing an exam question in the middle and trying another one: a fair amount of time has been wasted.

There are several ways that you can scope your study. Your background study of literature will naturally provide some useful material, as will regularly reviewing so-called 'grey' literature – such as digests of recent reports, summary publications of recent writing, and short-life discussion papers produced by institutes and professional bodies. Trying various different internet searches using different variants of the key terms will also bring forward many valuable potential avenues of thinking. And, of course, meeting (electronically or physically) with colleagues and discussing each others' dissertation ideas will be an important resource that should be formally included into the planning stages of your work.

All these will help you gain a clearer idea of why and how your issue matters to either the research or the professional community (or both). They will also help you begin to refine your use of the relevant terminology – the process of acquiring and using conceptual language effectively is an important indicator of learning at this level.

For scoping your study, discussion on a fairly low-key, flexible basis will provide you with many benefits. As well as making links with key members of your intended audience it starts the process of collecting information, however anecdotal, that will be important for you to satisfy the objectives you set yourself. But it also helps you get a better feel for the size and shape of the work you are proposing.

As you start talking (or emailing, or contributing to discussion forums, etc.) with people they will – often quite unconsciously – start making links between your subject and other aspects of the management field. This is almost inevitable given the multi-disciplinary nature of Business and Management. For example, if you were collecting evidence directly from one or more organizations, you may realise that one part of the study – which you might have thought could be resolved by reading certain documents and talking to a couple of key players about them – was not implemented as the senior decision-makers think. Therefore, to get a full picture, it will be necessary also to talk to people who have been running the system or process in question. Sometimes (more rarely) the opposite may be true, that an area that you thought needed a lot of primary data collection can be resolved by getting the right documents. Again, the discursive process might throw up the fact that the key stakeholders all have very different opinions about how an issue should be tackled – which indicates that you might need a wider survey than if there was a high degree of consensus.

May we issue one word of warning here. Sometimes electronic discussion lists receive an e-mail from a new participant which asks an unanswerable question. 'I am doing a dissertation on human resource strategies and I am wondering if anyone has any material which might help me.' That is just too broad a request. You are more likely to get responses when you ask something specific: 'has anyone been attempting to reconcile recent UK legislation about casual work with the European directive on the rights of part-time employees?'

You are even more likely to get responses when you have material to offer as well as questions to ask. There are other straightforward activities that will help you to estimate the scale of what you are doing but which also have an important psychological value in getting you moving on the dissertation.

One of these is to identify the key features of three or four typical or representative readers of your piece of work and prepare them as 'thumbnail' sketches (short accounts describing the person) This has the benefit that you will instinctively adjust your tone in the writing to make it accessible in terms of language and assumptions. It helps the scoping process because as you make these summary sketches you will think also of the kinds of questions they may have regarding the issue, the kinds of expectations they might have of such an inquiry, the kinds of challenge they might make to your argument. It also will help clarify how far your piece is research-based or practice-focused.

Another is to start writing the background section to the piece of work as soon as you have settled on a subject. Whatever you propose to do, you will need to give some background to it, in terms of the business context (be this at an industry or firm level), the reasons why this subject has been selected, the policy and operational implications of it, why it has a professional value, and so on. The intention here is that readers will be able to recognise not only why you have chosen the subject but also why you have set the objectives for the study in the way you have.

So far as scoping goes, the advantage of writing your background statement early is that it gives you a chance to focus on the issues. The interaction between your writing and your initial exploration of the issues will bring home to you many crucial factors – some directly related to your topic, some only contextual, indirect aspects – that will affect how you carry out the investigation and what kind of result you could reasonably hope to achieve.

> ### *To summarize*:
>
> In this section, then, we have seen that the actual choice of dissertation subject should be guided both by personal interests and also by what will add value for your intended audience – be this the research community or a group of professional business people. We have seen, too, that the best way of the establishing the scope of your investigation is to start communicating about it with relevant stakeholders at an early stage. Lastly, we have seen that getting your objectives right is very important indeed. The key thing here is to ensure that they are very specific.

● Progressing the investigation

> As this aspect will be considered in more detail in the next chapter we shall only cover it briefly at this stage. However, there are some practical issues which should be considered straight away. Amongst these are:
>
> - managing the timing of the investigation, especially knowing when to stop researching;
> - investigating ethically; and
> - when research can become an intervention in organizational life.

When to curtail further investigation

In the Assignments section we discussed how to decide when you have done enough research and reading. The same points apply here, though with greater force. There is no point at which you will be able to say definitively 'Right, I've clearly proved (or disproved) that such-and-such is the case.' Data is only ever an indication, never absolutely conclusive – this is true in physical science, and it applies equally with the study of human activities and institutions.

One danger is the desire to collect 'that extra little bit of information' that you hope will clinch your argument. Another is how much analysis to do if you have collected a lot of information. In the case of the former, we shall argue in the next chapter that you should set yourself in advance a target level of proof, and stop once you have got to that level. For example, you may decide to undertake a feasibility or pilot study of a certain process. In which case, you will want to collect a range of data that will indicate a good spread of possibilities. It is not necessary to demonstrate beyond reasonable doubt each of these possibilities. On the other hand, if you are going to try to establish a specific conclusion, then a higher level of proof might be needed.

The main points to bear in mind here are:

(i) standards of proof will vary depending on what you are trying to accomplish;

(ii) you will rarely get material that will establish matters beyond any doubt; and

(iii) once you have acquired sufficient material to meet your desired level of demonstration, stop.

In general there **is** an objectively best way to approach a major investigation, which is to plan the work systematically in the light of the time and resources available to you. Of course, many people have their own idiosyncrasies that affect the regularity of work, but even though this advice may be somewhat idealistic it remains the case that *a regular systematic approach is most likely to be effective*.

One factor affecting your timing is the 'slow-start' phenomenon. Many people take time to settle in to a subject, underestimate how much time the investigation may take, or simply lack the necessary sense of urgency to get started early. Whatever the cause of slow starting, it usually results in that person compensating by rushing towards the end of the process, as a submission date draws near, with the consequent errors or omissions due to hasty finishing.

There is one particular research method which often underestimates time, and which you should be careful of, namely the pilot and full questionnaire process. It can take a surprisingly long time to devise and pilot a questionnaire. Then when you have a good questionnaire, it is notoriously hard to get high proportions of returns, and you will need to invest a lot of time in this part of the process. Disaster will strike if you have used up too long on the piloting.

The resolution of timing problems is to begin by immediately drawing up a schedule of work, with realistic interim targets, including some that are already reasonably close. This will create a sense of drive and a recognition that time lost now cannot be found later. It does not especially matter if later you review and revise the schedule. The important thing is that it provides you with an impetus to get started. We would strongly suggest that, whatever the timetable of your course, you should be planning your research component from the day you start. At the beginning it may appear that you have plenty of time and can afford to worry about other things, and you may have to wait before your tutors publish the full details of this component of the course, but it is hard to rush good research, and the longer you allow yourself, the better the result is likely to be.

Slow starting is a flaw in the process, but this should not be confused with *quiet* starting – which is the sensible tactic of reading around the subject and mulling over the choice of topic before committing oneself too far. A failure to start quietly often leads to an individual making a choice too quickly. This in turn often means that a choice has to be revised or even abandoned later on, which is a waste of time. This can be avoided by the simple means of setting yourself a minimum period for mulling over your choice of topic for the dissertation before making any firm commitments.

Leaving oneself too much to do when competing a dissertation is probably the main outcome of poor time management. We have already looked at one kind of failure to finish properly. Another reason why you might fail to move on the concluding phase is the attraction of analysis. Once you have collected material – documents, interviews, questionnaires etc. – then you will want to look through it all and see what you can extract from it. If you have a lot of varied material then there can often be a feeling that buried within this is 'the answer'. Added to this is the fact that working with a lot of detailed information can be absorbing. It can appeal to the right side of the brain, which is more stimulated by feeling and less by hard inference. This can lead to people spending lots of quite enjoyable hours absorbed in their data, leafing through their notes and interviews, savouring the feeling of detective work as they (in their eyes) inch their way towards the hoped-for colossal discovery. It can be very enticing – it's what enthusiasts get out of studying something very intensively. But it will eat up your time.

The main solution is to set yourself two targets:

(a) a target for the appropriate level of proof that you need to progress your investigation, and
(b) a chronological target of when you should move on to the final stage of the working on the dissertation.

Ethics

Conducting business research sometimes raises ethical issues. If your subject is at all valuable for either the professional or research communities, then at the very least it might contribute to a debate affecting people's working lives and careers, and in the case of organization based work may have significant career implications for some people. As a basic human right people should know what is happening if it might affect their interests. But there is the countervailing issue that, when people do know what is going on, they may try to subvert it for their own ends. We have advocated a policy of early and open discussion, as this has a variety of benefits. It does have the potential shortcoming that people can see you coming, as it were, and thus might – consciously or unconsciously – try to subvert your investigation to make sure they come out of it well. Our view is that this happens anyway, and is less likely to be done deliberately if people realize that the study is genuinely independent. The alternatives involve some degree of deception which can backfire badly if during your research project people 'discover' what you are doing.

So our advice is: talk about things openly right from the start, whether this is with disinterested academics or other researchers, industry figures, or employees of a specific organization. People will get used to the idea, and will be more likely too find reassurance over time than if you restrict information and only tell people on a 'need-to-know' basis.

Do note that your research may well be subject to specific rules and regulations relating to ethics. Most universities have ethics committees nowadays that monitor the work of their academics, and often student work is also covered. Some companies that sponsor student dissertations may also have processes to monitor and approve research projects on ethical grounds. So check with your tutors about whether approval from the university ethics committee is required, and where appropriate do the same with any sponsor of your research.

Research as organizational intervention

There are additional difficulties with a research study based in one or more organizations. For any act of collecting material in an organization has some element of intervention into the workings of that organization, and this has consequential effects on people's attitudes towards what you are doing. People will get to find out what you are investigating, and may well start to draw conclusions – justified or not – as to what the outcomes will be. If you have communicated effectively with everyone, this will be no bad thing. But some people may have an incomplete idea of what you are doing, and may therefore build up inappropriate expectations and concerns about your work. Be prepared, therefore, for unexpected reactions. For example, someone looking at career patterns in an organization may find that people misunderstand what is being investigated, so that they think that the project is about career *development*, and from that falsely assume it will lead to their career *progression*. Difficulty will follow.

Communicating freely and openly to everyone about what you are doing is ultimately the right approach to diminishing this aspect of the research process. A useful follow-up exercise would be for you to think through the potential misunderstandings that key stakeholders might have of your proposed dissertation topic, and try to identify ways in which you could communicate your intentions so as to avert them. The sketches that you have made of typical readers of your work can be helpful here, in helping you focus on their potential issues and preconceptions.

To summarize:

The point at which your investigation should end is determined by your objectives – when you have enough information to satisfy these, then that is when to stop. Going beyond this will not only run you out of time but also overload you with data.

With issues of ethics and the organizational impacts of any research study, communicate openly and widely with all affected parties from the very start.

Concluding the investigation

When you have completed this section you will be able to critically evaluate the role of the six key elements of completing a research study:

(i) pulling together the final results of your researches into a set of justified conclusions;

(ii) making recommendations that address each of the main issues;

(iii) doing a 'reality check' on these by reference back to key decision makers to see (a) that you have not made a major misinterpretation of something and (b) that the draft proposals are acceptable;

(iv) defining an implementation plan for your recommendations – this may be detailed or in outline; the minimum requirement is that you demonstrate that you understand the issues involved in putting your proposals into practice;

(v) writing up the whole piece of work in the appropriate format, ensuring that arguments are properly supported, and that there is a clear link between each step, so that the reader sees the strength of your argument without being blinded to its potential shortcomings, (no matter what anyone may say to you, ALL research studies in management have shortcomings as well as strengths; this is structural, and thus a perennial and completely unavoidable occupational hazard of doing management research);

> (vi) producing and delivering the work to the canonical speci-
> fications set out in the course regulations.
>
> We will briefly comment on these below.

Conclusions

We have already said in an earlier chapter that there is an unfortunate tendency for people to think of the final elements of a professionally focused piece of work – be it dissertation, assignment, or management report – not as two distinct related sections but as one undifferentiated section called 'conclusions-and-recommendations' almost as if these are two terms that refer to the same thing. They do not, and it is extremely important that this is clear to you. If weak objectives are the first cause of poor performance in dissertations, the second is poor finishing, manifested particularly in sloppiness over distinguishing what you have found out (conclusions) from what you propose to do about it (recommendations).

When you have decided to end your investigation you will then need to bring together the key elements of what you have found out. 'Bring together' because you will have drawn the conclusions already as you have been analysing your research findings. But in the main body of your text they will appear in several places, not in one systematic presentation. The role of the conclusions section is to be just that – a systematic summary of all the key findings which you feel need noting or addressing in action. Depending on the nature of your investigation there may be different categories of these. Given that a dissertation involves both a professional problem-focused element and a conceptual, theory-testing element there should be some degree of each reflected in your conclusions section.

Although your dissertation is meant to evaluate material as objectively as you can, it is appropriate to present your results in a way that will make it easy for the reader to understand your points. If the argument has been complex, you will help the reader to understand what you are getting at if you make clear where the conclusions have come from – this might be simply by reference to the part of the main text where the particular inference is drawn e.g. 'there is strong evidence that induction processes are inconsistently applied (see ch. 3, sections 3.3–3.5)'. Here we see what has been concluded and also where to find it.

This example highlights that it is not merely a conclusion but an indication of how strong the evidence is. Readers of dissertations will adopt a *critiquing* perspective on your work. They will have noted how convincing is the evidence for the conclusions you draw. If you present a set of conclusions as if they all possessed a uniform level of validity they will be aware of the inconsistencies. It becomes all the stronger to state specifically how strong your evidence is. And how far the material you have collected may support your point(s). As discussed in an earlier chapter, there are several different levels of evidential support that a point may have:

(i) the point is *proved beyond reasonable doubt*,
(ii) the evidence *strongly supports* a point,
(iii) the evidence *confirms* the point,
(iv) evidence *indicates that, on the balance of probabilities*, your conclusion is valid.
(v) the evidence *suggests* your point.
(vi) evidence *is consistent with* your point.

This series goes in a declining order of certainty from one which is, for all practical purposes, almost certain down to something which is not at all certain, but worthy of further investigation. The point is: *state what kind of certainty your research has achieved* – it can never do your argument any harm. In a dissertation you are expected to demonstrate academic capabilities in this piece of work, and one of the most important of these is the ability to evaluate arguments, including your own.

The main things to bear in mind, then, regarding conclusions are:

- they summarize what you have discovered (they never introduce fresh material);
- they must directly be drawn from your preceding discussion and analysis;
- they are NOT to be confused with your proposals of what to do subsequently; and
- they are more convincing when there is an honest reflection of the degree of evidential support they carry.

Recommendations

We stated earlier that some research-based dissertations may not lead to any very specific recommendations. This is not to say that they make no recommendations – rather it is to indicate one of the strongest points of contrast between research- and practice-focused work, as the latter should always lead to some concrete proposals for what an organization and/or a managerial team should do.

The linkage between conclusions and recommendations is often a weak point in dissertations. Recommendations are often written at the end, when the writer has run short of time, perhaps because of too much attention to the collection and analysis of data.

Question

A poor link can happen when people do good research, use theory appropriately, analyse their findings suitably, draw justified conclusions, but then when the reader comes to read the recommendations it is as if they are looking at a different piece of work, for the proposed actions seem to have little clear relationship with the findings, and propose a very specific and only partially relevant plan.

Putting aside the possibility that the author is not very logical, what do you think might have happened here?

Answer

It can be the result of having poor objectives. The author may have not focused clearly enough at the start on what they might deliver to the reader at the end, and they therefore mistakenly think that what they are suggesting is acceptable. If a (weak) objective is 'to examine the marketing of the oil industry' then once someone has written out their conclusions they may well feel that they have fulfilled that objective and therefore they can propose something that would be useful partially for that issue but maybe for other reasons as well. This equivocation will likely lead to recommendations for which only half the justification is clear to the reader.

Alternatively the problem may stem from the researcher having made up their mind in advance. This will usually undermine the basis for a balanced evaluation of the findings, so that although the **reader** can see that the totality of evidence points in one direction, the **researcher** is predisposed to see the results as confirming their chosen option. When they come to formulate proposals for action, then they put down what they had always intended, without seeing that there is only a weak connection with the findings. This can also sometimes manifest itself in someone coming to a set of conclusions, and then proposing a very specific kind of proposal for action, so that the reader thinks 'Well, this proposal addresses the findings to some extent, but why do it in exactly *that* form?'

It should be made clear to the reader *how the recommendations arise from your findings*. With a practice-focused dissertation you might specify your proposals one-to-one against the conclusions. Usually this sort of approach only works when the conclusions are all of the same level of generality and do not overlap too much. More often you will want to give a range of proposals that jointly address the issues raised by the totality of the conclusions. It is important that the reader can see why this package is the appropriate response to what you have found out. This means that *recommendations must be justified*. There needs to be a rationale of the proposals – why this way of responding, rather than any one of a number of alternative approaches.

If your conclusions are particularly open, and could be addressed in a variety of ways, you might need to go through a process of identifying proposals, following what has sometimes been called the 'standard management model' – identify needs, generate a range of optional actions to meet those needs, evaluate each option, select the optimum.

What kinds of suggestions are appropriate as recommendations? Your proposals need to be justified, as we have seen. For a practice-based dissertation, they should also be substantial managerial options, not statements of what *should* happen but of what is *suggested*. For a research-based piece of work the requirement will naturally be less severe – but in this case too the statements should be about actions that could be undertaken.

The ideal way for your dissertation to end should be that every objective is clearly fulfilled. Your recommendations, as much as the conclusions, should make clear to the reader that this has happened. Some tutors on Masters programmes will mark dissertations in the order of objectives – conclusions – recommendations – the rest. In other words, they will try to assure themselves as to the extent to which your objectives have been fulfilled before evaluating the main body of the text.

What if you have not managed to fulfil all of your objectives? This is not ideal, but it can happen for a variety of reasons. It is rarely possible to ensure at the start of the research that you will be able to satisfy your objectives – the most interesting work is likely to discover things that had not been expected or appreciated before. It also can happen that the people whom you needed to survey were unexpectedly not available, or that the documentary data you were searching for is not accessible or ends up being not quite so illuminating as you hoped.

Again, the most important thing here is *to say what you have achieved and what you have not*. This will come into your conclusions, but in this case there may be some value in indicating what further research work would be necessary to fulfil the objectives. It is inappropriate to ignore the incompleteness of your investigation, for that can give the impression that you do not realise that you have not satisfied your objectives, which undermines the credibility of what you have done. *By evaluating what you have done and presenting this openly, you demonstrate again the key research skill of understanding academic arguments, and what they can and cannot achieve.*

Reality checking and implementation

If your dissertation is to have an impact on the relevant professional or research communities then it is important that the conclusions have some 'face validity'. that is, that they express the results in a manner that the key stakeholders can identify with and respond to. You must write in a language that your audience can read and understand. You must develop a 'voice' that your readers can hear – again referring back to your initial sketches of typical readers is valuable here. Equally, if you are going to make proposals, it is important that these are taken seriously. You may wish to challenge a strategy that has been adopted with strong support from senior figures. Making recommendations about this without preparing them is hopeless – in the normal course of things it simply will not be accepted, however strong your argument.

So it is important that as you are progressing with your investigation to check out your results and proposals with the key stakeholders. Doing this during the investigation is itself a legitimate research method – as we shall see in the next chapter. By the time you get to finishing the study it is important to ensure that there is some degree of acceptance. In this respect writing a dissertation is a balance between presenting what you have discovered and gaining acceptance for your argument.

As well as checking out how far your argument will find an audience, it is important at the very least to demonstrate how your proposals can be implemented. In some practice-based pieces of work this might need a full implementation plan, which might involve:

- the actions you are proposing;
- the benefit or outcome expected from these;
- who would be responsible for ensuring the actions are performed;
- what resources will be needed – human as well as equipment and consumables;
- how much the proposals will cost;
- the measure of whether the expected benefit has been obtained; and
- a contingency plan if the expected benefit is not achieved.

This much detail will not always be needed, even with practice-based dissertations, but it is useful to keep these aspects in mind when you formulate your recommendations. Many dissertations founder for the sake of a practical focus right at the end.

For consideration

Evaluate the following (from a dissertation on marketing an engineering company):

Conclusions

- The company has failed to market itself effectively to its target market.
- Compared with competitors, the marketing spend is deficient by nearly 35%.
- There is a need for a marketing director at Board level.
- Research has failed to establish clearly whether the new product offer should be progressed or not.

Recommendations

- Company to review and re-launch its marketing function.
- Increase spending in targeted areas, at least to the average of competitors.
- Appoint a marketing director at Board level.
- Further research is required to evaluate the new product offer.

Response

One advantage about this set is that there is a one-to-one matching between the conclusions and the proposals. But not much else about them is effective.

The statement about failing to market themselves effectively is so vague it could mean almost anything.

The financial conclusion is clear, though it would be even clearer if it simply said that the company spent 35% less than its competitors – the fact that it does not almost suggests that what is being stated here is not quite what has been demonstrated in the main text.

The 'conclusion' about a marketing director is a shamelessly disguised recommendation.

The conclusion that 'research has failed...' is misleading – it suggests that there was an objective about recommending whether or not to continue with the new product offer, but this is a proposal, not a finding. The research might have been about sales trends, customers' views on the new products, financial projections of returns, etc. These are areas that should be addressed in the findings, not whether the product offer should be progressed or not.

The recommendation to review the marketing department looks as if it is meant to address the general failure issue.

But it seems to presume what the outcome will be – a re-launch (how does the author know that the review will not lead to a decision to hand marketing over to an outside marketing consultancy, for example?) A great deal of argument is needed here to establish this proposal as the best way forward.

'Increase spending' is somewhat vague – it would be better to specify which areas to select.

Appointing the director is so bland that it underlines the inappropriateness of the statement made in the conclusions.

In the light of this discussion, you may wish to re-shape the conclusions and recommendations as a personal exercise, to test for yourself how they might be improved.

Writing up and presenting the dissertation

It is essential that in writing up the dissertation you follow the requirements as set out by your institution. These will most likely be issued to you or be available in course documentation or on an intranet page.

Typically there will be a specified word limit, such as no more than 20,000 words. Usually this limit will exclude annexes, appendices and references (as always, check documentation to make sure). Often there will be a specification of layout, including whether items such as an executive summary, abstract, lists of tables and figures, appendices, etc. are required, and sometimes what form and order they should take in the work.

One standard chapter layout is as follows:

- Introductory chapter, which will include all preliminaries such as background, aims and objectives, etc.
- Main body of your argument and investigation (often an early chapter will include your literature review and methodology).
- Final chapter – summary conclusions, recommendations, etc.
- Annexes, appendices, references and bibliography.

In some institutions there may also be a specification of binding. Electronic submission in addition, using specified file formats (to enable automatic plagiarism testing) is now becoming standard. For all these aspects make quite sure you have consulted your course regulations and documentation.

● Getting the work finished

> When you have completed this section you will be able to identify key actions that will add value to your dissertation in its final stages

You will probably be writing up your dissertation as you go along – in fact it would be extremely rash to leave everything in note form and then try to put into the appropriate form right at the end. But the final period when you get the whole piece written up is a crucial phase. Many dissertations have been improved beyond recognition by the process of final writing up and revisions of late drafts. There are various aspects that should be considered in this final phase of writing, including the following:

1   *Looking at the work as a whole.* The work as a whole moves from a statement of intent via a plan of what to do through evidence collection, findings and analysis to its completion (conclusions, recommendations, and implementation). With a large piece of work such as this, it is important to make sure that what you say in, for example, Chapter 2 squares with what is said in Chapter 8. People often write the chapters step by step – which helps with the progress of the work – but it does mean that the mindset within which you wrote Chapter 2 could have shifted significantly, in the light of what you have discovered, by the time you reach Chapter 8. Wholesale revision of the piece is usually essential before submitting a draft to your supervisor.

Look at what you proposed to do and see how far you actually achieved this. It is important to view your writing as a whole so that when the reader gets to the final sections they can see that what they have read is what they expected to read. If your objectives state that you will produce a review of quality control theories, for example, then you have to give one. Periodic review of what you are doing is thus important to make sure that at the end you do have the information you need to satisfy your objectives.

2   *Style.* This should be generally objective, but where you are putting forward a view that is uniquely yours then it is appropriate to make this clear, even in the first person (as long as there are not too many 'I's); evidence should be evaluated as honestly as you can; whilst you have a view and it is appropriate to register that view even at an early stage, it is important that the reader is given the argument

in a way that allows them to disagree; emotive terms should not appear, whilst value-laden ones should be carefully managed.

3   *Appendix.* What goes into an appendix is material that supports your argument but is not essential for it to flow: large bodies of data, for example. If a table is more than half a page, or if there are several tables of similar data, they go in an appendix. Appendices should never be used to subvert word count limits. *Main discussion material should therefore be in the main body of the text – if the text is too long then it needs editing.* Also appendices should contain material that is essential to the argument, not just things it would be 'nice' to include. If your argument works without the appendix then it is not necessary. Inclusion of items such as a company's annual report is usually unnecessary – whatever is really important can be taken out and extracted.

4   *Take the reader's perspective.* The reader is likely to approach your dissertation in his/her own way – there is no guarantee that they will start on page 1 and work through until they reach the end. But the argument must be structured in that way. You must have sign-posts at critical intervals – short summaries of where the argument has reached or statements of what the reader has just covered and what can be expected next. You have been working on this piece of work for months, and you know every page almost word for word, but the reader is coming to it afresh, so you must presume a degree of unfamiliarity with your argument. You should try to gently lead the reader through the line of your argument – and it is crucial that there is a line of argument to be taken through.

5   *Timing and scheduling.* In terms of timing your work, you should work backwards from the final submission date to the key stages. *A critical path analysis or similar charting mechanism is useful for this.* Bear in mind the following:

- When planning surveys and interviews, people may have difficulty meeting tight deadlines for seeing you – set aside a substantial lead-in time for these. Booked phone interviews can sometimes substitute if necessary.
- Writing up, especially of the later elements of the work, will take you longer than you expect, particularly if you check out your findings and proposals before finalizing them
- When you show your final draft to your supervisor, they may well have significant points that you should incorporate – in our experience students have improved poor dissertations to

excellent ones by responding cleverly to the final pieces of advice of their supervisors. This is one of the places where supervisors' advice could add most value to your work. So leave yourself a lot more than a week to make changes, and allow them sufficient reading time by recognising they have other calls on their time.

One of the most common experiences for a supervisor is when a student hands over their finished dissertation with the words: 'Now I have done all this work I realize how much better I could have made it if I had another week, or month!' In the light of this discussion about the dissertation, what do you think that sentence really means?

6   *Final production, printing and binding of the work takes time*. Make sure that you have fulfilled the specific requirements – if you are over the word count this will automatically lead to some level of penalty, for example. Check carefully the format of required elements such as title pages as well.

Make sure, too, that *the typographical style is uniform through*out – if the chapter headings in most of the chapters are in 16-point font, they will need to be in all the others as well. Don't forget that even with 'what you see is what you get' screen displays, there are sometimes glitches that mean that a paragraph that fitted neatly at the end of one page has an 'orphan' line that strays on to a page all on its own.

Make sure that you have adequate time to take account of unforeseen contingencies. Aim to *have the whole thing completed some days, if not more than a week, before the final submission date*. If you are desperately finishing it off on the last night, for example, then that is the time when a print cartridge will run out or a printer overheat and fail.

● What gets good marks in dissertations?

> When you have completed this section you will be able to state the main generic criteria used to grade dissertations.

The more you can estimate the marker's requirements the easier is it for you to evaluate how far you have met them so far (and hence what more you need to do).

As with other assessments, you should refer to the intended learning outcomes, as they are the basis for the criteria used to assess the piece. Below is a typical example of an assessment scheme for a dissertation – many institutions will use similar ideas, albeit phrased in different ways:

- *Defining the problem.* Was it clear? Did you consider its practicability and potential limits? Was the issue important, was it well delineated? Have all assumptions been drawn out? Did the problem have a sufficient background? Were the objectives clear?
- *Literature review.* Was the review focused and pertinent to the research subject? Did the proposed research build upon previous work in this area? Was there sufficient breadth and linkage with related disciplines?
- *Research methodology.* Was the research appropriate to the solution? Was the design of the research justified in terms of the research questions and practical conditions? Are potential weaknesses of the methodology recognised and taken account of?
- *Data collection and analysis.* Could another researcher replicate the study using the same procedures (if not, is there is a clear explanation of why this might be so)? Were population, sample and sampling method identified (if appropriate)? Was account taken of the range of relevant variable factors that might affect the research results? Are the results accurately recorded, analysed and presented? Have steps been taken to minimise bias in data collection and analysis? Remember the acronym DINA – description is not analysis. Ensure you have enough time to fully work through the material – do not simply present it as if it speaks for itself.
- *Discussion and conclusions.* Do the results support the conclusions? Are comparisons made with other relevant studies? Are the implications for practice clearly established? Were any shortcomings of the research honestly acknowledged? Have the conclusions and recommendations fulfilled the intentions expressed in the original objectives?
- *General report writing.* Are the title, organization and mechanics of the report good? Is the work properly referenced? (See next chapter's section on literature review for details on this.)
- *Summary.* Do the final components (summary, conclusions, recommendations) refer solely to the material collected and analysed in the main text?

Not all of these questions will apply to every dissertation, but they are the best benchmark you have as to what you should do, so you should pay careful attention to them. You will find a similar set of criteria in your course documentation – use them as your own checklist not only when you are writing up the work but as you are progressing through the investigation.

Levels, marks and standards

Let us assume you have produced a dissertation which meets all the criteria: that is essential – you cannot earn marks for missing elements. The tutors then have to make an assessment of how well you have met each of these criteria. You will need to search through the handbook to find the marking scheme – check if each criterion can earn the same proportion of marks, or if there are weightings which point to important and less significant criteria.

Then you will have to establish, within each criterion, what are the characteristics of work that has only just passed, work that is moderately good and work that is excellent. You might find a marking grid in your handbook, which defines levels and standards against criteria. The tutors will need such as grid to be able to make standardised assessments of your work.

Such grids, however, are very difficult to work with. Their purpose is to help tutors make very fine distinctions. Many use the 100-mark scale with a pass mark of 40, and they expect very few students to achieve over 80, so many tutors in practice only have 39 points on a scale to place your work. This is difficult, and marking is as much an art as a science.

You can help yourself greatly by understanding this process. The best way to do so is to bring a few colleagues together, debate and discuss what sort of evidence you would expect for the criteria, run marking exercises on each others' work, tackle the words on any marking grid or criteria list with the same academic challenge as you would any other subject, and gradually build up your mastery of this crucial subject.

The ideal you are aiming for is to end the course able to mark your own work, for yourself, and to know what you have done well and where you need to improve. That is true personal autonomy – you will then be independent and professional as a learner, as well as an expert in Business and Management.

Working with your supervisor

When you have completed this section, you will be able to identify points of good practice when working with your supervisor

You will be assigned a supervisor from the tutorial staff, whose role will be to support and advise you whilst you progress your investigation. Generally they will have a degree of specialist knowledge about the subject area that is the primary focus of your work.

A supervisor can be an extremely valuable resource, so long as you use them to best effect. As with all aspects of the course, it is best to (a) have a clear purpose when you contact your supervisor, and (b) come to an explicit agreement with them about how the two of you will work.

The key is to remember that the dissertation is the prime means that you have to demonstrate your attainment of Masters-level learning – with all that this implies in terms of autonomy in learning, taking responsibility for one's own choices as a professional, and making sense of material in the face of intrinsic uncertainties. Hence the relationship between you and your supervisor should approach that between peers, based on advice and dialogue, and NOT on directive judgement. If you seek for lists of sources, or if you expect detailed commentary on every paragraph you have written, then you may be trying to create an inappropriate relationship you're your supervisor. Your supervisor is a *resource*, not a surrogate dissertation assistant. Hence it is far better to contact them with a question about your work – 'I am proposing doing *x* or *y*, what do you think' than to ask 'what should I do now?' Also, make sure that you maintain steady contact – do not surprise them by sending unexpected and large chunks of material on their email.

Probably the most useful way to ensure that you have an appropriate relationship is to formally agree the way in which the two of you will interact. You should also include your observations of the relationship in the diary you keep on the dissertation. The relationship you have with your supervisor is individual, and therefore not comparable in any direct way with any of your colleagues' experiences – one of the more persistent and less justified complaints of many Masters students is that there is inequality of service provided by different supervisors. This mistakes equality for uniformity. Of course each supervisor-student relationship will differ from every other one: this is simply a result of it being a relationship between two human beings. But what matters is whether what happens in that relationship is what is expected and agreed, not whether it is the same as what other people are getting.

It is likely that supervisors in your Department will have previously debated what should be expected of them. They will have a copy of the module guide – good guides often have these protocols fully laid out. Supervisors will know the expectations of the module leader, and of their colleagues. They may have been allocated time for supervision. There may be policies and procedures to follow when first and second markers disagree, and how best to use the external examiner.

Your agreement with your supervisor should include expectations about the frequency and purpose of meetings, as well as about the nature of the support you expect or which will be offered to you. As at this stage of the course you will be expected to be mainly working on your own, such an agreement will be neither a wish-list on your part nor a set of imposed requirements on the supervisor's part, but rather it should be a negotiated agreement, demonstrating your ability to work with other researchers and profit from their advice and *critique*. And critique is the best service a supervisor can provide – they have extensive experience of the field, are likely to have conducted their own research projects, and probably will have seen many other dissertations, from which they have learnt a great deal as part of their supervisory activities. So they will be extremely well placed to critically evaluate your research activity.

To summarize:

In this chapter, we have looked at practical issues of completing a dissertation. The key points to remember are:

- Be clear as to whether your dissertation is addressing the research community or a professional audience.
- Select a subject that has the appropriate scope, and has some interest for you as well as value for your organization.
- Use course documentation and other sources to establish precisely what is required and how it will be assessed.
- Consult at an early stage and frequently as you progress the work.
- Set a clear aim and then SMART-like objectives.
- Distinguish carefully between different parts of the argument – especially conclusions and recommendations.
- Signpost the final work clearly.
- Learn to use your supervisor well.

7 Researching for your Dissertation

● Introduction

In the previous chapter we considered the logistic and practical matters that need to be resolved when conducting your research. In this chapter we shall look at the issues relating to the dissertation as a piece of management research.

Researching in an applied social science area such as Management is a complex matter, the difficulties of which should not be underestimated. For one thing, there is far less certainty than may be achieved in the natural sciences. For another, there is no consensus on the best way to conduct a research investigation in this field, with several general approaches being adopted which are fundamentally different in their assumptions. And thirdly the subject matter, comprising human beings, is continually interacting with one's study in one way or another, therefore presenting a major challenge to claims of reliability and validity of any study's conclusions.

There is, therefore, a wide spectrum of approaches, methods, and general evaluations of the nature and value of management research. So this chapter can only scratch the surface of what is one of the most problematic areas of business and management writing. It is not intended as a quick view of a difficult subject, more an indication of where the difficulties may lie. You are referred to the several texts identified in the bibliography that deal with research methods and methodology in detail, which you should use to help youthink through and progress your chosen methodology.

When you have finished the chapter, you should be able to:

- ● formulate a methodology that will be effective for carrying out the research necessary for your dissertation;
- ● use concepts and literature appropriately in your dissertation;
- ● identify what level of proof is needed in your investigation;
- ● evaluate different research designs;

- evaluate different research philosophies; and
- formulate criteria which will help you judge the value and use of an appropriate range of methods, designs and approaches for your own dissertation.

Each of these is covered in the following sections.

● Methods and methodology

> When you have worked through this section, you will be able to:
>
> • explain the difference between research methods and methodology; and
> • critically evaluate key elements of an effective methodology.

Your dissertation is an investigation and this needs to be carried out in a planned fashion. All research investigations involve some kind of planning phase, followed by some collection of material which is then analysed, evaluated, or interpreted – whether the researcher is clear about what they are doing or not. The more explicit you are in your thinking about what you are doing and what you might achieve, the more successful your dissertation will be.

The idea of research *methods* needs to be distinguished from research *methodology*. Methodology is a justification of your chosen approach, an argument that moves from a statement of what research question you wish to answer, through an overall design, down to a statement of the criteria used to adopt specific research methods. It makes critical use of theories of social research to help inform your solution to the practical questions of conducting social research, which include issues such as the scope of the data collection exercise, the kind of analysis adopted for data once it has been collected etc. Many dissertations make the mistake of jumping too readily to a specific choice of research methods, without constructing an argument that justifies their choice – often in doing this they may expand their understanding of what options are available to them. This chapter will focus on methodology rather than methods. It will help you to identify the key questions relevant to the construction of a sound and well articulated and justified methodology. In this area, where there are few unequivocally right answers as to how a question may be investigated, a key element to aim for is the depth of articulation of your methodology.

As we have said, management research has intrinsic shortcomings. Good research takes account of this, and makes clear to the consumer of the work (the readership) both advantages and disadvantages of the approach chosen in completing the research. Methodology is the conceptualizing of your research plan, justifying the plan in terms of this critical evaluation of choices, and relating the plan back to your question and to overall approaches to social research.

Methodology therefore comprises the following stages:

- conceptualizing the issues to help generate appropriate questions;
- clarification of research questions in the form of a statement of objectives;
- identification of what is needed to satisfy the objectives;
- a good argument justifying the choice of research design; and
- a statement of methods for data collection and analysis.

All this should be carried out critically, with an explanation of how weaknesses will be taken into account.

Conceptualizing your dissertation

> When you have worked through this section, you will be able to explain how concepts drawn from your reading will contribute to your dissertation

In Chapter 6 we looked at the early phases of research, including formulating clear research objectives. Following this, the next step is to conceptualize your objectives – developing them in terms of the concepts and models you have encountered in the literature, in order to develop the content of your research questions. This is achieved by your literature review – a chapter that critically discusses the main theoretical and professional ideas relevant to your dissertation subject. The review itself will normally appear in a dissertation just after the first chapter, which identifies objectives. However, the process of reading and critically reviewing what you read may well extend well into your data collection and analysis phases.

As we said in earlier chapters, reading should always be focused on a question. This is even more true at this stage, where you could go off in many different directions, given the very many potential linkages between your topic and other areas of management.

The key issues that you will be trying to resolve at this stage are about what you are trying to achieve (i.e. what is expressed in your objectives) and how your investigation will do this. So you will be considering issues such as:

- What do I need to know and understand in order to establish if I have the right objectives?
- What do I need to understand in order to satisfy my objectives?
- What information do I need to meet these objectives?
- What questions will enable me to meet my objectives?
- How far can these questions be investigated as they stand, or should they be divided into sub-questions?

There is an element of risk here that cannot be completely eliminated – you may do all the right things methodologically speaking, but still find that you asked the wrong question, because there was some unseen but crucial factor. The framing process – which is really a framing and subsequent *re-framing* process – helps to reduce that possibility, by highlighting the range of possibilities in terms of research outcomes, data collection options, conceptual distinctions and cross implications of your work. Keeping your literature review open for as long as is practicable helps with this aspect of risk, in that it increases opportunities for you to amend your plans in the light of discovering some new issue.

The process of conceptualizing your questions begins, as with all reading, with the search for material that deals explicitly with the subject matter. For example, if you are looking at the ways in which senior managers take decisions in a certain industry or sector then you trawl through indexes, databases, journal directories and other related sources of bibliographical information to identify material that includes some reference to 'managerial decision-making' or the like in that industry. Online searching is an art, where the choice of the wrong phrase can bring an unmanageably large set of references or none at all, though the most advanced engines do have sophisticated 'advanced' search options that will generally achieve better results than a straight search. This problem is less acute when physically searching through references (for example, in a library), but is still evident. Not all knowledge is, or probably ever will be, electronically accessible, and therefore you cannot rely on these sources exclusively. Before conducting searches electronically or physically, it is useful to begin building your own personal thesaurus of phrases or terms that for you seem to mean the same thing, so that if one does not work, you can try another – it will make sense to have this close to your dissertation diary (e.g. back of the same notebook). This thesaurus will naturally grow as your work progresses.

To be able to search effectively on-line requires you to effectively target specific words. The alternative activity is to browse. Before computing, 'browsing' was thought of as a casual, almost random activity. But nowadays it implies a process though which, by reading and thinking about texts and images, you make interesting connections and unexpected linkages which then you cluster into groups, and explore how others have engaged in the same processes by following references. This intellectual activity is now supported by web browsers which have the facility to open many panes within a master window, using tabs to move between them, which can be saved and continued in a future session. Explore both searching and browsing, and the various mixtures of the two, to see which is appropriate for you at the different stages of your knowledge of the various course topics.

As with reading for other assignments, the process of *chaining forward* applies, where you start with one question, and then find that your reading clarifies this and in doing so suggests fresh questions, which may go in the direction of greater depth or greater breadth of application. Sometimes both are involved. At each stage you will need to explore these fresh leads. Be aware that reading material which is interesting is seductive, and can draw you in, distracting from your key focus. The danger here is that unless you are very careful you will build up a 'to read' list that would take you several years!

It is at a stage like this that the value of your objectives comes out – for you can refer back to these and say *Given that I have somehow to satisfy my objectives, and in so doing produce a 20,000 word dissertation within the next 3 months, how much reading can I sensibly get through?*

In other words, by focusing on what has to be delivered one can estimate the scale of what you need to do to achieve those deliverables. Though this appears defensive it is an approach that does succeed in focusing people's minds on what is required. Incidentally, this mindset can also be helpful in managing not just your reading but other aspects of the process, writing for example – 20,000 words equals five or so chapters of about 4,000 words each. A chapter of 4,000 words would cover about eight pages (using a standard single spaced 12 point font such as Arial or Times New Roman). Whilst this might be an oversimplification, it helps to put your work into perspective.

Linked to the issue of how much reading to do is an additional consideration that can be useful in helping you draw lines around your work – *how much proof do I need?* By focusing not only on what questions you need to ask but also on how good your evidence needs to be, it can become clearer how much literature needs to be reviewed.

In the context of your dissertation, a review of the relevant literature does several things. Much the most important is helping to formulate the core concepts which will guide any field data collection and its analysis.

Additionally, a discussion of the literature places your investigation into an intellectual context, which will include issues such as:

- What questions are of concern to the research community?
- How far is this investigation within an existing trail of work, or is it asking fresh questions or taking the argument in a new direction?
- Are there precedents in the professional community for investigations of this kind?

In many ways, then, the literature review, as well as setting up the formulation of research questions, is also a precursor to the main body of the investigation.

So one important end result of your literature review will be a critically-established set of core concepts that will direct and inform your field research. This will be a small subset of what you actually discuss in the literature review chapter, which in turn will be a subset of what you actually accessed and looked at. (There will be a lot of redundant searching for material that looks as if it will be useful until you actually see it, when it becomes quite clear that it is not worth reading – this is inevitable.) The core concepts are those which will help you formulate more clearly your research questions and hypotheses. They will also help you in the analysis of the results you get from your field research.

Generally you will focus on a single model, theoretical statement or concept that will be the main driver of your research. This may be textual or diagrammatic in form (many of the key management theories in fields as diverse as strategy, HR, logistics, or leadership are expressed in logical diagrams that combine text and graphical structures). It is no exaggeration to say that the choice of model you use will have a determining effect on how successful your research is, so it pays you to read widely and critically. Whatever the form of your core concept, it will strongly influence the language you use to express your key research questions, as well as providing the structure of your analysis of whatever data you collect.

Then how do I know which models to use? This is an art rather than a science, so there is no formulaic response to this question. You will need to use several criteria to decide whether a concept will help you frame the key questions, and whether it will be effective as a basis for analysis, such as:

- Is this a well-established model, view or concept?
- Does the model or concept appear to have strong links with other issues so that if my investigation uncovers a wide range of factors this model can take account of them?

- Does the style of thinking reflected in the model seem to fit the culture of my organization?
- Is the model well evidenced in itself, or is it speculative?

These may not be the only criteria you might use. Hopefully they indicate the kind of issues that you will need to resolve whilst reading theoretical material in order to decide which concepts will drive your research activities.

The fact that some of your reading may be used as a central element in your research does not mean that the rest is not relevant. On the contrary, it is important that your literature review reflects the critique and comparisons between different approaches, so that the reader gets a full idea of where your thinking has come from. So, much of your reading will be critiqued and evaluated but not used any further than this.

In terms of the practicalities of your literature search, do not read without a means of recording your notes on the texts – notebooks, paper for files, audio tape, files and folders on your laptop or whatever is appropriate. Being properly prepared will save a lot of time later searching for references.

Also make sure to maintain records of the source of your material. Use a computer file (spreadsheet or database applications can work well for this purpose) to hold the details for each text you access. Use a referencing system such as the so-called *Harvard* or *Vancouver* approaches. The Curtin University Library and Information Service website (http://library.curtin. edu.au/referencing/) explains Harvard and Vancouver referencing systems, as well as other related conventions, notably those of the Modern Language Association, sometimes called MLA referencing, and the American Psychological Association, sometimes called APA referencing, not dissimilar to Harvard.

Institutions have different expectations for referencing – some will not mind what system you use so long as it is used consistently and correctly. Others will specify one that you *must* use. Do check your course handbooks on this. Whatever is the course protocol, some system of referencing is necessary and it should be applied throughout the whole of your work.

● Proof

> When you have worked through this section, you should be able to evaluate the importance of clearly acknowledging the degree of proof that is required in your research

The next stage of the methodology is to state the key research questions, from which you will be able to establish what information you will need to collect. Sometimes your research questions will be in the form of questions, such as: *'What are the average levels of variance between budgeted costs for major construction projects and their actual costs?'* Sometimes they may come in the form of hypotheses, such as a hypothesis that: *'actual costs of major projects exceed budgeted costs by an average of 10%'.* The advantage of the latter is that, being more specific, it is easier to test out. The disadvantage is that the discussion may lead to a purely categorical result, such as *'the evidence suggests that costs of major projects average just below 10%'* when what might be more useful would be some kind of breakdown of costs in different areas, for example. This is not a problem if you keep a vigilant eye not only on your research questions but also on the main aim and objectives. Thus, in reality, the biggest difference between research questions and research hypotheses is often one of focus – the one being on the statement, the other on the answer to the question.

A key item which very many dissertations miss is the issue about how much proof you need. This is important not only to help you monitor your progress as you are going along (and decide when to draw the line) but also to help you present the results of your work clearly. This is a much more difficult issue with management research than it is with, say, a study into the behaviour of the fruit fly. For management research is always at least partially evaluated by what people can do with it. So, even with a research based investigation, you have to decide how much is needed in order to support people's actions, and how much would still be left to them.

The levels of proof that are appropriate for research can be presented as a scale:

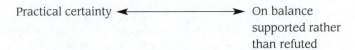

Practical certainty ⟵——————⟶ On balance
supported rather
than refuted

'Practical certainty' really means beyond all reasonable doubt. Complete certainty – beyond any possible doubt – is far too demanding a requirement: even the best natural science cannot meet this level of proof. For the other extreme, that on balance the question has been supported rather than refuted, one might say that the research had hardly produced anything that could support the question (note that anything less than this does not count as 'proof' at all: a study that led to an outcome that the question was on balance neither supported nor refuted would be inconclusive and therefore would not have demonstrated anything).

So the issue is: Where do you need to be on this scale? The further to the certainty end you want to be, the harder it is or the more restricted your questions will need to be in order to have much of a chance of realizing this level of proof.

For consideration

Here are four potential dissertation subjects that someone on a Management Masters course might choose to pursue. What level of proof do you think is necessary for each of them? Make a mental note of your views as we will return to these a little later.

A The feasibility of introducing an integrated information system for managing human resources at Tesco.
B Has the phenomenon of outsourced call centres improved customer satisfaction in the Dutch insurance industry?
C Knowledge management and the development of people in organizations – coordinated or opposed?
D What generic strategies are adopted by News International, and are these appropriate for the early 21st century?

From the formulations of the basic aims we can make the following observations about proof:

A 'Feasibility' implies that a management decision about introduction will be made on the basis of this report. Resources and time will be committed, and therefore a relatively high level of proof relating to this specific case is likely to be needed. There may still be uncertainties in the analysis, but these would only be at a relatively low level, concerning operational details, rather than at the macro level of whether to go for a particular system or not.
B The industry-focused question on call centres (still essentially a practice-based subject) has lower proof requirements, mainly because it will cover a number of different organizations, which will all vary significantly in their structure and behaviour.
C The research-based question on knowledge management has lower requirements still – what would probably be sufficient here would be to show that on a reasonable interpretation of the evidence the two processes (knowledge management and people development) are *probably* in such-and-such ways opposed and in such-and-such ways coordinated.
D The generic strategy question will require stronger levels of proof, but not to the same degree as the information systems question. Strategic choices can be applied in many different ways, and the potential for a basic mistake is less acute than with the choice of a computer system.

In the examples above we can see that the degree of proof varies depending on the kind of question being answered. In general one can make the following rough judgements concerning the required levels of proof required in a piece of research:

- Where the conclusion affirms that a general condition covers all examples of a certain category or type of organization, a high degree of proof confirming the conclusion is required, that covers all examples of that category.
- Where the conclusion refutes the idea that a general condition applies to a certain category, a high degree of proof is required but only as it applies to those cases that constitute the refutation (in the extreme this might even be just one good example).
- Where the conclusion indicates an undefined but positive degree of connection between two phenomena, then a median to low level of proof is required.
- Where the conclusion raises a question as to the potential influence of one factor upon another, a low level of proof is required.

This discussion indicates how and why different research aims will require different levels of demonstration. Broadly what we have seen in the above discussion is that *the more closely defined the research question is, the more likely it is to require strong evidential support.* This means that overall the degree of difficulty of research questions at this level can often balance out – the more openly defined ones are harder to research but a lower level of proof may be needed, whilst the more closely defined ones are more straightforward when it comes to collecting data, but they need more evidential support.

How much proof you need is a major factor in the determination of how much research you need to do, and therefore of when you will draw the line and say 'I've got enough information now', which is crucial for your time management of the dissertation process. It is also a critical – and often mishandled – issue when it comes to expressing the conclusions of your study. Many dissertations involve clear objectives, well thought through information gathering and discussion, but do badly at the final stage because they do not take account of the degree of support that their evidence provides for their answer to the research question. If the material you have collected only provides a limited degree of support, then it is safer to say so than to try to pretend that the question has been strongly confirmed. If in fact the question has NOT been strongly confirmed then all that has happened is that you have demonstrated to the examiner that you do not know the difference between strong and weak evidence.

● **Research designs**

> When you have worked through this section, you will be able to:
>
> • describe and evaluate some of the main research designs available to you; and
> • use criteria to evaluate the suitability of a particular research design for your dissertation.

Research design becomes important once you have identified what questions you need to ask and thus what information you need to collect. At this stage you will begin to consider which methods of collecting data are most suitable and how you will use them

It is important to recognize that there are two related but quite distinct issues:

●   the overall design of the research, and
●   the specific methods you will use to collect the information.

Research design refers to the overall strategy of your information collection. There are several types of research design, the following being amongst the more widely used:

1   *Survey designs, of which there are two basic forms:*

   ●   *Census* – you collect data from every member of the organization or unit being studied.
   ●   *Sample* – you define a method of identifying just a subset of the whole population under study and collect information just from them. Usually this is randomly identified, and is treated as representative of the whole. A great deal of statistics is devoted to the use of samples and representative results.

2   *Case studies.* This is where events affecting one or a small number of organizations are studied as a whole. Information is collected over a period of time relating to a variety of different elements, and then is analysed and presented as an interpretative narrative.

3   *Experimental research.* Experiment in the pure sense is very unusual in the study of human beings, as it presents many practical and

ethical difficulties. Far more frequent is action research, described in 9 below.

4   *Documentary analysis.* In a few cases it is not necessary to observe or gain testimony from members of the organization, but simply to read over a range of documents and form an overall view of them, usually writing this up as a narrative. It is essentially a historical method, and lends itself to explanation of events that happened in the past. It is sometimes encountered in connection with inquiries into management failures.

5   *Grounded theory.* Really a more elaborate approach to documentary analysis, this is a process of comparing documents, notes of interviews, memos, notes of observations, and allowing theory to emerge from the comparison. In the initial stages the 'theory' is tentative, but as more and more material is compared then the earlier theoretical statements are tested and refined.

6   *Secondary data analysis.* On some occasions it is not necessary to collect any fresh data but simply to analyse existing data. On this approach the originality and novelty often lies in the choice of data analysis instrument. Market analysis often employs elaborate statistical methods to *mine* information from large existing datasets.

7   *Longitudinal studies.* This is where a group of individuals are studied over an extended period of time. It is more likely to be carried out by a government body or a well-established university research centre, simply because it takes years, and in some cases decades. In its full embodiment, then, it is unlikely to be a suitable approach for your dissertation. However, an action research design (see 9 below) may involve a degree of observation of change over time.

8   *Participant research.* Based on the democratic view that all research into human behaviour should treat the participants as active members of the enterprise, this approach tries to break down the imbalances between researcher and researched by involving the 'subjects' of the research and getting them to help define the project, set objectives, conduct their own research, and contribute to the analysis of the findings, leading to full ownership of the end results. It is a lengthy and sometime politically fraught process – which is often an indication of how important the results of such work are to the main stakeholders of the process.

9   *Action research.* This last approach is closely related to participant research, and some writers seem to treat the concepts as almost interchangeable. Action research is an attempt to mirror the 'trying out' aspect of experimental physical science in the more complex

and dynamic human environment. It usually involves a description of the state of the organisation prior to some intervention being made, then a narrative of the intervention (usually some management action, maybe a consultation exercise, for example) and then an explanation of what happened as a result of this. It has some natural affinities with case-study research – indeed sometimes the two are combined. Key to its success is the process of evaluation and reflection which leads to further action. Because its focus is on processes of change, it frequently engages with those who are affected by the changes and acknowledges they have a part to play as the co-researchers.

Criteria for choosing a research design

The choice of which of these to use will be based on a variety of considerations:

- what you are hoping to establish in broad conceptual terms – e.g. develop a new approach to an aspect of management, critique the application of a technique to a particular organization;
- how much time you have available to conduct the research;
- what other resources you have available to support your research;
- the organizational dynamics and politics at the time of the research;
- your overall personal philosophy about what social research can achieve.

We shall deal with the last of these in the next section. What is important to acknowledge here is that there is a *balance* between these factors – it is not likely that they will all point unequivocally in the same direction. This is part of why social research is never as secure as physical research can sometimes be. For the research projects themselves work in a dynamic context, often compromising the various criteria of good research in order to be able partially to satisfy a range of requirements.

For consideration

Look back at the examples of dissertation subjects and levels of proof discussed in the previous section. Could you make judgements about which kinds of research design are most suitable for these?

Response for each question

A   *'The feasibility of introducing an integrated information system for managing human resources at Tesco.'*

This offers several possibilities. It could be investigated by means of a non-random survey, identifying key potential users of such a system and collecting their views of what information would be needed, and how to input and retrieve this. Some additional material might be drawn from other organizations, and there would be also some reliance on documentary sources to establish what the potential strengths and weaknesses of different systems might be. However, a more radical approach might be to take a participant research design, identify a key group of research collaborators (mainly employees at different levels) and allow them to reformulate the project in the light of their perception of what is needed.

B   *'Has the phenomenon of outsourced call centres improved customer satisfaction in the Dutch insurance industry?'*

This would fit very neatly into a random survey design – collecting views of a representative sample of customers. However, a case-study approach could also work well, so long as the cases selected provide a good spread across the industry.

C   *'Knowledge management and the development of people in organizations – coordinated or opposed?'*

This would probably benefit from a more hybrid design, incorporating some case studies, but also collecting opinions, via a non-random survey. A study that looked at developments over time – i.e. some form of longitudinal approach – could also be adopted. Being more research focused, this piece of work is likely to involve a larger degree of conceptual and literature-based material.

D   *'What generic strategies are adopted by News International, and are these appropriate for the early 21st century?'*

Conceivably this could be investigated using several distinct designs. For example, one could put together a group of the most influential stakeholders of the company and develop a participant approach. Alternatively, an external study might rely primarily on documents and secondary data, or a survey of the key decision-makers.

What we can see here, is that whilst some designs are often more directly suitable for some topics, these are not fixed categories. Additionally, hybrid designs incorporating elements of more than one of the types may be appropriate. The choice is not taken solely on the basis of content. Practical issues, such as how long it will take, how many people should be interviewed, whether there would be organizational implications, or security based restrictions on access, and so on, will influence your decisions.

Research approaches

> When you have completed this section you should be able to:
>
> • describe in broad terms a selection of philosophies of
>   management research; and
> • define certain key concepts of research, such as primary and
>   secondary research, and participant observation.

Your personal stance towards social research is an important feature of how
you will approach the investigation. Essentially, there is a range of different
attitudes or research philosophies that people may have. Guba and Lincoln
(1994) have identified three key questions that reflect the kind of choice a
researcher makes:

- **An epistemological question**: what kind of material does the
  researcher really acknowledge as 'knowledge'? For some this is
  hard factual material, for others it is beliefs and feelings.
  (Epistemology is the theory of knowledge, knowing about
  knowing.)
- **An ontological question**: what is business reality? Is it the
  culture and experience of organisational life? Is it performance?
  (Ontology is the study of the nature of existence.)
- **A methodological question**: what are the valid ways to collect
  information on organizations and business? (Methodology is the
  study of methods.)

The approaches that each individual takes to their research is in part defined
by their response to these three interlinked questions. It is very instructive to
reflect briefly on these three questions and think through one's own view on
each of them. The more explicit you are about your position the easier is it to
take account of this, deal with potential personal bias, and clarify what your
approach really establishes.

However, it would be misleading to see these stances as optional positions with you switching between them at will – it may be important to
explicitly stay with one stance, otherwise the research will end up being
inconsistent in tone, and potentially also in operations.

One way of categorizing research philosophies may be as follows:

Naturalism (sometimes called 'positivism' or 'realism' in the literature, which is misleading as these are particular versions of this overall approach) is the idea that social research is no different in essence from physical science, and therefore aims at the same things – i.e. proof or confirmation of what is 'out there'.

*Interpretivism (*sometimes called 'phenomenology' in the literature, again misleading, for much the same reason) is the view that social research differs fundamentally from physical research, in that the critical feature is the interpretation placed upon what is studied by the researcher.

Deconstructivism (associated at times with the idea of post-modernism) is the view that what is distinctive about social research is not the material that is collected but the relation between the questions that are asked and the social context in which people ask them.

Action based (identified most closely with the research designs of action research and participatory research) is the idea that all social research is essentially an intervention, a kind of interference in social experience, and therefore this should be made a key virtue rather than being seen as an occupational hazard.

For consideration

It may be useful for you to think through which of these four management research philosophies appeals to you most – the scientific aspect, the interpretation, the fact that it is societally based, or the fact that it represents a form of intervention.

Once you have decided upon an overall research design, which may have involved you thinking about how you personally feel about the key research philosophies, you will start to consider which specific methods of data collection you will want to use. It is worth noting the following issues (each of these is discussed in detail in the literature on business research methods, to which you will be directed as part of your course, and some examples of which are listed at the end of this chapter):

- *Primary and secondary research.* Primary research is material that you collect yourself, usually directly in the field; secondary is when you use the material collected and published by others. There are advantages and disadvantages about each, but most Business

Masters dissertations, whether research or professionally based, involve both to varying extents.

- *Observation*. It is often useful to collect information about an organization by watching what happens. This is nowadays often done with the explicit involvement of those who are observed. Neither the archetypal example of the old 'time and motion' efficiency experts who stood in factories jotting down notes on a clipboard nor the tactic of covert observation are effective, and some argue that the latter is not ethical either. Full participant observation often takes a long period of time whilst the researcher slowly becomes sufficiently accepted by the group within which they are researching to be trusted to observe their deeper interactions.

- *Testimony*. By far the most popular forms of data collection are those involving the testimony of others – getting people to say what they feel, what they do, what they know or believe about this or that phenomenon. This is generally based on interviews or questionnaires, though there are some quite complex elaborations of these approaches.

- *Surveys and samples*. Testimony is usually collected by means of a survey. Apart from the relatively unusual times when a survey of all members of a group may be conducted (a census survey) in general the researcher has to decide how to take an appropriate sample from the group being surveyed. Often a random sample is required, though it is worth noting that in some cases (e.g. establishing the weaknesses in a safety reporting system) a targeted sample may be more appropriate. Where randomness is sought, it is important to note that groups are rarely homogenous in nature – certain populations may be clustered in urban areas, others may have similar structured surnames (e.g. the prevalence in Scotland of people with surnames beginning 'Mac' or 'Mc'). So often a significant degree of ingenuity is required to actually get the membership of a group set out in such a way that a random selection may be taken. Also the size of the sample is problematic, though there are statistical methods for calculating optimal sizes: in practice the factors that matter most are (a) how much certainly you are looking or and (b) how variable the range of answers you expect. With both of these questions, the higher your answer the larger your sample is going to need to be. You are strongly advised to seek guidance from your tutor or supervisor before embarking on a sample survey.

- An additional aspect of social research is the idea of *triangulation*. This is the idea that if you collect information in one way, you may not detect potential flaws or biases in it. But if you collect the same information in two different ways and compare the results, then any bias should become apparent and can be eliminated. In practice what this implies is that you will need to consider all the data that you collect, whatever its origin, that relates to your research question, and you will make choices about how to reconcile data from different sources. Again ingenuity is needed here – aggregation of data collected and recorded in different ways is not always automatically valid, as the differences in collection method may undermine the assumption that the data really reflect the same phenomena at all.

For consideration

Below is an outline research design for a (fictitious) dissertation. Evaluate the suitability of the design, along with any potential strengths or weaknesses.

Aim: to evaluate the managerial process for ensuring the quality of maintenance services provided by XYZ Ltd to coastal boats based in a specific port.

Overall design:
(a) survey of boat/rig owners to establish satisfaction levels;
(b) interviews with maintenance managers to establish operational constraints;
(c) observation of maintenance processes, including interactions between maintenance workers and boat/rig owners, and maintenance operations;
(d) documentary analysis to establish general recorded trends of maintenance problems and their resolution;
(e) comparisons of XYZ's processes with those of other organizations and industries as to quality management of engineering maintenance.

Specific research methods:
(a) short questionnaire to a 30% sample of boat owners distributed quay-side and collected manually at a later date;
(b) structured interviews with the five main managers of XYZ Ltd, on an individual basis;
(c) non-participant observation of physical maintenance operations; tape/video recording (with participants' consent) of meetings between boat/rig owners and maintenance staff;
(d)   collection of documents from local offices;
(e) interviews with maintenance managers from three other organizations – one large shipping line, one transport department of a local authority, and one general electrical engineering company. →

Response

The first thing that might strike you is that for such an apparently low level subject a lot of field work might be needed to answer the research question. There is a counterbalancing advantage for this difficulty, in that the theory of quality management is relatively simple. There are basically two main variants – the ISO procedural approach and the more organizationally focused philosophy of Total Quality Management. For an area such as this, the organizational context is likely to be less complex than in a more integrated environment such as telecommunications.

What has been omitted from this research design (though we might be able to infer it) is the level of proof required. Given that there is quite an elaborate degree of field data to be collected it is reasonable to presume that specific policy decisions may be made on the basis of this research. Therefore the managers will want a high degree of probability that the conclusions arrived at from this study are indeed sound. Hence there will need to be a significant amount of data to support the conclusions.

As we have said several times, no social research design is perfect. Here there are potential problems with each stage:

- Boat owners are not known for being especially reflective types, and hence might need some convincing to take a questionnaire seriously at all. Also the collecting of questionnaires is not spelt out. This could be significantly more problematic than the researcher suspects – people will lose them, will have questions about them, will have forgotten them and do it perfunctorily in front of the researcher when he or she asks for them back.
- If you ask maintenance managers about their operational constraints, then they are likely to exaggerate these, as it can reflect well on them if they are seen to be battling against adverse circumstances.
- Overt non-participant observation is likely to produce the 'Hawthorne effect' where people act a-typically because being watched is unusual for them. Covert non-participant observation is high risk. Taping meetings can work so long as people forget the machine is on – it usually works if people are asked about it in advance and then their attention is not drawn to it too much when they come in.

With a subject such as quality management, documentary evidence is often crucial. The range of documents that would be relevant to this project will include safety records, accident reports, fault analyses, summaries of performance, statistical analyses of processes, non-routine reports on performance or shortfalls, etc. One advantage here is that the data itself does not contain researcher bias within it (such as can be alleged for interviews, for example). However, →

documents are always produced for a specific purpose and for a specific audience, and encountering them without knowledge of these can lead to misleading conclusions (e.g. a letter written by and for legal professionals will use terms in a different way from one written by and for engineers). To deal with this, you will find it useful to keep a written note of what you know about purpose and audience for each document you consider. The difficulty with documents is knowing exactly what they indicate. Typical questions are:

Are these complete? If so the material is extremely useful, if not then it is difficult to estimate what value they are, unless you know how incomplete they are.

Were they produced contemporaneously? If later than any events they relate to, then they are only as good as the memory of whoever produced them.

Perhaps the least problematic for this example are the comparative interviews. But one would need to question how far these are representative. The answer might be that they are the best that the researcher could organize via their contacts. This is not necessarily a weakness – what is important is that their degree of relevance is clearly flagged up in the chapter on findings.

● Collecting and analysing information

We are not going to go into the detail of the form and use of methods for collecting and analysing information for business research here. For one thing, the range of methods of both collection and analysis is vast, and we could do no more than hint at the depth and richness of this range. For another, the issues relating to even the most popular, and tried and tested methods, such as using a structured questionnaire in a sample survey, contains many more complexities than we could realistically cover in a text of this size and scope.

What we can do finally, however, is indicate some of the questions and issues that you need to resolve when selecting methods to collect or analyse research evidence.

● *Bias*: Each component in the collection of evidence needs to be carefully considered to avoid bias. For example, researchers conducting interviews present themselves in a certain way to those whom they are interviewing, and it is all too easy for presuppositions to creep into the minds of the latter based on the appearance, language and demeanour of the interviewer. Similarly, the visual appearance of pencil and paper research activities can significantly influence the attitudes of respondents to the activities they are asked to carry out (e.g. a highly glossy workbook may be impressive for some but intimidating to others)

- *Meaningless results*: Often a question or observation that appears straightforward when considered in the design phase of the research may turn out to have hidden complexities that undermine its value as a piece of evidence. For example, a question that contains terminology that is unfamiliar to the respondent or has a politically charged meaning within their organisational context, will lead to an answer that the researcher will not process correctly. Similarly, a series of questions or activities that someone is asked to carry out online may be fatally undermined by the time that they have available to complete these, so that they do it all in a rush without paying much attention to their responses.

- *Volumes of data*: Some methods can produce masses of information that can be difficult to process. One MA student we know of sent out an online questionnaire expecting to receive about 50 replies, and got 350! Clearly she could have processed just 50 of them, but that this could have introduced a further element of bias into the process (in the end she processed all 350, at the cost of a couple of sleepless nights). Another student decided to type up verbatim all of his unstructured (recorded) interviews, which led to him producing over 100 pages of close typed dialogue, again creating an unnecessary burden. Yet another sent out a simple online questionnaire, expecting about 30 responses, and only got 2! The moral here is simply to project the possible scope of activity your chosen data collection and analysis methods might commit you to, and then be ready to remedy the situation as circumstances unfold.

To summarize this chapter:

- Research into business and management issues can never be perfect – often the most important task of the researcher is to decide which weaknesses to control and which to accept, and then to decide how the latter may be taken account of.
- Methodology is the justification of a choice of research design and set of methods for collecting and analysing infor-

mation. A critical methodology sets out the benefits as well as the potential drawbacks of the chosen approach to research.

- An often ignored issue is the level of proof that is required to satisfy a researcher's questions or objectives: once you are clear on how much proof you need, make sure that this is reflected in the overall argument of your dissertation.
- Different researchers hold different research philosophies, and these are often not compatible.

Appendix Example of a piece of assessed coursework

In this appendix you will find an example of an assignment written by a typical MBA student, reproduced with their permission and our grateful thanks. It was completed in 2006, and received a high mark. Our choice of a good piece of work is to indicate the standard that is expected in most universities, and also to give you a standard to which you can and should aspire. It is not an unattainable target.

We have included the assessment requirements and criteria, and given a brief commentary on how these would have been used. We have not reproduced in full the comments of the marker, though when you look through the text and the criteria you should be able to see where the strengths and weaknesses of the piece lie.

Firstly note the brief for the assignment. The question is reasonably open-ended, in that it offers a choice of organization, and the student could exercise their own judgement as to which aspects of the field should be examined. Bear in mind that often this aspect of your own judgement may well be part of what is assessed (i.e. did you focus on the right issues for this organization?). This is especially important with dissertations, where the choice of issue and above all of what question to ask is a major component of the assessment.

In setting out the requirements, the tutor has indicated weightings of marks for each element. Obviously this is a really important indicator of what is required. Take care, however, to make sure that these are up to date – it is not uncommon for one tutor to have set an assignment, worked out assessment criteria and weightings, and then not teach the course, and a different tutor, with slightly differing interpretations, takes over. As we advised in our main text – if in any doubt, check out with the person who will actually mark your work.

The criteria used for this assessment are fairly generic – though remember that behind phrases such as 'correct use of relevant theoretical models' and 'quality and comprehensiveness of the literature' is the implied content of the subject matter.

One element that you might usefully explore is the link between these criteria and the learning outcomes that they are intended to measure, which is not as explicit here as we have suggested in the main text.

Assignment brief:
Corporate Social Responsibility report

You are required to write a report analysing corporate social responsibility in a business organization of your choice.

Word limit: 3,500–4,000 words.

Content:

The report should:

Identify and discuss the key corporate social responsibility issues faced by the organisation. (25 marks)
Identify and analyse the factors and initiatives outside the organization that will influence the development of these issues. (25 marks)
Critically examine the policies and activities that the organization has assumed to address the issues. (25 marks)
Develop a set of conclusions and recommendations arising from the above analysis. (25 marks)

Choice of organization:

Corporate social responsibility issues faced by organizations vary across industries. You may want to choose an organization from a particular industry that you are interested in, e.g. oil and gas, labour intensive industries, or pharmaceuticals.

Assessment criteria:

In addition to the general University marking criteria the following criteria will be applied to assess the report:

• Clear and intellectually sound structure and argumentation.
• The correct use of relevant theoretical models.
• The quality and comprehensiveness of the literature used.

You will find our comments on the assignment at the end. Read the assignment first and make you own decisions about it, then consider our opinions, then perhaps discuss your ideas with a colleague on the course.

● **Assignment**

---

1. Introduction

This report concerns with an analysis of corporate social responsibility (CSR) in British Airways (BA) from a practitioner's point of view. Its objectives are to assess the actions in BA to address the key CSR issues and develop recommendations in the light of this assessment. These objectives will be achieved, following a step-by-step process:

- Identifying key issues of aviation industry and then the particular matters related to BA, analysing recent developments and/or BA CSR Annual Report.
- Analysing external factors such as regulations, opinion trends and others that will influence the development of the identified key issues.
- Examining critically the policies and actions taken by BA to address these issues.
- Developing a set of conclusions in recommendations in the light of all of the above.

The approach to CSR follows the concept of Corporate Citizenship (CC), which is a two-way relationship between society and Corporations. (McIntosh et al, 1998). Other concepts/models related to CSR will also be used.

2. Key CSR issues in BA

2.1 CSR policies in BA

BA appears to recognise the importance of CSR. It bases its CSR policy on the concept on "Building a sustainable business" (BA-CSR, 2005). It appears to follow a triple bottom-line approach (Elkington, 1998), which suggest sustainability is a goal of business (Figure 1):

Table 1 shows evidence of this concept in BA:

Table 1: Triple-bottom line in BA

Dimension	Evidenced by
Economic	Goal: Increasing profit margin to 10%
Social	Working closely with employees and suppliers Working closely with local communities and government
Environmental	Action on environmental impacts on local communities around and on the global climate

Since 1990, BA publishes an annual report that identified BA's CSR initiatives. The report aims to explore initiatives in the report that have most impact on society. In order to have a broader picture other recent developments with CSR connotation not mentioned in the report will also be discussed.

2.2 Identification of issues

Waddock (2006) stated that CC has to be understood as a system characterized by ecological interdependence and mutuality among entities operating in different spheres of influence of a company. She presented a useful framework that help understand these spheres. It aids identification of issues and its location in the context of BA (Figure 1-next page):

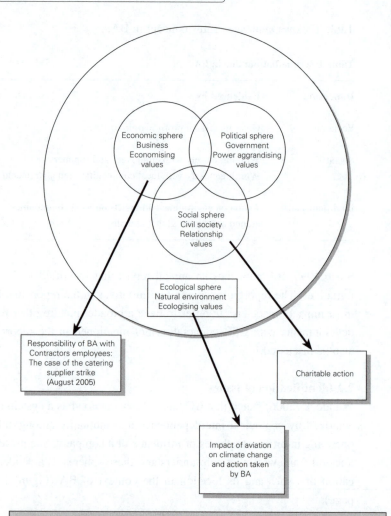

Figure 1: Spheres of influence of BA. Adapted from Waddock (2006)

The report will focus on three issues, although the framework can also be used for many other important issues, such as political-social sphere (lobbying for Terminal 5 construction-impact on local communities) and business-social sphere (impact of BA activities in Heathrow on local communities, e.g. noise-reduction), amongst many others. The first issue (Issue 1) chosen is the impact of aviation because as shown in the figure, the existence of other spheres depends on the environment. Issue 2 is a topical issue, the discussion over BA's responsibilities on contractors' employees. That led to industrial action that affected BA's flights in August 2005. Issue 3 is discussed because of the prominence of BA as a charitable giver; in the 2005 top-10 list in the UK (The Guardian, 2006). A description of these issues is detailed below.

2.3. Issue 1

Climate change is the most pressing environment issue facing humanity and aviation is a rapidly growing industry and the fastest growing source of climate change emissions (FOTE, 2005). Whilst there are two ways to address CSR issues, issues management and stakeholder management; it appears that the environment is too big an issue to be treated from a stakeholder perspective. It appears more appropriate to approach it from an issues management perspective (Carroll, 1979). For Carroll, environment is one of those issues, that can categorized as ethical and for which the company has a social responsiveness philosophy. In this case, BA has a corporate policy for environmental issues. This policy and the concrete actions that BA has taken will be examined in section 4, in the light of regulations and other external factors (section 3).

2.4. Issue 2.

Strike action by BA staff in support of 675 workers, summarily dismissed by Gate Gourmet (GG), BA's catering provider brought its flights to a standstill on 11/08/2005, with an overall cost of £40 million (Miller, 2005).

The question now is: Is BA responsible for the actions of its contractors and were BA staff right to go on strike for actions not handled directly by BA? The concept of stakeholders is relevant at this point. Freeman (1984) defined stakeholders as any group who can affect, or is affected by the achievement of the organisation's objectives. Therefore, after the strike, it is clear that GG employees are stakeholders. Mitchell et al (1997) developed a model that identifies importance of stakeholders dependent upon its salience. This depends upon the stakeholders' power, legitimacy and urgency.

These elements in the context of issue 2 are in Table 2:

Table 2: Stakeholder salience model for Gate Gourmet-BA case
Adapted from Mitchel, R.K.; Agle, B.R. and Wood, D.J. (1997)

Element	Evidenced by
Power	The ability to cause disruption: BA reputation affected-flights without food and loss of business
Legitimacy	Appropriate within socially constructed system of norms: Massive dismissals, without notice, perceived as unethical
Time-sensitive	GG took action in peak-activity season for BA. BA's revenue comes from Summer flights where fares and occupancy are higher.

Cooper (2004) stated that if the elements are evident in a stakeholder relationship, then management have a "clear and immediate mandate to attend and give priority to that stakeholder claims. The topic of how the issue developed and whether BA gave importance to the stakeholder and subsequent actions will be examined in next sections.

2.5 Issue 3.

The BA way (strategy) mentions being a respected company as one of BA's goals, evidenced by "Community stakeholders who respect British Airways". BA aims to support the communities in the destinations they serve both in the UK and overseas.

This is not just a philanthropic act. BA seems to have moved from just charity giving to also including collaboration with the Civil Society in the form of "partnership-based solutions to social and environmental problems" (Crane and Matten, 2004).

Table 3 shows the type of programmes and their significance in financial terms:

Table 3: Community relations, charitable giving and BA
Source: BA Annual Report on CSR 2005

Activities	Programme	Description	% as a total
Cash donations	Change for good	Customers giving loose change on board (UNICEF partnership), together with corporate donation of £0.5 m.	45%
	Employee donations	Race for life: raising money for Cancer Research Tsunami Relief	21%
In Kind	Community Learning Centre	Educational programmes for local children, young people and adult learners (Heathrow) Donation in cargo for Tsunami	15%
Corporate giving	Tourism for Tomorrow Awards	Recognition for world's leading examples in responsible tourism development	15%
	BA Environmental Awards	Programme for local school boroughs	
	Community volunt. awards	Donation to Charities supported by employees	
Management costs			4%
Employee time			1%

BA's total contribution for the year ending 31/03/05 was £6 million, up from £4 in 2004. Some of these programmes are part of wider-reaching initiatives. These will be discussed in section 2. More detail and attention to these activities will be given in section 4.

3. Factors outside BA that influence the development of issues

3.1 Climate change

Emissions from aviation directly contribute to the greenhouse effect. It stands at 2% of total carbon dioxide emissions from human activities, with the share projected to grow to 3% by 2050 (IATA, 2050) The most relevant initiative to limit or reduce greenhouse gas emissions is the Kyoto Protocol, a political commitment of developed countries (not endorsed by USA). This agreement and other developments will be examined below.

3.1.1 <u>Kyoto Protocol</u>.

The protocol in its article 2.2 reads: "The Parties included in Annex I shall pursue limitation or reduction of emissions of greenhouse gases not controlled by the Montreal Protocol from aviation and marine bunker fuels, working through the International Civil Aviation Organization and the International Maritime Organization, respectively". Although this constitutes an omission on the impact of aviation, other proposals directed towards addressing this issue, and they will be examined briefly below.

3.1.2 <u>UK presidency of the EU</u>.

The UK has suggested the inclusion of aviation into the European Union Emissions Trading Scheme in 2008. This scheme aims at reducing overall greenhouse-gas emissions and combat climate change.

3.1.3 <u>UK government</u>

The UK has taken a number of measures   From April 1 a major cross-Government programme will offset all aviation emissions from official air travel, providing support for a range of overseas projects, developed through the Kyoto Protocol's Clean Development Mechanism. This will offset some 0.5Mt of carbon dioxide over the next three years.

3.1.4 <u>Effectiveness of measures</u>.

The steps taken so far are not significant to reduce harmful emission. However, these are steps in the right direction; and affected parties, such as Europe's airports believe that "the total climate change impact should be addressed within an open emissions trading scheme wherein airlines in the EU will be able to trade permits to cover $CO2$ impacts" (ACI, 2005). On the other hand, the awareness of the public on these issues, constantly referred to in the media might constitute a factor that airlines should consider in their strategies.

3.2 GG case
Several external factors are antecedents to this case, of which key aspects will be examined below.

3.2.1 History
GG was in-house catering arm until it was sold off in 1997. Many of its employees are then ex-BA employees and have links with BA employees. This labour force is based around the Heathrow area, largely from one ethnic community, with several members of the same family (Coleman, 2005).

3.2.2 Competition
Due to the resurgence of low-cost carriers, and competition on all markets, maintaining downward pressure on yield (BA, 2005); BA has embarked upon a restructuring programme that includes substantial cost reduction in all areas. It included a £50 million-plus reduction in catering costs, with year-on year productivity improvements of 3%; and the contract makes "no allowance for even the most modest inflation-linked increase in wages".

3.2.3 Outsourcing
BA used to do its own catering, but outsourced it to cut costs (Coleman, 2005). It follows a strategy of focusing on core competences and outsourcing "non-core activities" to lower cost producers (Johnson et al, 2005). They warn; however, that many managers "take on board the principles of outsourcing but do not pay attention to the organisational implications of outsourcing". This is relevant in BA, since GG was in financial difficulties and they should have been aware of them, especially when BA had all its catering operations supplied by one contrac-

tor: GG (Coleman, 2005). Waddock (2006) exposed that outsourcing creates risks because boundaries between the firm and suppliers blur when the links are tight, as in this case.

On the other hand, Schnews (2005) presented an ethical dilemma on how outsourcing cut costs: "By passing responsibility for cutting wages, sacking workers, casualising jobs and upping the workload onto subcontractors. Contractors 'compete' to see who can impose the worst conditions on their workers, who are told to work harder for less or the company who buys their product will go elsewhere, and everyone will be out of a job. So the catering costs problems were passed on to GG. Their actions are examined below

3.2.3. GG management actions

GG is owned by Texas Pacific, a venture capitalist firm. These investors try to make profit quickly and then sell when the price is high. GG was losing £25m a year (BBC News, 25/08/2005). GG adduced that it had to reduce its workforce levels. However, they way they did it raised concerns. They dismissed the workers and replaced them with lower-cost agency-labour, "not exactly a recipe for industrial harmony" (Coleman, 2005). Schnews (2005) denounced that the plan to save £6.5m consisted in provoking a wildcat strike and workers without union backing could be sacked and replaced with agency staff, with the known consequences. They argue that there are double-standards when speaking about the urgency to reduce costs and commented that GG management awarded themselves significant pay increases.

3.3. Relationship with the civil society

Civil Society is called the third sector, distinctive from the market and the state (Crane and Matten, 2004). The concept of civil society, comprised of all citizens and their organizations has returned to popular use in the last decade (Reece, 2001). Heap (2000) notes that relations have moved beyond the strictly philanthropic causes to a point where business and civil sectors work in partnership to address various issues. This is normally done with Non-governmental-organizations (NGOs). BA appears to engage of own initiatives and others in partnership with NGOs.

3.3.1 Partnership with UNICEF

UNICEF is the world's leading organization working specifically for children. UNICEF is unique within the UN family in that it does not receive any funding from the United Nations (Unicef-UK, 2006). The organization has a global reach that allows them to share knowledge across borders. UNICEF staff work in developing countries. It means they deliver assistance where it is needed most (Unicef-UK, 2006).

3.3.2. Tourism for tomorrow.

This constitutes an award to examples of responsible tourism development (BA, 2005). This is embedded in the concept of sustainable tourism. Mowforth and Hunt (2000) defined tourism sustainability as the intersection among social/cultural, environmental and economic factors within globalization.

3.3.3 Heathrow activity's impact on local communities

Whoever lives Heathrow airport is affected by night-early morning flights that affect their sleep, congestion, all-year round noise-pollution, and so forth. On top of that local neighbours opposed to the construction of Terminal 5, which BA lobbied to the government. As the most prominent airline using Heathrow feels have to give back to the local community. This will be examined in next section.

4. Policies and activities that BA has taken to address issues

4.1 Climate change actions

4.1.1. General considerations

Even though, so far The Kyoto protocol has not made compulsory regulatory measures for aviation, BA appears to have taken a proactive stance, in response to the "growing interest of business in the environmental aspects of air travel" (BA, 2005). They consider several aspects such as local air-quality management, Waste and Resource use, Noise reduction, night movements and climate change. BA supports a long-term strategy to limit aviation's contribution to climate change based on robust science, sound economics and well-developed policy instruments (BA, 2005). Particular actions to tackle the issue are examined below.

4.1.2. Aircraft-fuel efficiency

BA contemplates a dual objective for minimising fuel consumption: reducing business costs and tackling climate change. The key factors to increase efficiency are fleet renewal, air traffic management and load factors. Combined work on these areas has achieved a reduction from 3.9 to 3.8 litres per passenger-kilometres over 2004-2005 (BA, 2005). This is significantly better than the agreement reached by airlines at a summit in 2004, where they committed to overall fuel efficiency of 4.0 litres per passenger-kilometre.

4.1.3. Emissions trading

BA has voluntarily participated in the UK Emissions trading scheme since 2002 covering emissions from domestic air services and properties. The results have been promising with a 23% reduction in carbon dioxide emissions. The trial scheme has been a learning experience and prepares BA for mandatory schemes that might be imposed by EU or at global level.

4.1.4 Does BA have a serious commitment towards climate change?

On 20/04/2006 Evening Standard cover page read that BA engaged in a price war, with prices as low as £29. Therefore, the modest gains by those measures are offset by the real problem: the increase in air travel. Marshall (2005) warned that climate change could cause irreparable damage that mount to apocalyptic dimensions and yet, BA engages in promotional activities that encourage flights where there is easy rail-access. In a survey to 1000 adults, 82% found that air-travel was a significant source of climate-causing pollution, 33% find that air-travel is too cheap and 52% that there should be a tax on fuel for air travel (CSN, 2005). It leads to considering that pressure group may constitute a major factor in the future. As stated in 2.3, the importance of the environment surpasses any stakeholder consideration. From an issue management perspective, a strategy of low-price, non-differentiated to no-frills airlines shows a double-standard posture towards climate in BA.

4.2. GG case.

4.2.1 Initial reactions

Rod Eddington, BA's CEO, in an interview expressed: "This is not our dispute". Barrow (2005) -of consultancy-firm People in Business disagreed: "If you appoint a supplier that uses business methods that are going to upset people, then, of course, it is your concern. As stated in 2.4 a stakeholder analysis highlighted the salience of GG employees as a prominent stakeholder, whose immediate attention was required. Eddington appeared to have ignored the expectations of key stakeholders: GG and BA's staff. It appeared to have caused the expectational gap shown in table 4:

Table 4: Expectational gap case Gate Gourmet-BA
Adapted from Gollner (1983)

Gap type	Description	What is	What should be
Conformance gap	What is V. What should be	GG is a contractor. BA has no legal responsibility over GG employees	GG workers were GG workers were ex-BA's workers and expect same standards.

Coleman (2005) stressed that this case raises deeper concerns about the "yawning gap" between the social responsibility and treatment of employees and practiced by major organizations like BA and the behaviour of their suppliers.

Waddock (2006) argued that when companies take a reactive stance, like in this case, denying responsibilities for establishing positive policies towards stakeholders and failing to anticipate problems from stakeholders, as a result, managers find themselves wondering how things evolved in such a negative fashion (BA's went on strike in solidarity).

4.2.2. When conflict escalated.

BA failed to anticipate the power that GG employees. Figure 2 shows the change of status of GG employees as BA's stakeholders:

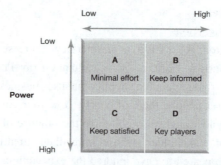

Figure 2: Interest-PPPower stakeholder matrix GG-BA case. Adapted from Johnson & Scholes 1999

From Eddington's first reaction, he felt little effort was needed because GG employees were powerless and perceived that it was entirely a GG management problem, with no interest on BA actions. After BA's employees went on strike, and passengers were stranded, it was for threat of this situation, with GG staff being key players in BA's business. Savage et al (1991) explained the strategies followed when stakeholders pose a threat to companies (Figure 3):

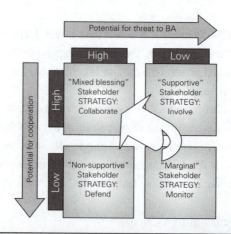

Figure 3: Strategies followed by BA during GG strike depending on perception about stakeholder. Adapted from Savage *et al.* (1991)

BA started with the position that GG strike was not their problem. They just monitored it but as soon as BA staff expressed active solidarity; they started to engage in conversations with GG, understanding GG's financial difficulties. BA agreed to increase from £130m to £140m a-year and extended contract period by two years.

4.2.3 Are BA's actions reasonable?
There is no evidence that BA accepted responsibility for their contractor's employment conditions. They just addressed a business issue: GG could not be a feasible business under the previously agreed conditions. The only intervention they made that all improvements to GG contract were subject to solving their staff issues. However, there was no enforcement of BA procedures when dealing with employee relations, applied to their contractors. Thus, BA's position does not appear to criticised GG methods and the reasons for conflict are still latent, whether GG or any other is its catering contractor. The principle of outsourcing as a strategy, amongst other "amoral theories" (Ghoshal, 2005) is the underlying justification for BA's position towards this conflict; and from an ethical point of view, it can be seriously criticised.

4.3 Giving back to the community
4.3.1 Change for good
BA has used the magnificent opportunity of accessing their customers and persuading them to give unwanted loose change on-board for a good cause. This programme has won awards because of its longevity, scale and active participation of cabin-crew. The scale of the programme is impressive: £2.7 million and 45% of total charity-investment. The choice of partner and the causes they have supported (Tsunami relief, crisis in Darfur, etc) are excellent.

4.3.2 Tourism for Tomorrow
Even tough the money involved in the programme compared to other may be small; it has great symbolic significance: the involvement in sustainable tourism. This is a topical theme in the tourism-receiving developing countries. There is much more than sponsoring a category of an award. The impact of tourism upon these communities deserves a

more dedicated treatment, especially because it is directly related to BA's activities. Porter (2002) emphasised that corporations "can use their charitable efforts to improve their competitive context". A more profound involvement of BA with the cause of sustainable tourism can enhance BA's competitive advantage and their image as a responsible tourism promoter.

4.3.3 Local community programmes.

BA claims to consult with and share their community strategy with their partners in boroughs surrounding Heathrow. They also work on developing partnership programmes in order to enable assess the impact of their "investments" with the community. The programmes (see 2.5) appear to be focused and show continuity, a sign of success. The perception of community giving as an "investment" is also a positive sign of engaging in positive action with the local community, besides working on problems such as noise reduction, local air-quality and so forth.

5. Conclusions and recommendations

5.1. Has BA acted responsibly at all times?

Previous sections have shown a mixture of good actions, contradictions, and even a "laissez-faire" approach to ethics. For example, their actions on climate change are offset by their encouragement on increasing air travel, particularly short-haul. On the other hand, their handling of the GG conflict shows a negative aspect. Their lack of involvement and understanding with contractors' employees can be perceived as "let-it-be" approach, and when the conflict escalated their undecided actions were unhelpful. On the other hand, they have displayed the behaviour of a good neighbour and responsible corporation by engaging actively in local community programmes and in a high profile programme in partnership with UNICEF. However, it is considered that their involvement with sustainable tourism is timid and more should be done in that respect.

5.2. What should BA do?

The case of GG showed unpreparedness in the event of unexpected conflicts. BA's marketing strategy engaging in price-war with short-haul, low-price airlines needs revision as well as their involvement with sustainable tourism. All of these issues suggest a plan of action, to be examined below.

5.2.1. Codes of conduct.

In respect of suppliers, BA just mentioned the ethical issue of paying them on-time to in their CSR report. A way to prevent conflict will be to compile a Code a Conduct, regarding employees' relationships, extended to their suppliers. It should include a clause of consultation with labour force before engaging in massive redundancies and to assure that workers are treated fairly.

5.2.2 Appointment of issues manager.

In order to prevent conflicts, mitigate their impacts, the appointment of a manager in a position to monitor stakeholders' relations is a practical measure. It is suggested that this person work independently from the Public Relations function, since his function precedes their work; otherwise its function would be seen as "window-dressing". Waddock (2006) defined the functions of an issues-manager:

- Identify emerging issues relevant to corporate concerns
- Identify expectational gaps between stakeholders and company.
- Analyse the potential or actual impact of issues to the company.
- Determine what kind of responses the company should make.
- Implement measures or ensure that others implement it.

She also explained that for issue analysis, it was necessary to assess the history of the issue, forecast how it might develop; perform a scenario analysis of different possibilities and the actual analysis of the issue on the company.

All the above would have been relevant to handle conflicts such as the GG case, but also will help with a variety of issues, involving different stakeholders or the environment.

5.2.3. <u>Crisis management units</u>

If an issue has not been forecasted, it might create a crisis. Waddock (2006) explained that even though companies might not predict that a crisis will occur, they need to know what to do, and more importantly, how to do it quickly. Actual rehearsal of implementation plans is a crucial component of good crisis management. It is evident that acting decisively in the GG case, instead of waiting for it to develop into a major crisis would have diminished its effects.

5.2.4 <u>Focus on long-haul flights and fight against climate change</u>

BA's CEO Rod Eddington CSR report urged the global aviation industry to work together to reduce the industry impact on climate or risk additional taxation (BA, 2005). The UK government has made promises on climate change that can cause "a major knock to the UK's £10bn a year aviation industry" (McErlean, 2006). BA should take active measures and lobby actively against unnecessary short-haul flights, a sector which is unprofitable to Ba and in which BA appears uncompetitive. This will show that BA is really fighting against climate change because in addition to their initiatives to reduce greenhouse-gas emissions and participating voluntarily in emissions trading programme, recognises that limiting air travel is a major step. This involves a change in strategic direction that has to be weighed carefully.

5.2.5. <u>Support to sustainable tourism.</u>

UN Commission Sustainable Development (1999) alerted that the true proof of sustainable tourism will be the sustainable development of local communities that serve as tourism destinations. BA should work participate in true programmes, like the ones mentioned below, adapted from UN-Commission paper (1999):

- Investment in programmes of local water and soil quality, with direct impact on local health as a result of inadequate infrastructure.
- Raise awareness in travellers about the fact that high consumption lifestyle of these tourists, with high levels of energy and water consumption are globally unsustainable.

The participation in real programmes will give BA an image of fighting a problem of which they are part of the problem but they can also be part of the solution, rather than sponsor awards that may be perceived of making-believe that somebody else has to do something about it.

[End]

● How far does the assignment satisfy the requirements?

There is a clear structure to the work, based around sections addressing the four tasks set out in the requirements. The author identifies three main issues and these are then followed through thematically in each section, thus forming a second tier of the structure. This has a number of advantages: firstly, the reader (i.e. the marker) can easily navigate through the piece, secondly they can see where they are in the argument, and thirdly it is easy for the reader to see exactly how and where each task has been addressed. This bears out our advice that use of the language in which a question is expressed can be part of the basis of your answer.

Even though you may not (yet) be familiar with the models used by the author, it should be clear whether or not they are relevant – if they are then they will help the argument move forward a step. This is as good a test as any for which models to use in a piece of work, and when to use them.

Look at the models used in the assignment to help analyse the issues initially (fig 1) and then to analyse stakeholders (table 2 and figures 2 and 3). Evaluate how far they take the reader further forward in the argument.

Similarly, whilst you may not know the literature in this field yet in your studies, you can see if it is used effectively to take the argument forward. Note the referencing system used is consistent – Harvard style (though the assignment bibliography has been omitted from this Appendix).

The role of literature and models in the argument illustrates an important feature of assessment criteria: they are not always discrete, distinct, aspects that can be independently evaluated; often a strength in one area, such as use of literature, also strengthens other areas, such as argument, and vice versa. So it is quite misleading to think of these criteria as 'ticks' that can be picked off one by one. This is also why part of the expertise of the tutor is in their judgement in forming an overview of the piece of work in general, which they may then analyse in terms of the assessment criteria.

And what areas could be stronger? Bearing in mind that this attracted a high mark, it should be noted that most of what is required has indeed been achieved. But it is very rare for there to be no points of improvement at all. One aspect with this piece of work goes back to the SOLO model – this answer could be read as a fine piece of multistructural writing, although in fact it does include some relational material as well. But it does not explore a great deal at the extended abstract end of this spectrum. There could be more critique of models used, more reflection on the formulation of the models and whether any adaptation of models is appropriate, as well as more generalization of the outcomes of the discussion. This would bring the piece up into the very high marks indeed. Would you have awarded it a distinction? You will need to find your own course assessment criteria and levels to properly answer this question.

References

Adair, J. (1973) *Action Centred Leadership*. New York: McGraw-Hill.

Belbin, M. (1982) *Management Teams: Why they Succeed or Fail*. London: Heinemann.

Biggs J. (2003) *Teaching for Quality Learning at University: What the Student Does*. Buckingham: Open University Press.

Brown, J. S. and Duguid, J. (2000) *The Social Life of Information*. Boston: Harvard Business School Press.

Checkland, P. (1984, 1999) *Systems Thinking, Systems Practice*. New York: John Wiley.

Dall'Alba, G. (1991) 'Foreshadowing Conceptions of Teaching', in *Research and Development in Higher Education*, vol. 13, pp. 293–7.

Guba, Egon G., and Yvonna S. Lincoln (1994) 'Competing Paradigms in Qualitative Research,' in Denzin, Norman K., and Yvonna S. Lincoln, (eds), *Handbook of Qualitative Research*. Thousand Oaks, CA: Sage Publications, Inc., pp. 105–17.

Joint Information Systems Committee, www.jisc.ac.uk

Prosser, M. and Trigwell, K. (1999) *Understanding Learning and Teaching: The Experience in Higher Education*. Buckingham: Society for Research into Higher Education and Open University Press.

Useful Resources

Books

Of the very wide range of texts on research in the social sciences, the following are distinctive:

Management Research – An Introduction, M. Easterby-Smith and R. Thorpe. London: Sage, 2003.
  This is a popular and fairly comprehensive introduction not only to the practicalities of research into management but also into some of the theoretical issues.

Research Methods for Managers, J. Gill and P. Johnson, 3rd edition. London: Sage, 2003.
  This is a close competitor of the Easterby-Smith and Thorpe text. It is more accurate, but also a little more dense and therefore not quite so easy to read.

Research Methods for Business Students, M. Saunders, 4th edition. London: FT–Prentice-Hall, 2006
  Another very popular text. It is more practically focused than the previous two, though not so specifically focused on postgraduate research

Researching and Writing a Dissertation for Business Students, C. Fisher. London: FT-Prentice Hall, 2004.
  A thorough guide, especially useful for the more professionally focused piece of work.

Business Research, J. Collis and R. Hussey. Basingstoke: Palgrave Macmillan, 2003.
  A workhorse text used by many students. Again a tendency to talk in undergraduate-style terms, but doctoral students have used this to good effect.

The Student Assignment and Dissertation Survival Guide, G. Ajuga. London: GKA Publishing, 2001.
  Based on a great deal of experience supporting students at all levels, this is not so much a comprehensive introduction to research so much as a very clever (if slightly dubious) bluffer's guide to getting good marks – but students say it works!

Essential Quantitative Methods for Business Management and Finance, L. Oakshott. Basingstoke: Palgrave Macmillan, 2001.
A thorough introduction to 'quants' for managers. It is not specifically about quantitative research but the techniques are basically the same.

Statistics Without Tears, D. Rowntree. London: Penguin, 1991.
A shorter introduction, but explains each concepts very clearly, and strongly recommended for anyone who feels that stats is 'not for them'.

Quantitative Methods for Business Decisions, 5th edition, J. Curwen and R. Slater. New York: Thompson Learning, 2001.
Again a general management quantitative analysis book. A well-established text which has been updated several times.

Websites

There are many websites that can support your research. We have picked just three that may be of general value as sources in their own right:

http://trochim.human.cornell.edu/pointers/pointers.htm
Full of tips and references to other sites concerning social research.

http://www.library.miami.edu/netguides/psymeth.html
An internet resource list, again providing many useful further references.

http://www.sosig.ac.uk
The website of a UK-based academic social science interest group (hence the acronym name) which covers a number of topics relevant to social research methodologies.

Index

A

Academic
  culture, 4
  work, 1ff
  writing, 107–15
Action
  learning, 4
  research, 209
Active learning, 18, 39, 41
AMBA (Association for MBAs), 65
Argument, 5, 22, 49, 71, 72, 82, 110ff, 124
Assessment, 65, 68,140
  criteria 103–4, 164, 195
Assignments, 23, 31, 46, 56–7, 103, 109,
    116, 138, 179

B

Bibliography, 53, 60
Brainstorm, 77, 99

C

Case study research, 208
Cheating, 115
Classes, 35
Competence
  management, 27
  professional, 9
Course
  documentation, 36, 94, 190
  handbooks 204
Critical analysis, 2–5, 67, 124
Critique, 2, 4, 184, 197

D

Debate, 15, 99, 115
Dissertation, 163 ff, 198ff
  aims and objectives, 174–6
  marking, 187, 193ff

practice-focused, 164ff, 174, 185, 187
presentation, 190, 193
research-focused, 164ff, 174, 185,
    187

E

Essays, 97, 109, 130
Ethics, 181–2
  regulations, 182
Examinations, 24, 65, 87, 100, 103
  case study, 100
  open book, 101
  questions, 99
Experience, 3

G

Ground rules, 146, 151, 159
Grounded theory, 209
Group effectiveness, 143
Group work, 32, 44, 47, 97, 124, 141ff,
    177
  feedback, 149–51
  international students, 144
  learning, 142
  marking 195
  revision in, 98
Groups, task, 142
Groupthink, 152

H

Handouts, 19, 22

I

International students, 15, 31, 158
Interviews, 214

K

Kolb's experiential learning cycle, 132

L

Learning, xi, 5, 24, 34, 46, 69, 84
  approach to, 10
  conceptions of, 12, 15, 39, 43,
  outcomes, 15, 36, 67, 68, 97, 104, 105,
    164, 194
  students' conceptions of, 11
  tutors' conceptions of, 11
Lectures, 35, 39, 41, 43, 46
Literature review, 200, 203

M

MA in Business and Management, ix, 165
Marking, 84
  criteria, 99
Marks, dissertations, 164
Masters level, ix, xi, 6–8, 39, 40, 43, 44,
    52, 53, 67, 74, 82, 86, 93, 96, 101,
    105, 106, 107, 118, 163, 196
  generalist, 9
  specialist, 8
MBA, ix, 9, 111, 141, 166, 170
Memory, 24
Mind mapping, 16, 117
Module guides, 31, 196
MSc in Business and Management, ix,
    111, 165

N

Notes, 19–21, 37, 40, 48, 49, 50, 70, 101,
    119

O

Objectives, 201
Observation, 214

P

Paragraph, construction of, 22, 49
Participant research, 209
Personal development, 13, 34
Plagiarism, 51, 115
Practice, 2
Presentation, assignments, 121, 126
Professional competence, 9

Q

Quality Assurance Agency, 6, 8, 68
Questionnaire, 214, 217

Questions, 10, 11, 66, 69, 72, 73, 75,
    77, 81, 94, 97, 100, 101, 102, 168,
    202

R

Reading, 16, 23, 38, 48, 54, 57, 118
Referencing, 51, 115
Reflection, 132ff, 148–9
Regulations, academic, 31
Reports 109, 130, 166
Research, 116ff, 198ff
  bias, 217
  design, 208ff
  methodology, 199ff
  methods, 199ff
  objectives, 200
  primary and secondary, 213
  questions, 207
Resources, electronic, 160
Return to study, xii, 31
Revision, 21, 92 ff, 102
  groups, 100

S

Seminar, 35
SOLO (Structure of Observed Learning
    Outcome) taxonomy, 40, 41, 72,
    105–6
Sources, 52, 56, 119, 196
  online, 58ff
Structure, 104–6
Students, learning from other, 14
Subject Benchmark Statement, 9
Supervisor, 171,195ff
Surveys, 214, 208
Syllabus, 35, 93, 95, 102
Syndicate groups, 47, 141ff

T

Teaching, 15, 41, 45
  conceptions of, 11, 12, 37, 39, 43
  objectives, 36, 37
  students' conceptions of, 11
  tutors' conceptions of, 11
Testimony, 214
Thesis, 166
Time management, 27, 30, 134ff, 180
Tutors, use of, 5

U

UKCOSA (Council for International
Education), 18

V

Virtual Learning Environments (VLE), 15,
154, 160

W

Writing, 22, 110, 126